Handwriting Without Tears®
by Learning Without Tears

Kick Start Kindergarten
Teacher's Guide

GRADE TK

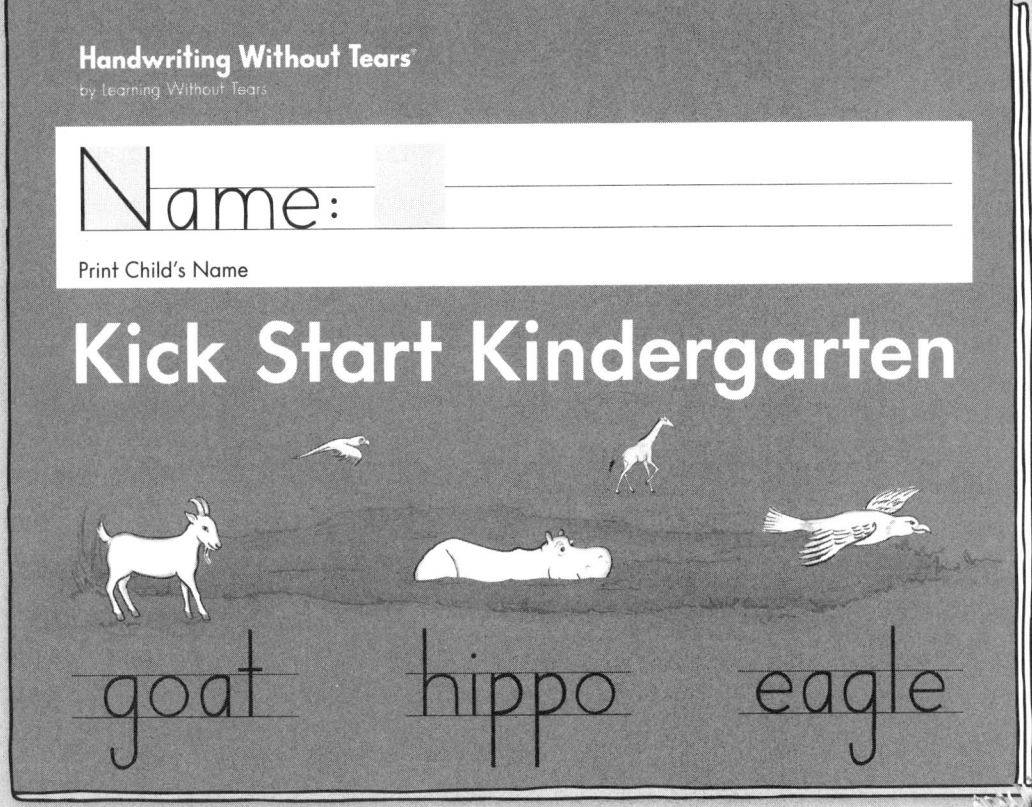

Guide to Student Edition Lessons
and Multisensory Activities

by Jan Z. Olsen, OTR

LEARNING
Without Tears®

8001 MacArthur Blvd.
Cabin John, MD 20818
LWTears.com | 888.983.8409

Author: Jan Z. Olsen, OTR
Curriculum Designers: Dr. Christina Bretz, OTD, OTR/L and Tania Ferrandino, OTR/L
Content Advisor: Elizabeth DeWitt, Ed. D.
Illustrators: Jan Z. Olsen, OTR and Julie Koborg
Graphic Designers: Sammie Simon and Julie Koborg
Editors: Annie Cassidy, Kathryn Fox, and Megan Parker

Copyright © 2022 Learning Without Tears
Second Edition
ISBN: 978-1-952970-82-5
123456789BRB242322
Printed in the USA

Welcome

Welcome to Handwriting Without Tears® by Learning Without Tears and to teaching handwriting.

This is your teacher's guide, not only for the student edition, but for a way of teaching handwriting that is effective for children. Your children will be moving, singing, and playing with you as they build and write letters.

That's how good handwriting starts—with hands-on materials and teaching that bring the curriculum to life.

For this reason, explicit, multisensory handwriting instruction is crucial, and we are committed to ensuring students can access it regardless of where they are learning. We are excited to offer an integrated print and digital approach, so students can learn handwriting actively and joyfully in any learning environment.

Handwriting Without Tears is part of the Learning Without Tears family. We started in the 1970s and have evolved based on our continued and direct experience with students, teachers, occupational therapists, and administrators across the country. Our 35 years of experience and ongoing collaboration solve the problems associated with early writing skills and do so in a way that is joyful, effective, and innovative.

Our materials and teaching strategies make learning a positive, successful experience for children in just 15 minutes a day. You will help your students build strong printing skills for writing letters, words, and sentences. Every lesson includes a multisensory element and has additional, optional connections to tie handwriting to other parts of the school day.

We support teacher directed learning. We believe you'll enjoy using our program and are excited to have you bring it to life in your classroom.

Jan Z. Olsen

Table of Contents

1 – INTRODUCTION
- 4 This Is Handwriting Without Tears!
- 6 Simply Smart Student Materials
- 8 Features of the Student Edition
- 10 Get to Know the Teacher's Guide
- 12 Accessing Digital Products in + Live Insights
- 14 Teaching Handwriting in All Settings

17 – TEACHING HANDWRITING
- 18 Stages of Learning
- 19 Intent to Prevent
- 20 Handwriting in the Literacy Block
- 21 Emergent Writing: A Developmental Progression
- 22 Scope & Sequence

25 – TEACHING GUIDELINES
- 26 UNIT 1: F E D P B R N M
  Numbers 1–3
- 27 UNIT 2: H K L U V W X Y Z
  Numbers 4–7
- 28 UNIT 3: C O Q G S A I T J
  Number 8
- 29 UNIT 4: c o s v w – t
  a d g
  Numbers 9–10
- 30 UNIT 5: u i e
  l k y j
- 31 UNIT 6: p r n m h b
  f q x z

33 – GET READY! POSTURE, PAPER & GRIP
- 34 Preparing for Paper & Pencil
- 35 Stomp Your Feet
- 36 Paper Placement & Pencil Grip
- 37 The Correct Grip
- 38 Picking Up My Pencil
- 39 Grasping Grip

41 – CAPITALS
TEACHING STRATEGIES
- 42 Developmental Teaching
- 43 Student Edition Design
- 44 Capital Teaching Order
- 45 Help Me Write My Name

FROG JUMP CAPITALS
- 46 Frog Jump Capitals
- 47 F
- 48 E
- 49 D
- 50 P
- 51 B
- 52 R
- 53 N
- 54 M
- 55 Review

STARTING CORNER CAPITALS
- 56 H
- 57 K
- 58 L
- 59 U
- 60 V
- 61 W
- 62 X
- 63 Y
- 64 Z
- 65 Review

CENTER STARTING CAPITALS
- 66 C
- 67 O
- 68 Q
- 69 G
- 70 S
- 71 A
- 72 I
- 73 T
- 74 J
- 75 Review
- 76 Capitals for Me

79 – LOWERCASE LETTERS, WORDS & SENTENCES

TEACHING STRATEGIES
- 80 Student Edition Design
- 81 Double Line Success
- 82 Lowercase Teaching Order
- 83 Lowercase Alphabet

SAME AS CAPITALS AND t: c o s v w – t
- 84 c + words
- 86 o + words
- 88 s + sentences
- 90 v
- 91 w
- 92 t + sentences

MAGIC c LETTERS: a d g
- 94 a + words
- 96 d + words
- 98 g + words

MORE VOWELS: u i e
- 100 u + words
- 102 i + words
- 104 e + words

TRANSITION GROUP: l k y j
- 106 l
- 107 k
- 108 y + sentences
- 110 j

DIVER LETTERS: p r n m h b
- 111 p
- 112 r + sentences
- 114 n + words
- 116 m + words
- 118 h + words
- 120 b + words

FINAL GROUP: f q x z
- 122 f + words
- 124 q
- 125 x
- 126 z + sentences
- 128 Name

131 – NUMBERS
- 132 Numbers on the Slate Chalkboard
- 133 Number Stories
- 134 1–10
- 144 Numbers Review
- 145 About Reversals

147 – MULTISENSORY ACTIVITIES
- 148 Multisensory Cues
- ♪ 149 Songs for Readiness
- 150 Shake Hands With Me
- 151 Sign In, Please
- ♪ 152 "Where Do You Start Your Letters?"
- 153 Top to Bottom
- 154 Mat Man® – Build
- 155 Mat Man® – Draw
- 156 Wood Pieces – Set
- 157 Wood Pieces – Trade, Polish & Sort
- 158 Wood Pieces – Positions & Body Parts
- 159 Wood Pieces – Curves & Circles
- 160 Wood Pieces – Vertical, Horizontal & Diagonal
- 161 Wood Pieces – Capital Letter Cards, Show Me Magnetic Pieces for Capitals
- 162 Wood Pieces – Capitals on the Mat
- 163 Capitals on the Door
- 164 Wet-Dry-Try for Capitals
- 165 Mystery Letters on the Slate Chalkboard
- ♪ 166 Songs for Capitals
- ♪ 167 Songs for Lowercase
- 168 Letter Stories
- 170 Air Writing
- 171 Laser Letters
- 172 Digital Formation Tools: Letter & Number
- 173 A+ Worksheet Maker
- 174 Wet-Dry-Try App
- 175 Hand Activity
- 176 Wet-Dry-Try for Lowercase Letters
- 177 Voices
- ♪ 178 "Sentence Song"
- 179 Syllables

181 – RESOURCES
- 182 School-to-Home Connections
- 183 Sentence School
- 184 Remediation Tips
- 191 Strategies for English Language Learners
- 194 Strategies for Children with Special Needs
- 197 Handwriting Standards for Written Production
- 200 References
- 201 Index

This Is Handwriting Without Tears®!

The award-winning Handwriting Without Tears curriculum draws from years of innovation and research to provide developmentally appropriate, multisensory strategies for early writing.

Whether you're using a physical, digital, or integrated approach to teach handwriting, our superior teacher and student materials provide an effective and engaging experience for all learners.

Explicit, thoughtful, and targeted handwriting instruction:

- Multisensory teaching strategies appeal to all learning modalities
- Child friendly, simple language to reach every student
- Large step-by-step models provide a clear example
- Innovative, developmentally appropriate letter order promotes easy learning
- Cross-curricular connections reinforce content being taught in other subjects
- Lefty-friendly design ensures all students can succeed in handwriting
- Easy-to-use assessments track students' progress and supports instruction

This Is Handwriting Without Tears®!

Teacher's Guides and Student Editions
The teacher's guides provide scaffolded instruction that allow educators to differentiate lessons for various learners and learning styles. Multisensory strategies to reach every learner are integrated in every lesson, as well as cross-curricular connections. The Student Editions feature child friendly language and a clean, simple, and intuitive approach that invites personalization and fosters handwriting success. Every page has large step-by-step models that show students how to sequence the letter. Double lines and line generalization activities promote legible writing that will transfer to success on all paper styles.

Manipulatves
A wide range of thoughtful and purposefully created manipulatives engage multiple modalities while bringing learning to life. The Handwriting Without Tears hands-on manipulatives are proven to stimulate and strengthen visual, tactile, kinesthetic, and auditory learning styles, while teaching children to build and sequence their letters prior to writing on paper.

Interactive Digital Teaching Tool (IDTT)
IDTT includes pre-loaded lesson plans aligned with the Handwriting Without Tears developmental order, and the ability to change the order of letter instruction to align to ELA curriculum. Digital teacher's guides and student editions make planning easy, and educators can also access, and assign, digital letter formations, teaching videos, and fun animations students will love. IDTT supports group or individual instruction. Educators can easily assign lessons remotely.
Plus, the reporting feature easily identifies when students have completed assignments.

Digital Student App
Using the Digital Student App, students can complete lessons and receive music, videos, and messages from their teacher. They'll also have access to a digital toolbox, including Letter and Number Formations, Wood Pieces, and Wet-Dry-Try, they can use anytime.

Simply Smart Student Materials

ABOUT THE *KICK START KINDERGARTEN* CURRICULUM

Our intuitive and engaging student materials make learning handwriting joyful and fun. The materials below were created to fit into your daily routine. As you become familiar with the program, gradually incorporate new activities and choose those that suit your students' needs.

Kick Start Kindergarten Student Edition
The Student Edition is loaded with capital, lowercase, word, sentence, and number practice. Your students will love the fun activities, which develop their handwriting and sentence skills. We developed 36 weeks of teaching guidelines in this teacher's guide to help you plan your lessons.

The Digital Student App
Our Digital Student App allows students to access the full Handwriting Without Tears curriculum virtually. In a student friendly digital environment, they complete lessons assigned by their teacher that include, music, animations, and digital formation tools. The physical Student Edition and Digital Student App work together to provide a perfectly integrated print and digital solution for handwriting.

Wood Pieces Set for Capital Letters
Included are the four basic shapes used to build capital letters: 8 Big Lines, 6 Little Lines, 6 Big Curves, 6 Little Curves. Children polish, sort, stack, and learn the names of the Wood Pieces. When they use Wood Pieces in teacher-directed play, they learn size, shape, and position concepts.

Capital Letter Cards & Mat for Wood Pieces
Next, students use the Wood Pieces to build letters. For example: they make B with a Big Line + Little Curve + Little Curve. The Mat and Letter Cards use a ☺ icon on the top left corner for orientation.

Simply Smart Student Materials

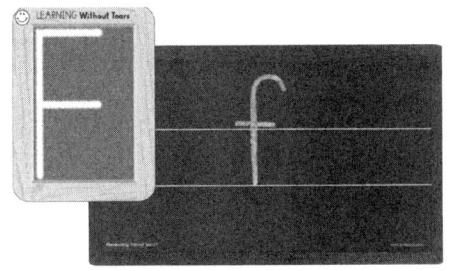

Slate Chalkboard & Blackboard with Double Lines
Use the Slate Chalkboard to teach capitals and numbers and the Blackboard with Double Lines to teach lowercase letters. Incorporate our Wet-Dry-Try technique to add endless opportunities to trace, write, and learn to form letters and numbers.

Individual Student Manipulative Kits
The individual manipulative kits include essential multisensory materials so students can access our hands-on learning activities from any learning environment.

Magic C Bunny
Make the puppet your teaching assistant. Access A Click Away ☺ for directions to make your own Magic C Bunny out of a paper napkin. Your students will form letters correctly when they learn the Magic C way.

Music & Movement
Music promotes movement, and movement positively affects cognitive development. Whether children are tapping Big Lines or writing letters in the air, our music and movement activities will enliven your lessons and catch your students' attention. You'll find our lessons are loaded with active learning, like Syllable Moves- a fun, stand-up-and-move activity that teaches students to hear and distinguish syllables.

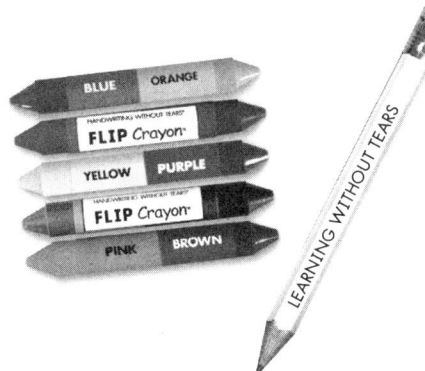

FLIP Crayons® & Pencils for Little Hands
FLIP Crayons help children develop hand coordination and fine motor skills. They will love flipping them over and over to change colors. Our golf-size pencils are perfect for kindergarten children because they can write with pencils that fit their hand size.

Features of the Student Edition

We carefully plan every student edition page and everything that's on it. Our student editions are accessible and friendly, yet also promote excellence. We want children to practice correctly, which is why our student edition pages promote efficient, effective practice for each letter.

Child Friendly, Simple Language
When teaching letter formation, we eliminate language that assumes children understand left/right orientation, clockwise/counterclockwise, or forward/backward circles. We make it easy by using a few carefully selected words that all children know and understand.

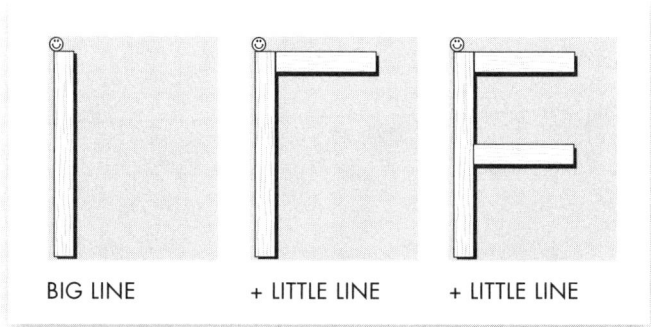

Large Step-by-Step Models
It is much easier for children to understand how to form letters if you show them how. Our student editions contain large step-by-step images that show students how to make each part of every letter.

Lefty Friendly
Teaching pages provide models on the left and right so left-handed children can easily see the model they are copying. Lefties never have to lift their hands or place them in an awkward position to see a model.

Developmental Teaching Order
Our developmental approach helps children master skills and boosts confidence. We teach the easiest skills first, then build on prior knowledge. We teach capitals first and follow with lowercase letters. We also teach in small groups of similar formation.

Features of the Student Edition

Black & White, Clean Design, and Thoughtful Illustrations
The black and white pages in our student editions are clean and clear. We deliberately avoid visually confusing backgrounds, colored graphics, crowded pages, and multicolored lines. Our simple student edition pages are appealing and invite children to color and draw when they have finished a lesson.

Our illustrations promote left-to-right directionality. This is a unique feature of our student editions. The car, helicopter, horse, and other drawings move left to right across the page to encourage correct visual tracking and writing direction.

Continuous, Meaningful Review
Children retain skills better if they have continuous, meaningful review. That's why each new letter is used in words and sentences that emphasize practice of the new letter and help children review and practice previously learned letters.

Cross-Curricular Connections
In addition to handwriting, we want the pages to have connections to other grade-appropriate curricula. We created activities that help you teach handwriting and review other grade-appropriate skills.

Simple Spatial Organization
We begin by teaching capital letters and numbers with Gray Blocks, which prevent reversals and help children learn how to place letters and numbers.

As children move to lowercase, our double lines foster handwriting success. The mid line is for size, and the base line is for placement. The middle space is for small letters, the top space is for tall letters, while the bottom space is for descending letters.

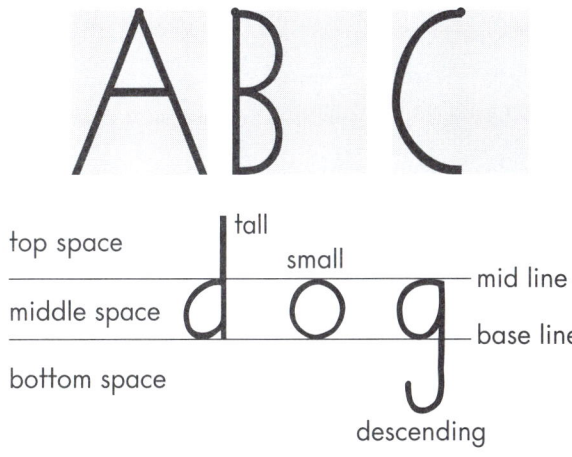

When children are learning to print, they need extra room to write. Our landscape style student editions give them the space they need to write and develop good spacing habits.

Line Generalization: Success on All Paper Styles
Our student editions provide activities for children to experience different types of lined paper. We start them with simple double lines, then teach them to master all lines.

Get to Know the Teacher's Guide

Lesson Overview
There is a lesson plan for every student edition page. Below is a sample of how a letter formation lesson is organized.

STARTING THE LESSON
Letter, student edition page, and objectives are shown in the top corner. Start each lesson with the suggested multisensory activity.

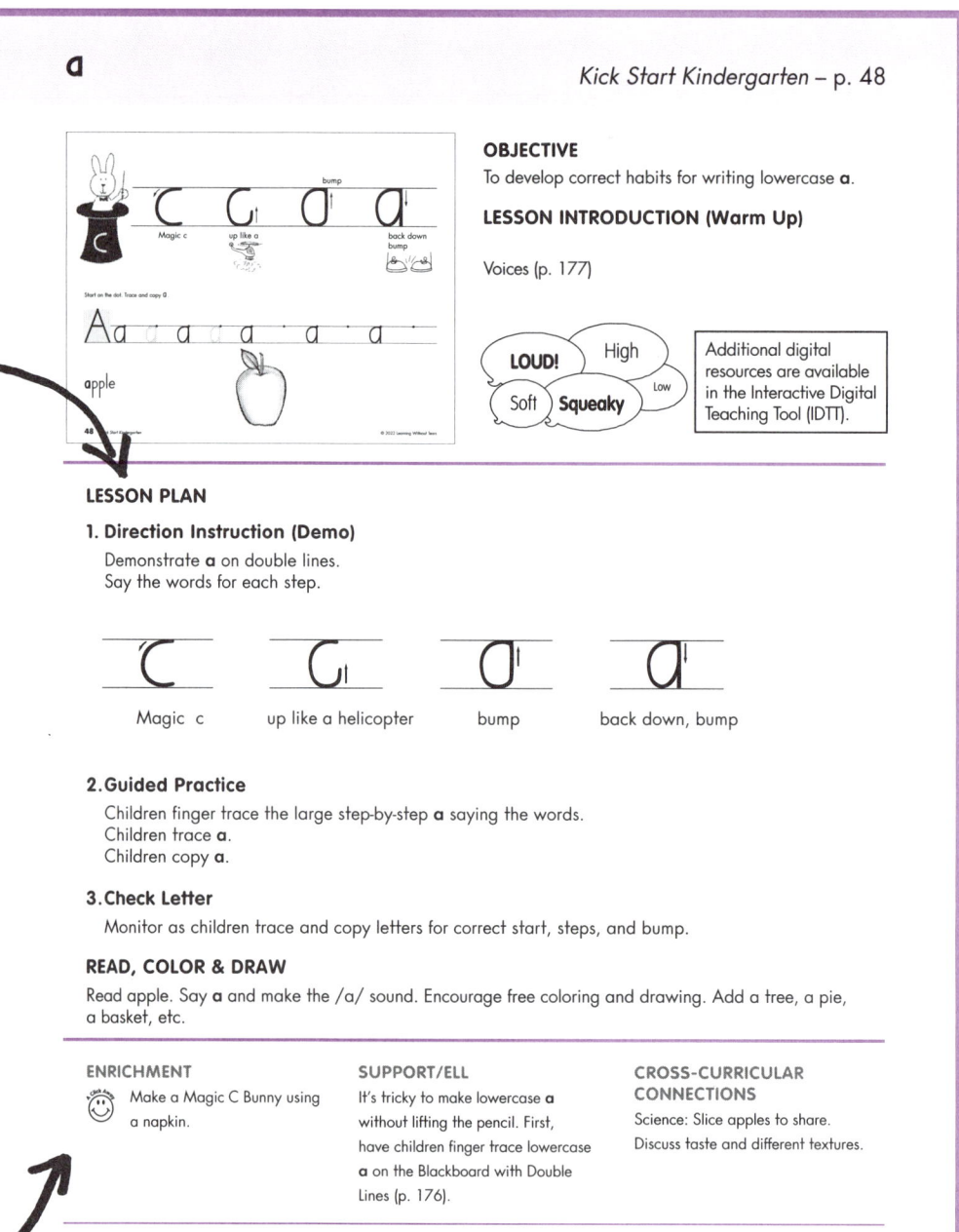

TEACHING THE LESSON
Lesson Plan
The letter lesson follows these steps:

1. **Direct Instruction (Demo)** – Actively demonstrate the letter for children to finger trace and then copy.

2. **Guided Practice** – Children finger trace and copy the letter.

3. **Check Letter** – Children check their letter and evaluate formation.

Read, Color & Draw
You and your children read the sentence. Children color and draw.

EXTENDING THE LESSON
Differentiated Instruction

Enrichment
Ways to extend learning by adding complexity or variety.

Support/ELL
Suggestions for adapting or simplifying the activity.

Cross-Curricular Connections
Connects the lesson to another subject.

Get to Know the Teacher's Guide

Multisensory Activities

Many multisensory activities for handwriting practice are implemented repeatedly throughout the curriculum. Below is an example of the step-by-step directions we provide for each activity. These multisensory activity pages can be found starting on p. 147.

ABOUT THE ACTIVITY
Introduction gives you background and guidance for the activity.

MATERIALS
Materials list helps you organize and plan for the activity.

ACTIVITY PLAN
Step-by-step directions along with illustrations to guide you through.

Wet-Dry-Try for Lowercase Letters

Wet-Dry-Try is an innovative teaching strategy. We use a slate chalkboard for capitals and numbers. For lowercase letters and words we use the Blackboard with Double Lines. This is the physical version. The digital version is available on the Interactive Digital Teaching Tool and Digital Student App. The latest research on brain development supports this activity. This research calls for fewer elements (just two lines), modeling, sensory engagement, and immediate feedback (Sousa 2011).

Materials
- Blackboard with Double Lines* (1 per child)
- Little Chalk Bits (1")
- Little Sponge Cubes (1/2")
- Little cups of water
- Paper towel pieces

Activity

1. **Prepare Blackboards**
Write letter with chalk as a model to trace.

2. **Teacher's Part – Write f with Chalk**
Use chalk to write a letter on double lines.
Say the step-by-step directions.

3. **Child's Part – Wet-Dry-Try**
As the child does each part, say the step-by-step directions to guide the child. The child is encouraged to join in, saying the words.
Wet: The child uses a Little Sponge Cube to trace the letter.
Dry: The child uses a little piece of paper towel to trace the letter.
Try: The child uses a Little Chalk Bit to write the letter.

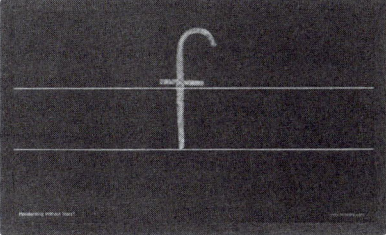 

*If you don't have a Blackboard with Double Lines, consider using our Double Line Writer on your whiteboard. This product is available at LWTears.com.

Digital Version

 Interactive Digital Teaching Tool: Share via your interactive whiteboard or smartboard

 Digital Student App: Integrated in lessons and on "My Tools" for additional practice

176 Kick Start Kindergarten Teacher's Guide: *Multisensory Activities*   © 2022 Learning Without Tears

Accessing Digital Products in +Live Insights

Go to +Live Insights at **pli.LWTears.com** to manage and access all of your digital Learning Without Tears products. The Interactive Digital Teaching Tool and Digital Student App are located in +Live Insights.

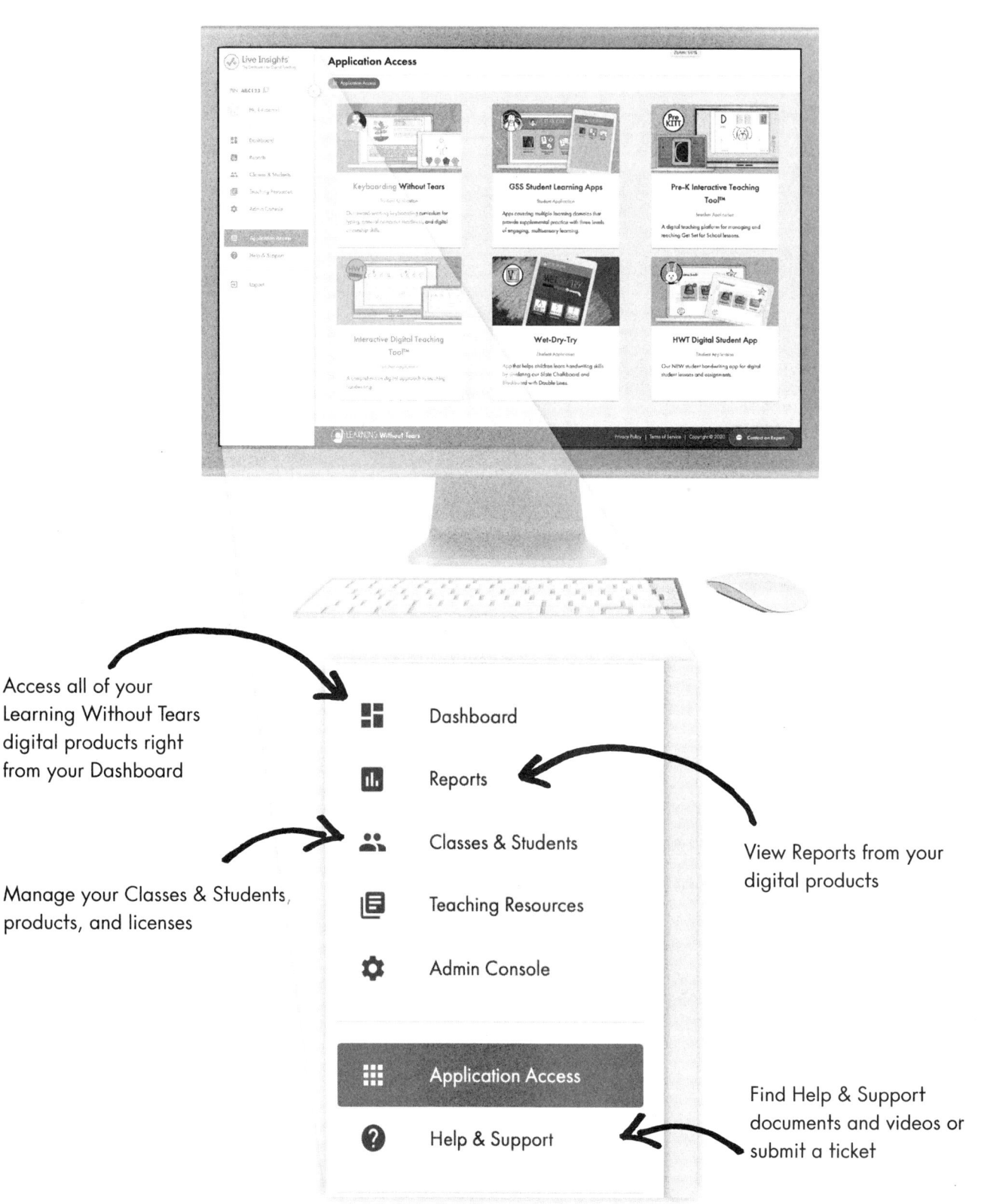

Access all of your Learning Without Tears digital products right from your Dashboard

Manage your Classes & Students, products, and licenses

View Reports from your digital products

Find Help & Support documents and videos or submit a ticket

Using the Interactive Digital Teaching Tool

The Interactive Digital Teaching Tool (IDTT) makes planning Handwriting Without Tears lessons effortless, and provides digital resources to engage students in any learning environment.

Teachers send lessons and activities to students.

Students access lessons in their student app.

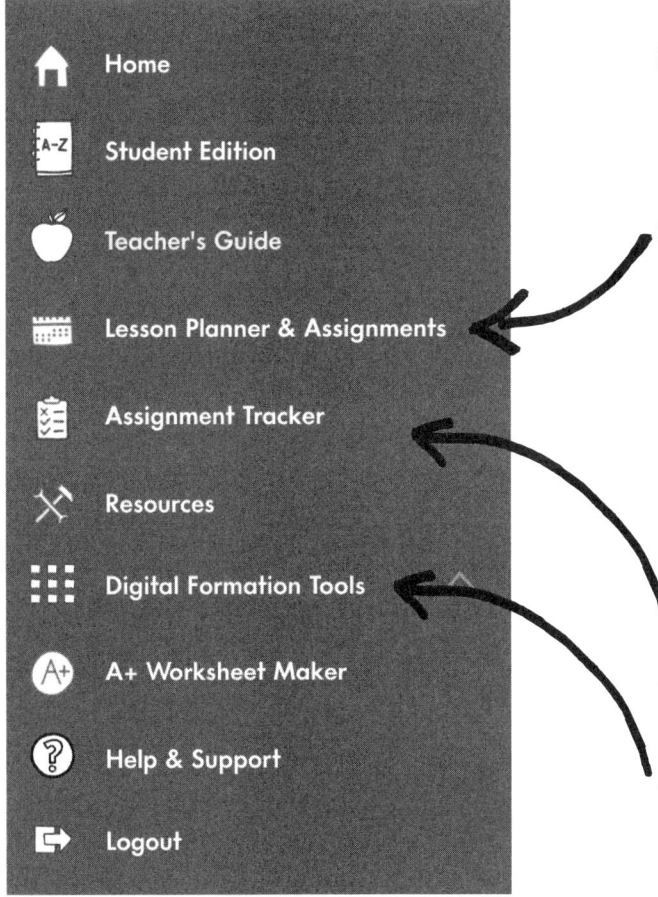

In IDTT, educators can:

1. Access digital student editions and teacher's guides

2. Plan and assign handwriting instruction
   - Choose from dozens of pre-loaded lesson plans aligned with the Handwriting Without Tears developental order, or choose your own order
   - Create lesson plans lessons that include animation, music and model lessons taught by master teachers
   - Assign Lessons directly to students they can easily access via the Digital Student App

3. Track whether student assignment has been completed

4. Access digital formation tools
   - Wet-Dry-Try
   - Letter & Number Formations
   - Wood Pieces

Teaching Handwriting in All Settings

The print and digital components in Handwriting Without Tears support a variety of different use cases. The Lesson Planner in the Interactive Digital Teaching Tool (IDTT) contains lessons pre-populated with recommended activities. However, you can easily customize a lesson to best fit your needs.

	In-Person: All learning is happening in the classroom—whether it's hands-on activities, a teacher projecting on a whiteboard, or students working on the Digital Student App on a computer during center time.
Lesson Time	10–15 mins
Lesson Introduction (Warm Up)	**Hands-on Learning** Choose one or more of the following activities: Wood Piece Play, Music, Capitals on the Mat for Wood Pieces, Wet-Dry-Try on the Slate, Wet-Dry-Try on the Blackboard with Double Lines, Air Writing, or Hand Activity. **Digital: IDTT** Share one or more of the following activities via smartboard, or send to students via the Digital Student App: Animations, Letter & Number Stories, Wood Pieces, Hand Activity.
Direct Instruction (Demo)	**In-Class Demo** Demonstrate letter formation via the Interactive whiteboard, Slate or Blackboard with Double Lines, flip chart, or whiteboard or **Digital: IDTT** Share and demomonstrate letter formation via smartboard, or send to students via the Digital Student App: Letter & Number Formations, Wet-Dry-Dry, or Live Teaching videos.
Practice	Students complete appropriate lesson pages in their Student Edition.

Teaching Handwriting in All Settings

Hybrid: Instruction and practice are split between school and at home.	**Virtual:** All instruction and practice is happening at home via the computer.
5–10 mins home/independent 5–10 mins in class	Lesson Time: 10–15 mins
Hands-on Learning (live in the classroom) Choose one or more of the following activities: Wood Piece Play, Music, Capitals on the Mat for Wood Pieces, Wet-Dry-Try on the Slate, Wet-Dry-Try on the Blackboard with Double Lines, Air Writing, or Hand Activity. **Digital: IDTT** Assign one or more of the following activities to the Digital Student App: Animations, Letter & Number Stories, Wood Pieces, or Hand Activity.	**Hands-On Learning** (Not recommended for virtual learning unless students have access to manipulatives at home.) **Digital: IDTT** Assign one or more of the following activities to the Digital Student App: Animations, Letter & Number Stories, Wood Pieces, or Hand Activity.
Digital: IDTT Demonstrate letter formation by assigning one or more of the following activities to the Digital Student App: Letter & Number Formations, Wet-Dry-Dry, or Live Teaching videos.	**Digital: IDTT** Demonstrate letter formation by assigning one or more of the following activities to the Digital Student App: Letter & Number Formations, Wet-Dry-Dry, or Live Teaching videos.
Students complete the appropriate lesson pages in their Student Edition in the classroom.	If students have access to their student edition at home, they can complete the assigned lesson pages. There is also the option to print the assigned pages from the Digital Student App.

TEACHING HANDWRITING

Children's handwriting matters. Handwriting skills affect school success (Feder and Majnemer 2007). When children master handwriting, they are free to focus on the content of their writing instead of the mechanics. With our easy-to-teach, easy-to-learn curriculum, you will be empowered to teach handwriting efficiently and well. With your guidance, children will learn correct letter formation and good handwriting habits that will serve them well in every subject.

The Handwriting Without Tears curriculum draws from years of innovation and research to provide developmentally appropriate, multisensory tools and strategies for your classroom.

"Writing fluency frees attention for content."

(Lichsteiner et al., 2018)

Stages of Learning

PRE-INSTRUCTIONAL STAGE – PRE-K, TRANSITIONAL KINDERGARTEN, AND KINDERGARTEN

The focus is on building readiness skills essential for learning. Pre-instructional readiness activities promote social-emotional learning, fine motor skills, drawing, coloring, alphabet knowledge, pre-writing, writing, number, and counting skills. Most handwriting lessons will begin with multisensory hands-on learning, which will boost these skills prior to writing letter and numbers.

INSTRUCTIONAL STAGES

Because research shows that children can imitate months before they can copy lines and shapes, the first stage of handwriting instruction is demonstration-imitation. When you demonstrate, children can see your physical motions. They imitate how you move to write a letter or number. For handwriting success in your classroom, use these three stages.

Stage 1 – Direct Instruction (Demo)

The child watches as the teacher writes and then imitates.
Ready for next stage?

- No: Do more multisensory activities.
- Yes: Let children finish a student edition page by copying models.

Stage 2 – Guided Practice

The child looks at the completed model of a letter, word, or sentence and copies it to match the model.
Ready for next stage?

- No: Go back to demonstrating the letter.
- Yes: Supervise copying.

Stage 3 – Independent Practice

The child writes unassisted, without a demonstration or a model.

You will know when your children are ready for independent writing when they can:

- Write their names correctly.
- Write letters and numbers from memory.
- Write dictated words (assist with spelling).
- Enjoy free writing.

The Intent to Prevent

THE HANDWRITING PROCESS

Good handwriting skills result from your thoughtful attention and instruction. Students need deliberate instruction to develop good habits and overcome bad ones.

With this guide and Handwriting Without Tears® materials, you will be prepared to help students make writing a natural and automatic skill. You'll find that their handwriting abilities and habits vary. Regardless of where they start, you can help them develop and improve their skills:

TEACH	TO FIX
How to hold the pencil correctly	Awkward pencil grip
Letters/numbers that face the right way — 3 cats	Reversals — Ɛ ƨʇɒɔ
Letters/numbers that start at the top — top	Starting at the bottom — bottom
Letters/numbers that are formed correctly and consistently — 10 right	Incorrect letters/numbers — 9 wrong

© 2022 Learning Without Tears — Kick Start Kindergarten Teacher's Guide: *Teaching Handwriting*

Handwriting in the Literacy Block

Handwriting is an essential component of a complete literacy curriculum, and can be integrated within daily literacy activities. Our handwriting lessons take 10–15 minutes a day. It's easy to connect your handwriting lessons to parts of your literacy block. Below are some possibilities:

Guided & Independent Reading
Instruct students on the formation of letters and words from the text after shared reading.

Guided & Independent Writing
Take turns practicing a specific letter's formation during interactive activites.

Word Work & Phonics
Provide direct instruction on features of the letters in target words. Utilize Handwriting Without Tears mulitisensory activities to practice correct letter formation while writing words.

Integrating Handwriting & Reading

The three options below work best because they adhere to the fundamental principles of each discipline and incorporate lesson work from each in a way that fully supports skill development. Find one that works best for you. In the Lesson Planner in the Interactive Digital Teaching Tool (IDTT), you can modify the lesson order to align to any one of the following sequences.

1. **Separate the handwriting and reading teaching order**

Teach both programs in the recommended orders. Keep instruction separate until familiar letters appear. Then remind children of letters they know from handwriting or reading instruction.
- During handwriting, remind students of letter sounds they know.
- During reading, remind students how to write letters previously taught.

2. **Integrate the handwriting and reading teaching orders**

Teach both programs in the recommended order, but make connections between them to facilitate learning.
- During handwriting, integrate reading instruction for that letter by saying, "We are learning to write letter a. Letter a makes the /a/ sound."
- During reading, integrate handwriting instruction for that letter by having students finger trace the letter in their handwriting books while you say the letter's formation. Or, print additional practice pages using A+ Worksheet Maker.

3. **Follow the reading teaching order**

Teach both reading and handwriting in the reading teaching order. During handwriting, simply go to the letter teaching page you are covering in reading. Complete the word and sentence pages after you have taught all the letters.

Emergent Writing: A Developmental Progression

Children will develop emergent writing skills in a developmental sequence from scribbling to conventional spelling. This begins with young two-year old's random marks and scribbles, progressing to children forming lines and shapes in preparation for writing letters. Between four and five years of age there is an obvious interest in forming letters through exploration.

2–3 year old
(random marks)

3–4 year old
(starting to draw person, letters)

4–5 year old
(writing letters, name)

Supportive Ways to Promote Emergent Writers
- Provide natural opportunities to explore strokes and shapes, for example, drawing at an easel.
- Include movement and play activities to teach position in space, left-right discrimination and basic foundation skills.
- Include intentional multisensory letter play as part of your daily routine.
- Teach grip and provide tools to promote an effective grip.
- Boost children's vocabulary and listening skills through books and storytelling.
- Encourage children to draw pictures to express themselves and tell a story.
- Ask children to tell you about their pictures and write their response. This allows children to see how print has meaning. (see below).

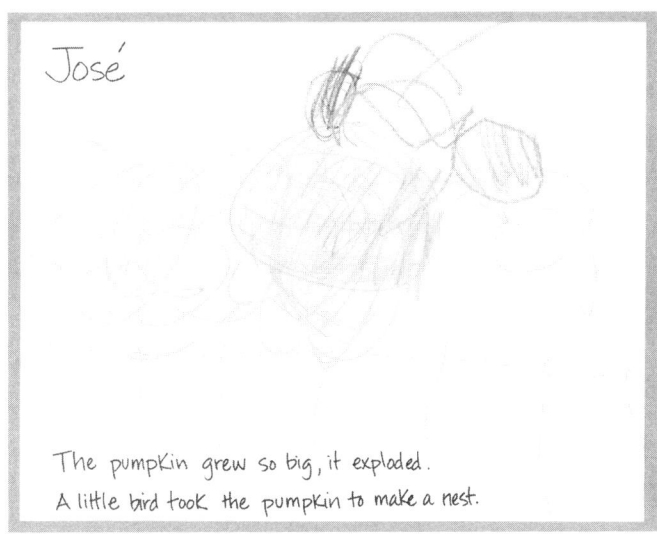

Scope & Sequence

The Scope & Sequence of Printing defines the content and order of printing instruction. The skills needed for printing develop as early as Pre-K. Although we do not teach printing formally at the Pre-K level, we can create an environment and encourage activities to develop good habits that students need in kindergarten. The secret is to teach skills in a way that makes learning natural, easy, and fun.

Type of Instruction

Informal/Structured: A variety of activities address the broad range of letter and school readiness skills.
Formal/Structured: Teacher-directed activities are presented in a more precise order with specific objectives.

Handwriting Sequence

Pre-Strokes: These are beginning marks that can be random or deliberate.
Shapes: These are often introduced before letters and are a foundation for letter formation skills.
Capitals/Numbers: These use simple shapes and strokes. They have the same size, start, and position.
Lowercase Letters: These are tall, small, and descending symbols with more complex strokes, sizes, starts, and positions.

Stages of Learning

Pre-Instruction Readiness: Attention, behavior, language, and fine motor skills for beginning writing.
Stage 1–Direct Instruction: Watch someone form a letter first, and then write it.
Stage 2–Guided Practice: Look at a letter and then write it.
Stage 3–Independent Practice: Write without watching someone or even seeing a letter.

Physical Approach

Crayon Use: Crayons prepare children to use pencils. Small crayon use encourages proper grip.
Pencil Use: Proper pencil grip facilitates good handwriting. In kindergarten, children transfer their crayon grip to pencils.
Posture: Good sitting posture promotes good handwriting. This is taught in kindergarten.
Paper Placement: Correct paper placement helps children move the writing hand across the page. Paper placement is different for left- and right-handed children.

Printing Skills

Primary Skills
 – Memory: Remember and write dictated letters and numbers.
 – Orientation: Face letters and numbers in the correct direction.
 – Start: Begin each letter or number correctly.
 – Sequence: Make the letter strokes in the correct order.

Secondary Skills
 – Placement: Place letters and numbers on the base line.
 – Size: Write in a consistent, grade-appropriate size.
 – Spacing: Place letters in words close, put space between words.

Functional Writing

Letters/numbers, words, sentences, paragraphs, and writing in all subjects

Scope & Sequence

SCOPE & SEQUENCE OF PRINTING					
	Pre-K	Transitional K	Kindergarten	1st Grade	2nd Grade
Type of Instruction					
Informal/Structured	✓				
Formal/Structured		✓	✓	✓	✓
Handwriting Sequence					
Pre-Strokes	✓				
Shapes	✓	✓			
Capitals/Numbers	✓	✓	✓	✓	✓
Lowercase Letters	*See note below	✓	✓	✓	✓
Stages of Learning					
Pre-Instruction Readiness	✓	✓	✓		
Stage 1–Direct Instruction	✓	✓	✓	✓	✓
Stage 2–Guided Practice		✓ Emerging	✓	✓	✓
Stage 3–Independent Practice		✓ Emerging	✓	✓	✓
Physical Approach					
Crayon Use	✓		✓		
Pencil Use		✓ Emerging	✓	✓	✓
Posture		✓ Emerging	✓	✓	✓
Paper Placement			✓	✓	✓
Printing Skills					
Primary Skills					
– Memory	✓	✓	✓	✓	✓
– Orientation	✓	✓	✓	✓	✓
– Start	✓	✓	✓	✓	✓
– Sequence	✓	✓	✓	✓	✓
Secondary Skills					
– Placement		✓ Emerging	✓	✓	✓
– Size		✓ Emerging	✓	✓	✓
– Spacing			✓	✓	✓
Functional Writing					
Letters/Numbers	✓	✓	✓	✓	
Words		✓ Emerging	✓ Short	✓ Short	✓ Long
Sentences			✓ Short	✓ Short	✓ Long
Paragraphs				✓ Short	✓ Long
Writing in All Subjects			✓	✓	✓

*Children in Pre-K are taught lowercase letter recognition and introduced to lowercase letters. They may be taught to write the lowercase letters in their names.

TEACHING GUIDELINES

We have provided teaching guidelines to help you plan your instruction. Units include a set of letters, numbers, and/or writing skills to teach in a developmentally appropriate manner. You have flexibility to stay on a unit until students have success with those skills and are ready to move ahead.

- **UNIT 1:** Readiness & Name
  Frog Jump Capitals: **F E D P B R N M**, Numbers: **1–3**

- **UNIT 2:** Starting Corner Capitals: **H K L U V W X Y Z**, Numbers: **4–7**

- **UNIT 3:** Center Starting Capitals: **C O Q G S A I T J**, Number: **8**

- **UNIT 4:** Lowercase – Same as Capitals and t: **c o s v w – t**,
  Magic c Letters: **a d g**, Numbers **9–10**

- **UNIT 5:** Lowercase – More Vowels: **u i e**, Transition Group: **l k y j**

- **UNIT 6:** Lowercase – Diver Letters: **p r n m h b**, Final Group: **f q x z**

Each of the six units has daily lessons with multisensory activities.
On days that indicate Review/Multisensory, choose one of the activities from pp. 147–179.

When the student edition is complete, maintain good habits with Handwriting All Year Activities. Visit ☺ A Click Away for free Handwriting All Year downloads.

UNIT 1: Capitals F E D P B R N M Numbers 1–3

Unit Summary:

1. Preview **CAPITAL ALPHABET**
2. Teach **NAME**
3. Teach **CAPITALS**
   Frog Jump Capitals   F E D P B R N M
4. Teach **Numbers**   1 2 3

Week	Monday	Tuesday	Wednesday	Thursday	Friday
1	Capitals p. 44 Get Ready! Posture, Paper & Grip pp. 33–39	Help Me Write My Name p. 45	Capitals p. 44 Get Ready! Posture, Paper & Grip pp. 33–39	Help Me Write My Name p. 45 Use template on ☺ A Click Away	Number 1 p. 134 For Educators: pp. 131–133 (teaching numbers)
2	F p. 46-47 (Begin Frog Jump Capitals) For Educators: pp. 41–44 (teaching capitals)	E p. 48	Help Me Write My Name p. 45 Use template on ☺ A Click Away	D p. 49	Number 2 p. 135
3	P p. 50	B p. 51	R p. 52	Help Me Write My Name p. 45 Use template on ☺ A Click Away	Number 3 p. 136
4	N p. 53	M p. 54	Review the letter with a multisensory activity (Select from pp. 147–179).	F E D P B R N M Review p. 55	Review the NUMBERS with a multisensory activity (Select from pp. 147–179).

*Handwriting Without Tears assessment: The Screener of Handwriting Proficiency includes evaluation of children's posture and grip along with capital and lowercase letters. We recommend administering this assessment at the beginning of the year to help drive instruction. You will need 15–20 minutes to prepare for the assessment and 20–30 minutes to administer and score. Full directions can be found on **LWTears.com/screener**.

☺ Handwriting Record **idtt.LWTears.com/ext/TGKSK/2022** (resources section)

UNIT 2: Capitals H K L, U V W X Y Z   Numbers 4–7

Unit Summary:
1. Guide **NAME**
2. Teach **Capitals**
   Starting Corner Capitals   H K L U V W X Y Z
3. Teach **Numbers**   4 5 6 7

Week	Monday	Tuesday	Wednesday	Thursday	Friday
1	H p. 56 (Begin Starting Corner Capitals) **Get Ready! Posture, Paper & Grip** pp. 33–39	K p. 57	L p. 58	Number 4 p. 137	Number 5 p. 138
2	**Help Me Write My Name** p. 45 Use template on ☺ A Click Away	U p. 59	V p. 60	W p. 61	Number 6 p. 139
3	X p. 62	Y p. 63	Z p. 64	Review the Letter Group with a multisensory activity (Select from pp. 147–179). **H, K, L, U, V, W, X, Y** p. 65	Number 7 p. 140

UNIT 3: Capitals C O Q G, S A I T J — Number 8

Unit Summary:

1. Guide **NAME**
2. Teach **CAPITALS**
   Center Starting Capitals   C O Q G S A I T J
3. Teach **Number**   8
4. Review **CAPITAL ALPHABET**

Week	Monday	Tuesday	Wednesday	Thursday	Friday
1	C p. 66 (Begin Center Starting Capitals) **Get Ready! Posture, Paper & Grip** pp. 33–39	O p. 67	Q p. 68	G p. 69	**Help Me Write My Name** p. 128 Use template on ☺ A Click Away
2	S p. 70	A p. 71	I p. 72	T p. 73	Number 8 p. 141
3	J p. 74	Review the Capital Letter Group with a multisensory activity (Select from pp. 147–179).	C, O, Q, G S, A, I, T, J p. 75	**Capitals for Me** p. 76	**Help Me Write My Name** p. 128 Use template on ☺ A Click Away

UNIT 4: Lowercase c o s v w – t, a d g   Numbers 9–10

Unit Summary:

1. Preview **Lowercase Alphabet**

2. Teach **Numbers**   9–10
   Review Numbers   1–10

3. Teach **Lowercase**
   Same as Capitals and t   c o s v w – t
   Magic c Letters   a d g

Week	Monday	Tuesday	Wednesday	Thursday	Friday
1	**Lowercase** p. 83 **For Educators:** pp. 79–82 (teaching lowercase) **Get Ready! Posture, Paper & Grip** pp. 33–39	**Lowercase** p. 83 **Hand Activity** p. 175	c p. 84 (Begin Same as Capitals and t)	**Words C c** p. 85	Number 9 p. 142
2	o p. 86	**Words O o** p. 87	s p. 88	**Sentences S s** p. 89 **Sentence Song** p. 178	Number 10 p. 143
3	v p. 90	w p. 91	t p. 92	**Sentences T t** p. 93	**Numbers on the Slate Chalkboard** p. 132
4	a p. 94 **Words A a** p. 95 (Begin Magic c Letters)	d p. 96	**Words D d** p. 97	g p. 98	**Words G g** p. 99

UNIT 5: Lowercase u i e, l k y j

Unit Summary:

1. Teach **Name in Title Case**

2. Teach **Lowercase**
   Vowels   u i e
   Transition Group   l k y j

Week	Monday	Tuesday	Wednesday	Thursday	Friday
1	u p. 100 (Begin vowels) **Get Ready! Posture, Paper & Grip** pp. 33–39	Words U u p. 101	i p. 102	Words I i p. 103	Help Me Write My Name in Title Case ☺ A Click Away For Educators: pp. 79–82 (teaching lowercase)
2	e p. 104	Words E e p. 105	Review the Letters with a multisensory activity (Select from pp. 147–179).	l p. 106 (Begin Transition Group)	k p. 107
3	y p. 108	Sentences Y y p. 109 **Sentence Song** p. 178	j p. 110	Review the Letters with a multisensory activity (Select from pp. 147–179).	Help Me Write My Name in Title Case ☺ A Click Away

UNIT 6: Lowercase p r n m h b, f q x z

Unit Summary:

1. Guide **Name in Title Case**

2. Teach **Lowercase**
   Diver Letters   p r n m h b
   Final Group   f q x z

Week	Monday	Tuesday	Wednesday	Thursday	Friday
1	p p. 111 (Begin Diver Letters) **Get Ready! Posture, Paper & Grip** pp. 33–39	r p. 112	Sentences R r p. 113 **Sentence Song** p. 178	n p. 114	Help Me Write My Name in Title Case ☺ A Click Away For Educators: pp. 79–82 (teaching lowercase)
2	Words N n p. 115	m p. 116	Words M m p. 117	h p. 118	Words H h p. 119
3	b p. 120	Words B b p. 121	f p. 122 (Begin Final Group)	Words F f p. 123	Help Me Write My Name in Title Case ☺ A Click Away
4	q p. 124	x p. 125	z p. 126	Sentences Z z p. 127	Congratulations! – Name p. 128

GET READY! POSTURE, PAPER & GRIP

Grip is one of the foundations of handwriting. Children need to hold and use a pencil correctly (Dennis and Swinth 2001). We've planned pre-writing and grip guidelines for you so your students will be ready to learn and engage through three-dimensional, musical, joyful learning that supports your teaching all year long.

To make sure children are ready to learn, begin the year with readiness activities that focus on pre-writing and pencil grip. The proper grip will develop the hand muscles and build the fine motor skills that are needed for successful handwriting. We begin with simple kinesthetic activities and work toward seated writing practice.

In this section, we include activities to develop, promote, and solidify good habits for grip and posture.

- Paper Placement & Pencil Grip

- The Correct Grip

- Picking Up My Pencil

- Grasping Grip

Preparing for Paper & Pencil

THREE EASY STEPS

When it comes to handwriting, children must be taught everything, including how to sit, position the paper, and hold a pencil. This is the physical approach to handwriting. Sometimes it's the physical approach, not the letters and numbers, that causes a child to struggle with handwriting. Think of it like playing a musical instrument; if you don't know how to position yourself and hold the instrument correctly, how can you play beautiful music? The same is true with writing letters and numbers. The ability to position yourself and hold your pencil correctly has a lot to do with being able to write legibly.

Important questions:
- What affects children's posture?
- How should the paper be placed?
- What is the secret to a good pencil grip?

STEP 1 – POSTURE

Does the furniture fit? The right size and style of chair and desk affect school performance. Children don't come in a standard size. Check that every child can sit with feet flat on the floor and arms resting comfortably. Children who sit on their feet often will lose stability in their upper torso. On the following page, we show you how good posture can be fun. We have a secret for getting children to stop sitting on their feet.

STEP 2 – PAPER PLACEMENT

There's a misconception that people should slant their paper to make slanted writing. Not true. In fact, we slant paper so that it fits the natural arc of the forearm. Children who slant their papers properly can write faster because the arm moves naturally with the paper.

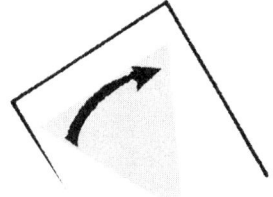

STEP 3 – GRASPING GRIP

The most important thing to understand about pencil grip is it doesn't develop naturally—it is learned. Based on our years of experience helping children, we developed our own theories about how to develop good pencil grip habits effectively. Because children are born imitators, demonstration will lead to success.

On the next few pages, you will find fun strategies to help you teach posture, paper, and pencil skills.

Stomp Your Feet

Stomping is fun and really works because it keep students' feet on the floor and parallel in front of them. The arm movements make their trunks straight. The noise lets them release energy, but it's under your control. When you have them stop stomping, they'll have good posture and be ready to pay attention. Use "Stomp Your Feet" a few times a day.

Materials
- "Stomp Your Feet" from *Rock, Rap, Tap & Learn* music album

Activity

1. Sit down and show the children how to stomp their feet and wave their arms.
2. Have them shout, "Na, na, naaaah, na, na naaah," with you as they wave and stomp.
3. Have children push and pull their hands. Have them hug themselves.
4. End by having children raise their shoulders up, pull shoulders back, and let them down.

Push palms

Pull hands

Hug yourself tightly

Raise shoulders

Pull shoulders back

Let them down

ENRICHMENT
 Video Lesson: View "Stomp Your Feet" at **idtt.LWTears.com/ext/TGKSK/2022**

SUPPORT/ELL
While doing the motions, say the words out loud: "stomping," "pulling," "pushing."

Paper Placement & Pencil Grip

PLACE THE PAPER

How do you position paper correctly? Some children may lean over in an awkward position to write. Children who put their paper in front of them and slant it properly can write more efficiently because they position their arms naturally with the paper. You need to teach them how to place their papers appropriately. Have your students turn to p. 6 in *Kick Start Kindergarten*, and teach them how to slant their papers for their handedness.

Children who are able to print sentences across the page are ready to tilt the paper at a slight angle to follow the natural arc of the writing hand. The correct way to tilt the paper is easy to remember (see illustrations below). For right-handed children, put the right corner higher; for left-handed children, put the left corner higher. The writing hand is below the line of writing. This practice encourages a correct, neutral wrist position.

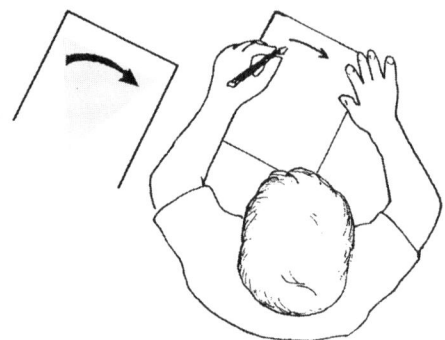
Left-Handed Students

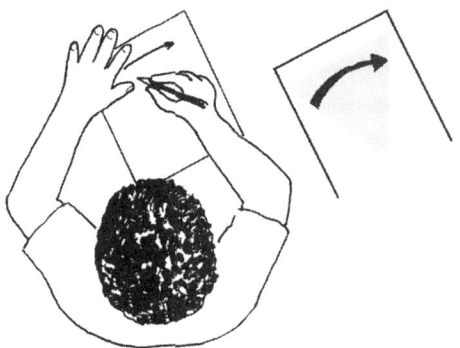
Right-Handed Students

LOOKING OUT FOR LEFTIES

 You might observe some left-handed children slanting their papers too much. They do this to prevent their wrists from hooking. Allow them to exaggerate the slant on their papers if it doesn't cause speed or neatness trouble. Visit **idtt.LWTears.com/ext/TGKSK/2022** for more information about the left-handed writing position.

Cross Strokes

When writing, we typically travel from top to bottom and left to right. At times, left-handed children may choose to cross letters by pulling their writing hand from right to left. This is natural. Model it for them in their student editions for the letters below.

Mark arrows → for right-handed students. Mark arrows ← for left-handed students.

A E F G H I J T - f t

The Correct Grip

The standard way for children to hold their pencil is illustrated below. If you write using a grip that is different than tripod or quadropod, alter your grip for classroom demonstration.

Tripod Grip
Standard grip:
Hold pencil with
thumb + index finger.
Pencil rests on middle finger.

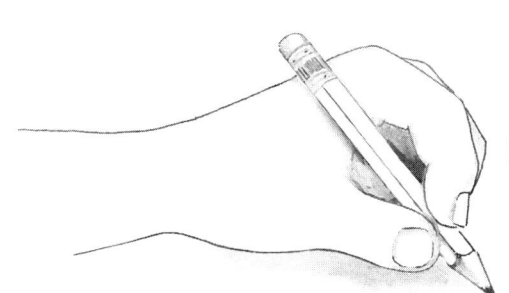
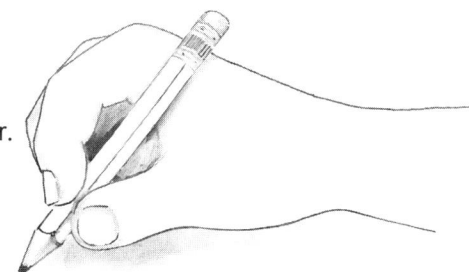

Quadropod Grip
Alternate grip: Hold pencil with
thumb + index and middle fingers.
Pencil rests on ring finger.

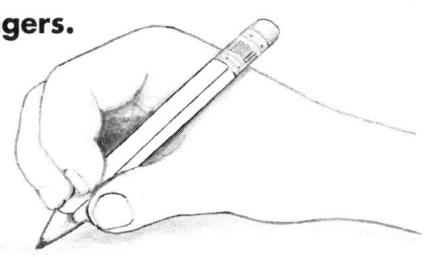

A Note About Pencil Size

Start by using golf-size pencils. As children gain handwriting experience, their control will improve. Typically, as children gain more control in first grade, they will be ready for a standard-size pencil.

Flip the Pencil Trick
Here is another method that someone introduced to us at a workshop. It's such fun that we love to share it. Children like to do it and it puts the pencil in the correct position. (Illustrated for right-handed students.)

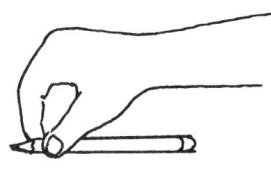

Place pencil on table pointing away from you. Pinch the pencil on the paint where the paint meets the wood.

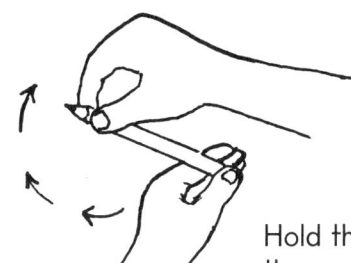

Hold the eraser and twirl the pencil around.

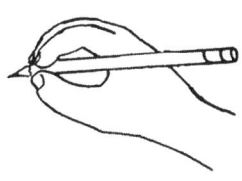

Voilà! Correct grip.

Picking Up My Pencil

Use this song from the *Rock, Rap, Tap & Learn* music album to make your pencil grip lessons more memorable. You sing the first verse, and students will join in the second.

Materials
- "Picking Up My Pencil" from *Rock, Rap, Tap & Learn* music album

Activity

1. Listen to "Picking Up My Pencil" as background music a few times with your students.
2. For fun, review the names of the pencil grip fingers: thumb, pointer, tall man (middle finger).
3. Without the music, sing and demonstrate the first verse.
4. In the second verse, children will sing with you. They pick up their pencils, check their own grip, and their neighbor's too.

Note: The fast pace of the song is to encourage students to pick up the tune quickly, and to inspire them to sing it on their own.

ENRICHMENT

 Additional practice for Pencil Pickups

SUPPORT/ELL

If a child struggles to position the pencil, place it in their fingers correctly. Name their fingers as you position them on the pencil.

Grasping Grip

Educators often have questions about pencil grip, such as why awkward pencil grips happen and how to correct them. We seldom hear about how to prevent them. A good pencil grip does not develop naturally. In fact, several factors affect how a child learns to hold a pencil correctly. Below are 10 things we often think about regarding grip:

1. **Experiences**
   We develop pencil grip habits while we are young. Children who are encouraged to feed themselves have more fine motor experiences than those who are spoon fed. Those who have early self-feeding experiences may have an easier time learning how to hold their crayons and pencils.

2. **Toys**
   Today's toys are very different from those with which we grew up. We should always encourage and remind families about non-battery operated toys because they help build hand strength.

3. **Imitation**
   Children are born imitators. When they are watching you write, always demonstrate a correct grip because they tend to do as you do.

4. **Early Instruction**
   Help children place their fingers. Teach Pre-K children and kindergartners their finger names and finger jobs and show them how their fingers should hold writing tools.

5. **Tool Size**
   Choose appropriate writing tools. We prefer little tools: Little Sponge Cubes, Little Chalk Bits, FLIP Crayons®, and Pencils for Little Hands. These tools promote using the finger tips naturally. Big tools elicit a fisted grip; little tools, a more mature grip. As adults, we write with pencils that are in proportion to our hands. Children should do the same.

6. **Timing**
   It is difficult to correct the grips of older children because we have to re-teach their motor patterns. Older children need time to get used to a new way of holding a pencil. It takes repetition, persistence, and practice.

7. **Blanket Rules**
   Avoid blanket rules about pencil grip devices. Some devices may work for a child. If they are motivating and work, use them. Use grip devices as a last resort and use them for older children who understand their purpose.

8. **Acceptance**
   Some awkward pencil grips are functional. If the child is comfortable and doesn't have speed or legibility issues, let it go.

9. **Joints**
   We are all made differently. Some of us have joints that are more relaxed. Therefore, expect slight variations in what is considered a standard grip. If a child is unable to use a standard grip, you may consider an altered grip.

10. **Summer**
    This is the perfect time to change an awkward grip. Take advantage of the child's down time to create new habits.

CAPITALS

Capitals are big, bold, and important. They deserve a very important place in developing strong handwriting skills. Teachers agree and task analysis shows that capitals are easier to learn than lowercase letters (NAEYC and IRA 1998).

We teach developmentally, so we teach capitals first. We teach capital letters as a group, separate from lowercase. Instead of teaching 52 letter symbols with a mishmash of different sizes, positions, and confusing starting places, we divide and conquer. We cut the learning task in half and begin with 26—not 52—letters.

In this section, children will:

- Build good habits for capital letter formation in a developmentally appropriate sequence

- Be provided with ways to enrich or support each lesson

We have carefully planned the curriculum to help you develop strong handwriting skills for every child, from the very first lesson.

Developmental Teaching

HANDWRITING SKILL PROGRESSION

When children learn to write their capitals, they develop a strong foundation for printing. Children learn to:
- Start letters at the top.
- Use the correct stroke sequence to form letters.
- Orient letters and numbers correctly—no reversals!

When capitals are taught first, learning lowercase letters is a breeze. Think about it: **c**, **o**, **s**, **v**, **w**, and **x**, **y**, and **z** are the same as their capitals; **j**, **k**, **t**, **p**, and **u** are also similar to their capital partners. If we teach capitals correctly, we have already prepared children for nearly half of the lowercase alphabet.

Some capitals are developmentally easier to write than others. Children gradually develop the ability to copy forms in a predictable order (Gesell 1940).

| up to 3 years old | up to 4 years old | up to 6 years old |

Developmental Analysis – Capitals Vs. Lowercase Letters

This is the capital/lowercase analysis that informs our developmental teaching order.

Capital Letters Are Easy
- All start at the top.
- All are the same height.
- All occupy the same vertical space.
- All are easy to recognize and identify (compare **A**, **B**, **D**, **G**, **P**, **Q** with **a**, **b**, **d**, **g**, **p**, **q**).
- All are big, bold, and familiar.

Lowercase Letters Are More Difficult
- Lowercase letters start in four different places (**a**, **b**, **e**, **f**).
- Lowercase letters are not all the same size:
    - 14 letters are half the size of capitals.
    - 12 are the same size as capitals.
- Lowercase letters occupy three different vertical positions: small, tall, descending.
- Lowercase letters are more difficult to recognize because of subtle differences (**a**, **b**, **d**, **g**, **p**, **q**).

Let's Do the Math

You can see at a glance that capitals are easier for children. Students have fewer chances to make mistakes when they write capital letters. They aim their pencil at the top and get it right. With lowercase, there are many more variables.

CAPITAL & LOWERCASE LETTER ANALYSIS		
	Capitals	Lowercase
Start	1	4
Size	1	2
Position	1	3
Appearance	• Familiar • Distinctive A, B, D, G, P, Q	• Many similar • Easy to confuse a, b, d, g, p, q

Student Edition Design

USING THE *KICK START KINDERGARTEN* STUDENT EDITION

Our student editions use child-friendly language and large step-by-step models to promote excellence and efficient, effective practice for each letter.

Kick Start Kindergarten is divided into three major sections: Capitals, Lowercase Letters, and Numbers. The sections also include word and sentence activities that combine letter practice with age-appropriate language arts activities.

Capital Letter & Word Pages

Our capital letter pages show large step-by-step instructions for letter formation with Wood Pieces and on the Slate Chalkboard. Capital letters are explained to children using real world examples of capitals. Children practice forming capital letters on Gray Blocks to prevent reversals.

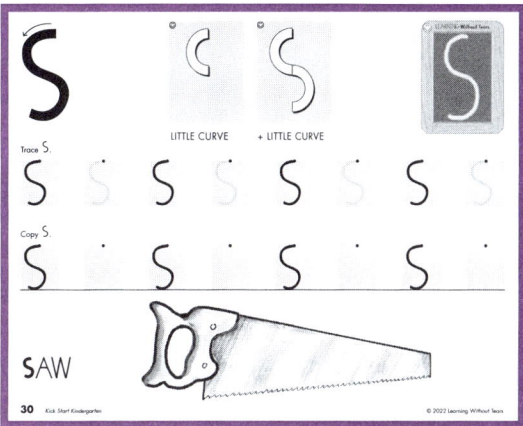

Gray Blocks and Simple Spatial Organization

We begin by teaching capital letters and numbers with Gray Blocks to prevent reversals and help children learn how to place letters and numbers. Our simple letter and number teaching strategies are reversal-proof and enable children to form letters and numbers correctly.

When children are learning to print, they need extra room to write. Many student editions and worksheets are poorly designed, requiring students to cram their words into spaces that are too small. Our landscape style student editions give them space to write and develop good spacing habits.

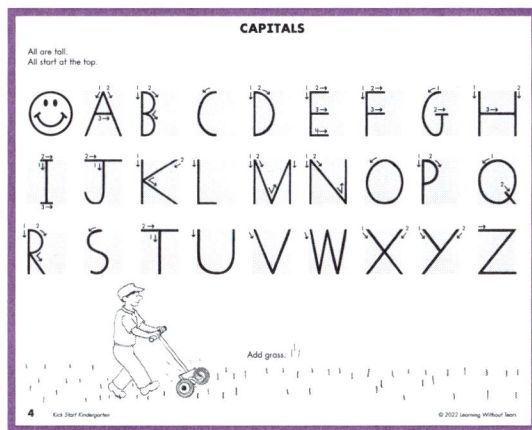

Capital Teaching Order

DEVELOPMENTAL TEACHING ORDER

The Handwriting Without Tears® teaching order is planned to help children learn handwriting skills in the easiest, most efficient way. It's also developmentally planned to start with a review of the easy letters: the capitals. They are the first letters children should learn. Your kindergartners may know them, but you want to be sure they print them correctly. The capital teaching order will help you teach:

1. Correct formation: All capitals start at the top. Strokes are made in the correct sequence.
2. Correct orientation: No reversals.

To do this, start by teaching letters in groups on Gray Blocks:

Frog Jump Capitals

Starting Corner Capitals

Center Starting Capitals

These letters start at the top left corner with a Big Line on the left. When the first line is on the left, the next part of the letter is on the right side. This prevents reversals and teaches good stroke habits.

Reviewing these letters ensures that children start at the top left and use the left-to-right formation habit. The good habits children form with **U, V, W, X, Y, Z** will carry over to **u, v, w, x, y, z**.

C, O, Q, G start with a Magic C stroke. The good habits children learn here with **C, O, S, T, J** will make learning **c, o, s, t, j** much easier. There will be no problems with stroke direction or reversals.

Help Me Write My Name

Objective

To write name in capitals with correct formation.

LESSON INTRODUCTION (Warm Up)

Sign In, Please (p. 151)

Additional digital resources are available in the Interactive Digital Teaching Tool (IDTT).

LESSON PLAN

1. Direction Instruction (Demo)

Demonstrate child's name on Gray Blocks. Say the step-by-step formations for each letter. Model one letter at a time.

 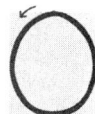  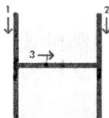  

2. Guided Practice

Draw a starting dot for each letter. Children copy one letter at a time.

3. Check Name

Monitor as children write their names for correct start and steps.

READ, COLOR & DRAW

Pencil Pick-Ups: Have children use appropriate grip for adding stars. Encourage free coloring and drawing.

ENRICHMENT

Have children practice writing their names on Gray Block paper.

SUPPORT/ELL

 Help Me Write My Name. Remind families to model one letter at a time.

CROSS-CURRICULAR CONNECTIONS

Language Arts: Identify and discuss the names of all the children in the class.

Frog Jump Capitals

Kick Start Kindergarten – p. 6

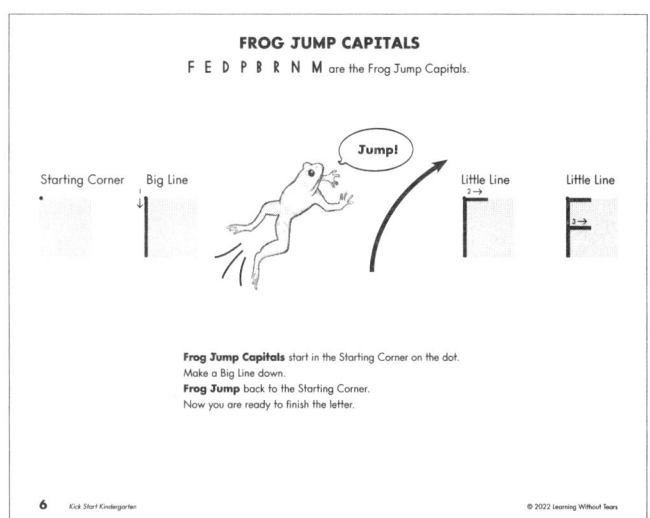

Objective
To learn the steps for writing Frog Jump Capitals: **F, E, D, P, B, R, N,** and **M**.

LESSON INTRODUCTION (Warm Up)
Positions and Body Parts with Wood Pieces (p. 158)

Additional digital resources are available in the Interactive Digital Teaching Tool (IDTT).

LESSON PLAN

1. Direction Instruction (Demo)
Demonstrate **F** on the Slate Chalkboard or Gray Blocks.
Say the words for each step.

Lesson F:

Start in the Starting Corner | Big Line down | Frog Jump | Little Line across the top | Little Line across the middle

2. Guided Practice
Children finger trace step-by-step models on the page while saying the words.

3. Check Letter
Monitor to see if they follow the steps and finger trace **F** correctly.

ENRICHMENT
Have children point to the top of the Frog Jump Capitals as you discuss starting all capitals at the top.

SUPPORT/ELL
Jump! Have students crouch down and jump when you say, jump! Add a "ribbit" for fun.

CROSS-CURRICULAR CONNECTIONS
Science: A frog's back legs are big and strong for jumping. Find other facts about frogs as a class.

p. 7   F

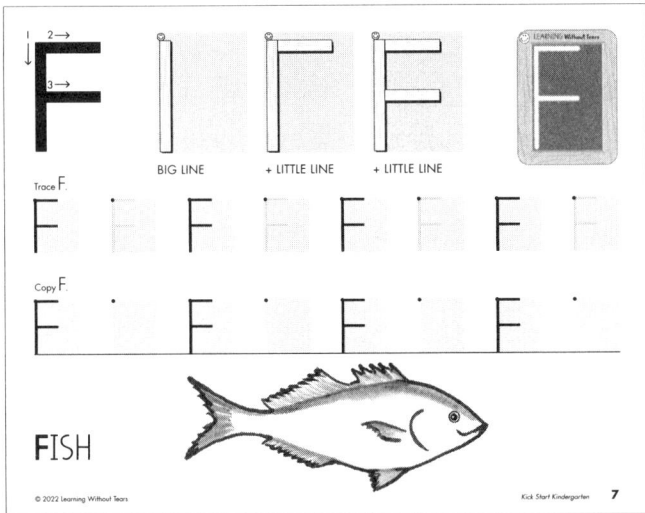

OBJECTIVE
To develop correct habits for writing capital **F**.

LESSON INTRODUCTION (Warm Up)
Capital Letter Cards for Wood Pieces (p. 161)

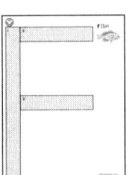

> Additional digital resources are available in the Interactive Digital Teaching Tool (IDTT).

LESSON PLAN

1. Direction Instruction (Demo)

Demonstrate **F** on the Slate Chalkboard or Gray Blocks.
Say the words for each step.

Lesson F:

Start in the Starting Corner   Big Line down   Frog Jump   Little Line across the top   Little Line across the middle

2. Guided Practice

Children finger trace step-by-step models on the page while saying the words.
Children trace **F**.
Children copy **F**.

3. Check Letter

Monitor as children trace and copy letters for correct start and steps.

READ, COLOR & DRAW

Read FISH. Say **F** and make the /f/ sound. Encourage free coloring and drawing. Add water, other fish, etc.

ENRICHMENT
Ask children to locate capital **F** in the classroom, on a label, or in a book.

SUPPORT/ELL
Have children make a Frog Jumps after the Big Line. Say "ribbit" when it's time to jump to the top.

CROSS-CURRICULAR CONNECTIONS
Science: Compare and contrast frogs and fish. Discuss the characteristics of amphibians and fish.

E

Kick Start Kindergarten – p. 8

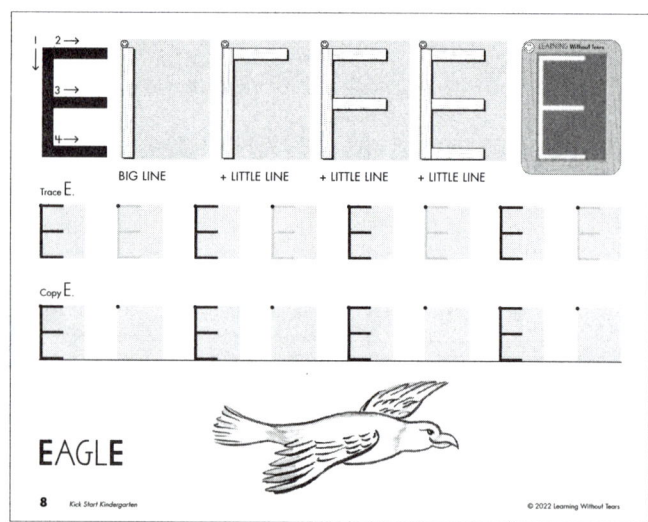

OBJECTIVE
To develop correct habits for writing capital **E**.

LESSON INTRODUCTION (Warm Up)
Capitals on the Mat for Wood Pieces (p. 162)

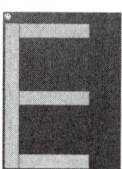

Additional digital resources are available in the Interactive Digital Teaching Tool (IDTT).

LESSON PLAN

1. Direction Instruction (Demo)

Demonstrate **E** on the Slate Chalkboard or Gray Blocks.
Say the words for each step.

Lesson E:

Start in the Starting Corner | Big Line down | Frog Jump | Little Line across the top | Little Line across the middle | Little Line across the bottom

2. Guided Practice

Children finger trace step-by-step models on the page while saying the words.
Children trace **E**.
Children copy **E**.

3. Check Letter

Monitor as children trace and copy letters for correct start and steps.

READ, COLOR & DRAW

Letter **E** makes two sounds. Stretch long /e/ at the beginning of eagle. Stretch short /e/ at the beginning of edge.

ENRICHMENT

Have children identify capital **E** in an EXIT sign. Look for other signs/words with capital **E**.

SUPPORT/ELL

Have children practice top, middle, and bottom positions with Wood Pieces (p. 158).

CROSS-CURRICULAR CONNECTIONS

Social Studies: Bring in a picture book about eagles. Explain that the bald eagle is the national emblem of the USA.

p. 9   D

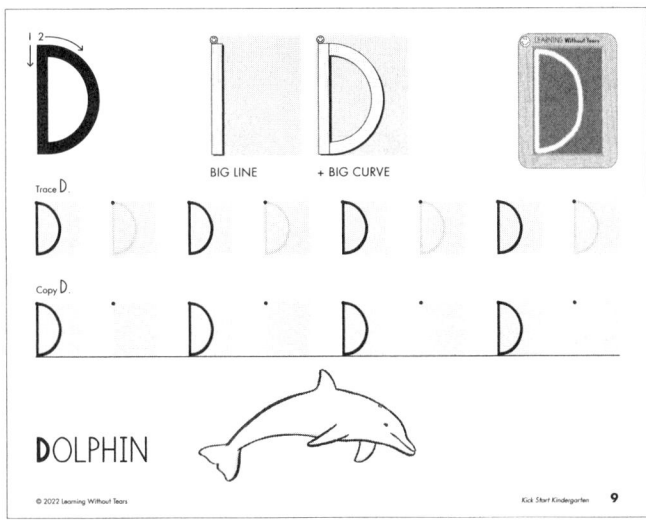

OBJECTIVE
To develop correct habits for writing capital **D**.

LESSON INTRODUCTION (Warm Up)
Wet-Dry-Try on Slate Chalkboard (p. 154)

> Additional digital resources are available in the Interactive Digital Teaching Tool (IDTT).

LESSON PLAN

1. Direction Instruction (Demo)

Demonstrate **D** on the Slate Chalkboard or Gray Blocks. Say the words for each step.

Lesson D:

   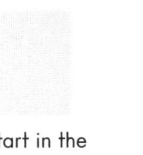      D

Start in the Starting Corner   Big Line down   Frog Jump   Big Curve to the bottom

2. Guided Practice

Children finger trace step-by-step models on the page while saying the words.
Children trace **D**.
Children copy **D**.

3. Check Letter

Monitor as children trace and copy letters for correct start and steps.

READ, COLOR & DRAW

Read DOLPHIN. Say **D** and make the /d/ sound. Encourage free coloring and drawing. Add water, other dolphin, etc.

ENRICHMENT
D is for day. Let children say "day" after you start saying the days of the week: Mon___, Tues___, etc.

SUPPORT/ELL
If children are not ready to copy letters, write the them with a highlighter in Gray Blocks, so children can trace.

CROSS-CURRICULAR CONNECTIONS
Science: Compare dolphins and sharks. Create a class pictograph to illustrate the class favorite.

P

Kick Start Kindergarten – p. 10

OBJECTIVE

To develop correct habits for writing capital **P**.

LESSON INTRODUCTION (Warm Up)

"Frog Jump Capitals" from *Rock, Rap, Tap & Learn* music album

Additional digital resources are available in the Interactive Digital Teaching Tool (IDTT).

LESSON PLAN

1. Direction Instruction (Demo)

Demonstrate **P** on the Slate Chalkboard or Gray Blocks.
Say the words for each step.

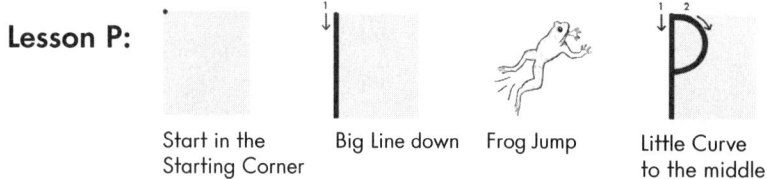

Lesson P: Start in the Starting Corner / Big Line down / Frog Jump / Little Curve to the middle

2. Guided Practice

Children finger trace step-by-step models on the page while saying the words.
Children trace **P**.
Children copy **P**.

3. Check Letter

Monitor as children trace and copy letters for correct start and steps.

READ, COLOR & DRAW

Read PIG. Say **P** and make the /p/ sound. Encourage free coloring and drawing. Add a barn, grass, etc.

ENRICHMENT

Have children gather the Wood Pieces they need before they make capitals **F**, **E**, **D**, or **P** on the Mat. Ask, "What do you need for **F**?"

SUPPORT/ELL

Make **P** with Wood Pieces. Show children how the Little Curve ends in the middle.

CROSS-CURRICULAR CONNECTIONS

Language Arts: Show children how capital **P** makes a /p/ sound. What other words have a /p/ sound?

p. 11   B

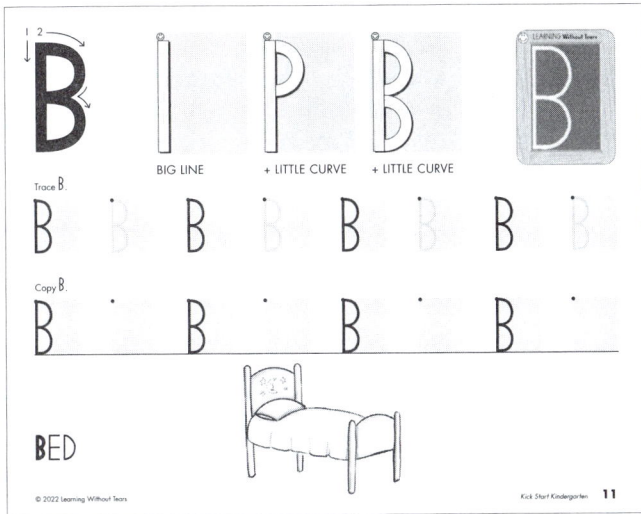

OBJECTIVE
To develop correct habits for writing capital **B**.

LESSON INTRODUCTION (Warm Up)
Capital Letter Cards for Wood Pieces (p. 161)

Additional digital resources are available in the Interactive Digital Teaching Tool (IDTT).

LESSON PLAN

1. Direction Instruction (Demo)
Demonstrate **B** on the Slate Chalkboard or Gray Blocks.
Say the words for each step.

Lesson B: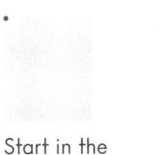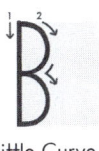

Start in the Starting Corner | Big Line down | Frog Jump | Little Curve to the middle | Little Curve to the bottom

2. Guided Practice
Children finger trace step-by-step models on the page while saying the words.
Children trace **B**.
Children copy **B**.

3. Check Letter
Monitor as children trace and copy letters for correct start and steps.

READ, COLOR & DRAW
Read BED. Say **B** and make the /b/ sound. Encourage free coloring and drawing. Add person, toys, dresser, etc.

ENRICHMENT
 Alphabet Show and Tell

SUPPORT/ELL
Use Wet-Dry-Try (p. 164) to demonstrate how the Little Curves in capital **B** are the same size.

CROSS-CURRICULAR CONNECTIONS
Language Arts/Math: Read *5 Little Monkeys Jumping on a Bed* by Eileen Christelow. Discuss story. Have children practice counting to five.

R

Kick Start Kindergarten – p. 12

OBJECTIVE
To develop correct habits for writing capital **R**.

LESSON INTRODUCTION (Warm Up)
Capitals on the Mat for Wood Pieces (p. 162)

Additional digital resources are available in the Interactive Digital Teaching Tool (IDTT).

LESSON PLAN

1. Direction Instruction (Demo)
Demonstrate **R** on the Slate Chalkboard or Gray Blocks. Say the words for each step.

Lesson R:

 Start in the Starting Corner

 Big Line down

Frog Jump

 Little Curve to the middle

 Little Line slides down

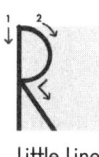

2. Guided Practice
Children finger trace step-by-step models on the page while saying the words.
Children trace **R**.
Children copy **R**.

3. Check Letter
Monitor as children trace and copy letters for correct start and steps.

READ, COLOR & DRAW
Read RAINBOW. Say **R** and make the /r/ sound. Encourage free coloring and drawing. Add clouds, raindrops, etc.

ENRICHMENT
Encourage observation. Red is the top color on a rainbow. Red is also the top color on a traffic signal.

SUPPORT/ELL
Have children make capital **R** with sand or shaving cream in a tray with a smiley face in the top left corner to indicate starting position.

CROSS-CURRICULAR CONNECTIONS
Arts: Mix red and yellow to make orange. Mix blue and yellow to make green.

p. 13

OBJECTIVE
To develop correct habits for writing capital **N**.

LESSON INTRODUCTION (Warm Up)
Vertical, Horizontal, and Diagonal Positions with Wood Pieces (p. 158)

Additional digital resources are available in the Interactive Digital Teaching Tool (IDTT).

LESSON PLAN

1. Direction Instruction (Demo)
Demonstrate **N** on the Slate Chalkboard or Gray Blocks. Say the words for each step.

Lesson N:

  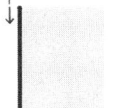  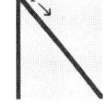 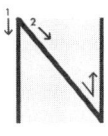

Start in the Starting Corner | Big Line down | Frog Jump | Slide down | Big Line up

2. Guided Practice
Children finger trace step-by-step models on the page while saying the words.
Children trace **N**.
Children copy **N**.

3. Check Letter
Monitor as children trace and copy letters for correct start and steps.

READ, COLOR & DRAW
Read NEST. Say **N** and make the /n/ sound. Encourage free coloring and drawing. Add eggs, a bird etc.

ENRICHMENT
Call out the letter that makes the /n/ sound and have children write it on Gray Block Paper.

SUPPORT/ELL
Use a highlighter on student edition page for children to trace capital **N**.

CROSS-CURRICULAR CONNECTIONS
Science: Discuss how and why birds build a nest. Look at pictures of different nests.

M

Kick Start Kindergarten – p. 14

OBJECTIVE
To develop correct habits for writing capital **M**.

LESSON INTRODUCTION (Warm Up)
Digital Letter and Number Formations (p. 172)

Additional digital resources are available in the Interactive Digital Teaching Tool (IDTT).

LESSON PLAN

1. Direction Instruction (Demo)

Demonstrate **M** on the Slate Chalkboard or Gray Blocks.
Say the words for each step.

Lesson M:

 Start in the Starting Corner
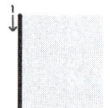 Big Line down
 Frog Jump
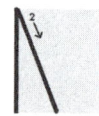 Slide down to the middle
 Slide up
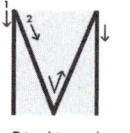 Big Line down

2. Guided Practice

Children finger trace step-by-step models on the page while saying the words.
Children trace **M**.
Children copy **M**.

3. Check Letter

Monitor as children trace and copy letters for correct start and steps.

READ, COLOR & DRAW

Read MONKEY. Say **M** and make the /m/ sound. Encourage free coloring and drawing. Add bananas, a tree, etc.

ENRICHMENT
Have children write the word "ME" and draw a picture of themselves.

SUPPORT/ELL
Have four children make capital **M** with their bodies.

CROSS-CURRICULAR CONNECTIONS
Language Arts: Read *Curious George* by H.A. Rey. Discuss the different situations that George gets into throughout the book.

p. 15

Frog Jump Capitals Review

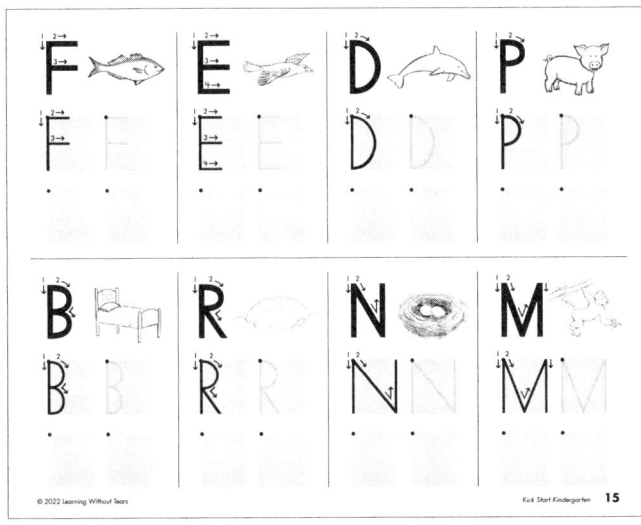

OBJECTIVE
To develop correct habits for writing the Frog Jump Capitals.

LESSON INTRODUCTION (Warm Up)
SONG: "Frog Jump Capitals" from *Rock, Rap, Tap & Learn* music album

Additional digital resources are available in the Interactive Digital Teaching Tool (IDTT).

LESSON PLAN

1. Direction Instruction (Demo)
Demonstrate Frog Jump Capitals on the Slate Chalkboard or Gray Blocks. Say the words for each step.

 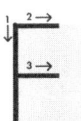 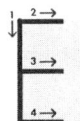     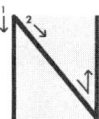 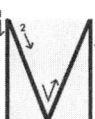

2. Guided Practice
Children trace and copy Frog Jump Capitals.

3. Check Letter
Monitor as children trace and copy letters for correct start and steps.

ENRICHMENT
 Home Link:
Frog Jump Capitals

SUPPORT/ELL
Have children say the directions for each out loud. Children like to "ribbit" for the Frog Jump.

CROSS-CURRICULAR CONNECTIONS
Science: Ask children if the different items on the page belong in the sky, land, or water: fish - water, eagle - sky, etc.

H

Kick Start Kindergarten – p. 16

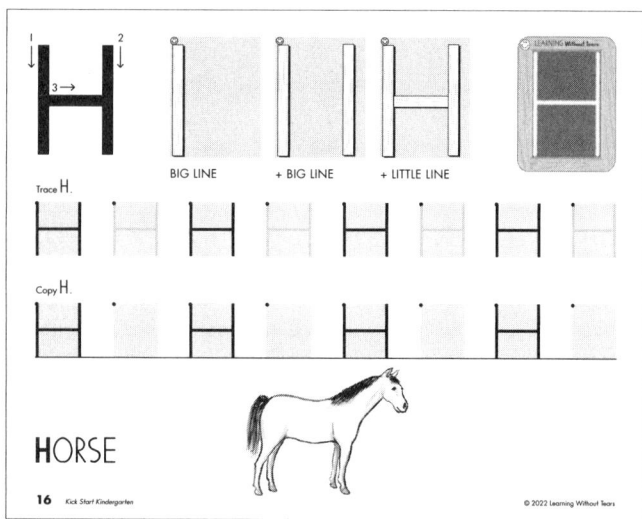

OBJECTIVE
To develop correct habits for writing capital **H**.

LESSON INTRODUCTION (Warm Up)
Capitals on the Mat for Wood Pieces (p. 162)

Additional digital resources are available in the Interactive Digital Teaching Tool (IDTT).

LESSON PLAN

1. Direction Instruction (Demo)

Demonstrate **H** on the Slate Chalkboard or Gray Blocks.
Say the words for each step.

Lesson H:

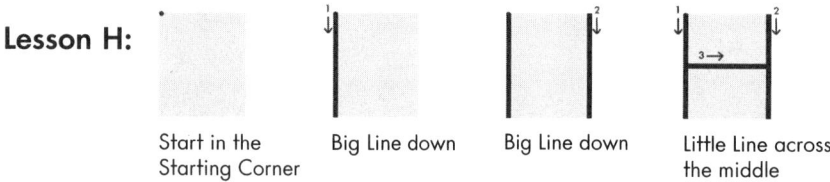

Start in the Starting Corner | Big Line down | Big Line down | Little Line across the middle

2. Guided Practice

Children finger trace step-by-step models on the page while saying the words.
Children trace **H**.
Children copy **H**.

3. Check Letter

Monitor as children trace and copy letters for correct start and steps.

READ, COLOR & DRAW

Read HORSE. Say **H** and make the /h/ sound. Encourage free coloring and drawing. Add a saddle, grass, hay, a carrot to eat, etc.

ENRICHMENT
Call out the letter that makes the /h/ sound and have children write it on Gray Block Paper.

SUPPORT/ELL
Help left-handed students write cross strokes from right to left by guiding their hand.

CROSS-CURRICULAR CONNECTIONS
Math: Bring in a toy horse. Have children count legs, mouth, nose, tails, feet, etc.

OBJECTIVE
To develop correct habits for writing capital **K**.

LESSON INTRODUCTION (Warm Up)
Wet-Dry-Try App for Capitals, Numbers & Lowercase (p. 174)

Additional digital resources are available in the Interactive Digital Teaching Tool (IDTT).

LESSON PLAN

1. Direction Instruction (Demo)
Demonstrate **K** on the Slate Chalkboard or Gray Blocks. Say the words for each step.

Lesson K: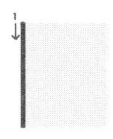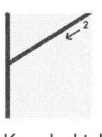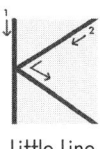

Start in the Starting Corner · Big Line down · Karate kick to the middle · Little Line slides down

2. Guided Practice
Children finger trace step-by-step models on the page while saying the words.
Children trace **K**.
Children copy **K**.

3. Check Letter
Monitor as children trace and copy letters for correct start and steps.

READ, COLOR & DRAW
Read KITE. Say **K** and make the /k/ sound. Encourage free coloring and drawing. Add more kites, clouds, sky, sun, etc.

ENRICHMENT
Have children make the capital **K** out of pipe cleaners.

SUPPORT/ELL
Build capital **K** with Wood Pieces to reinforce the little diagonal lines of **K**.

CROSS-CURRICULAR CONNECTIONS
Arts/Language Arts: Make paper kites and have students describe their kites.

L

Kick Start Kindergarten – p. 18

OBJECTIVE
To develop correct habits for writing capital **L**.

LESSON INTRODUCTION (Warm Up)
Capital Letter Cards for Wood Pieces (p. 161)

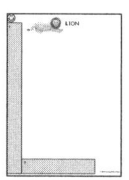

Additional digital resources are available in the Interactive Digital Teaching Tool (IDTT).

LESSON PLAN

1. Direction Instruction (Demo)
Demonstrate **L** on the Slate Chalkboard or Gray Blocks. Say the words for each step.

Lesson L:

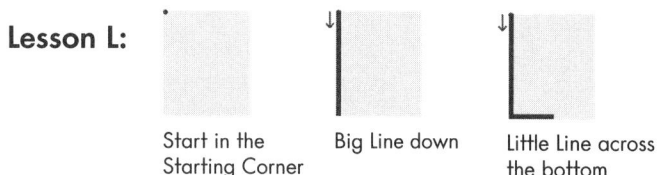

Start in the Starting Corner | Big Line down | Little Line across the bottom

2. Guided Practice
Children finger trace step-by-step models on the page while saying the words.
Children trace **L**.
Children copy **L**.

3. Check Letter
Monitor as children trace and copy letters for correct start and steps.

READ, COLOR & DRAW
Read LION. Say **L** and make the /l/ sound. Encourage free coloring and drawing. Add grass, hills, dirt, etc.

ENRICHMENT
Have children finger trace capital **L** on top of a book: down and across.

SUPPORT/ELL
If children lift up the Little Line of **L**, remind them to come to a full stop before writing the Little Line.

CROSS-CURRICULAR CONNECTIONS
Science: Discuss how lions are kings of the jungle. Discuss other animals you would find in the jungle.

p. 19

OBJECTIVE
To develop correct habits for writing capital **U**.

LESSON INTRODUCTION (Warm Up)
Digital Letter and Number Formations (p. 172)

Additional digital resources are available in the Interactive Digital Teaching Tool (IDTT).

LESSON PLAN

1. Direction Instruction (Demo)

Demonstrate **U** on the Slate Chalkboard or Gray Blocks.
Say the words for each step.

Lesson U: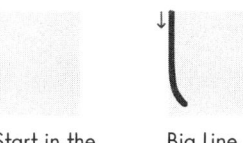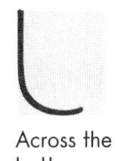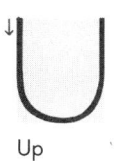

Start in the Starting Corner | Big Line, turn | Across the bottom | Up

2. Guided Practice

Children finger trace step-by-step models on the page while saying the words.
Children trace **U**.
Children copy **U**.

3. Check Letter

Monitor as children trace and copy letters for correct start and steps.

READ, COLOR & DRAW

Read UNICORN. Say **U** and make the /u/ sound. Encourage free coloring and drawing. Add clouds, sun and rainbow, etc.

ENRICHMENT
Have children trace capital **U** on a tray with salt or sand by going down, under, and up.

SUPPORT/ELL
Do not make capital **U** with Wood Pieces because it ends up an odd shape and size. Instead tell a Letter Story: **U** go down, **U** walk on the bottom, and **U** go up.

CROSS-CURRICULAR CONNECTIONS
Language Arts: Read *Where the Wild Things Are* by Maurice Sendak. While reading, discuss why the book is a fantasy.

V

Kick Start Kindergarten – p. 20

OBJECTIVE
To develop correct habits for writing capital **V**.

LESSON INTRODUCTION (Warm Up)
Capitals on the Mat for Wood Pieces (p. 162)

Additional digital resources are available in the Interactive Digital Teaching Tool (IDTT).

LESSON PLAN

1. Direction Instruction (Demo)

Demonstrate **V** on the Slate Chalkboard or Gray Blocks.
Say the words for each step.

Lesson V:

 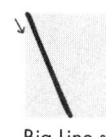 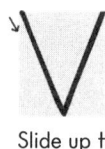

Start in the Starting Corner   Big Line slides down to the middle   Slide up to the corner

2. Guided Practice

Children finger trace step-by-step models on the page while saying the words.
Children trace **V**.
Children copy **V**.

3. Check Letter

Monitor as children trace and copy letters for correct start and steps.

READ, COLOR & DRAW

Read VOLCANO. Say **V** and make the /v/ sound. Encourage free coloring and drawing. Add rocks and lava, etc.

ENRICHMENT
Bring in popsicle sticks and have children form **V**, then write **V** on Gray Block Paper.

SUPPORT/ELL
Show children how **V** needs a sharp point at the bottom or people will think it's a **U**. Use your hands to make **V** and have children imitate.

CROSS-CURRICULAR CONNECTIONS
Science: Have children make their own volcanoes. Fill a plastic bottle with half water, half vinegar and then one teaspoon of baking soda.

p. 21

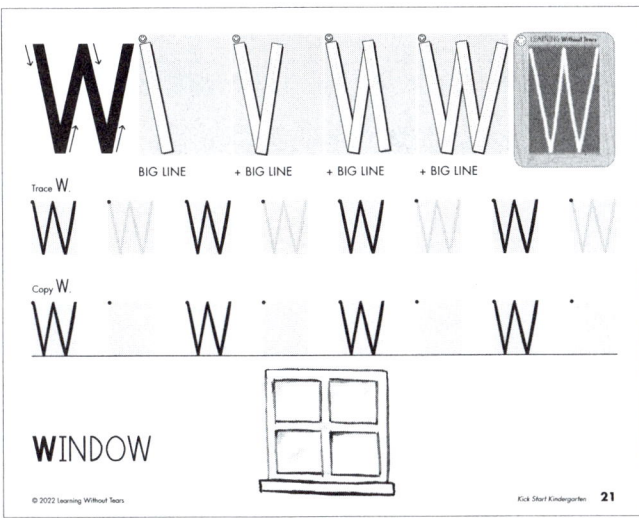

OBJECTIVE
To develop correct habits for writing capital **W**.

LESSON INTRODUCTION (Warm Up)
SONG: "Sliding Down to the End of the Alphabet" from *Rock, Rap, Tap & Learn* music album

Additional digital resources are available in the Interactive Digital Teaching Tool (IDTT).

LESSON PLAN

1. Direction Instruction (Demo)

Demonstrate **W** on the Slate Chalkboard or Gray Blocks.
Say the words for each step.

Lesson W:

 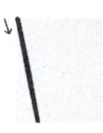   

Start in the Starting Corner | Big Line slides down | Slide up | Slide down | Slide up

2. Guided Practice

Children finger trace step-by-step models on the page while saying the words.
Children trace **W**.
Children copy **W**.

3. Check Letter

Monitor as children trace and copy letters for correct start and steps.

READ, COLOR & DRAW

Read WINDOW. Say **W** and make the /w/ sound. Encourage free coloring and drawing. Add curtains, the sun, etc.

ENRICHMENT
Write **WE** on Gray Block Paper. Say, "We," and have children add a verb, i.e., we wave, we talk, we laugh.

SUPPORT/ELL
Give each child two Big Lines to hold together at the bottom and then open. Next, have children hold **V**s together to make **W**.

CROSS-CURRICULAR CONNECTIONS
Language Arts: **W** is for WET. Show children signs for WET PAINT and WET FLOOR. Point out the pictures that go with the signs.

X

Kick Start Kindergarten – p. 22

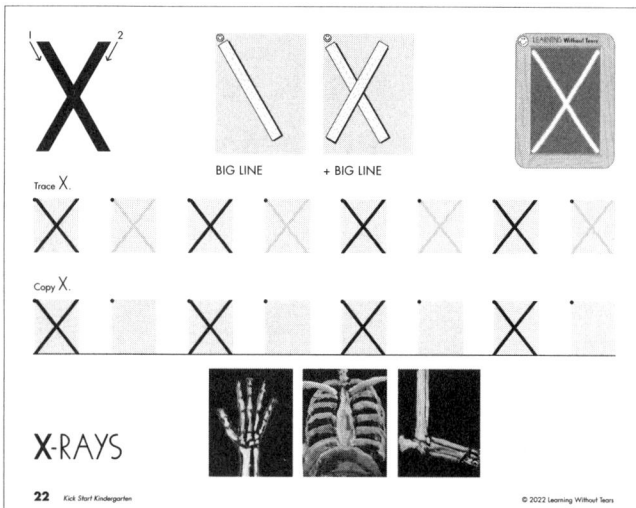

OBJECTIVE
To develop correct habits for writing capital **X**.

LESSON INTRODUCTION (Warm Up)
SONG: "Diagonals" from *Rock, Rap, Tap & Learn* music album

Additional digital resources are available in the Interactive Digital Teaching Tool (IDTT).

LESSON PLAN

1. Direction Instruction (Demo)

Demonstrate **X** on the Slate Chalkboard or Gray Blocks.
Say the words for each step.

Lesson X:

Start in the Starting Corner   Big Line slides down   Big Line slides down

2. Guided Practice

Children finger trace step-by-step models on the page while saying the words.
Children trace **X**.
Children copy **X**.

3. Check Letter

Monitor as children trace and copy letters for correct start and steps.

READ, COLOR & DRAW

Read X-RAYS. Say **X** and make the /x/ sound. Encourage free coloring and drawing. Add more bones, etc.

ENRICHMENT
Draw the letter **X** on a carpet square or another square surface.

SUPPORT/ELL
Use Wood Pieces (two Big Lines) to make an **X** in the air. Tap the Big Lines together and have children say, "**X** marks the spot."

CROSS-CURRICULAR CONNECTIONS
Science: Show pictures of an X-ray and discuss when these are needed.

p. 23

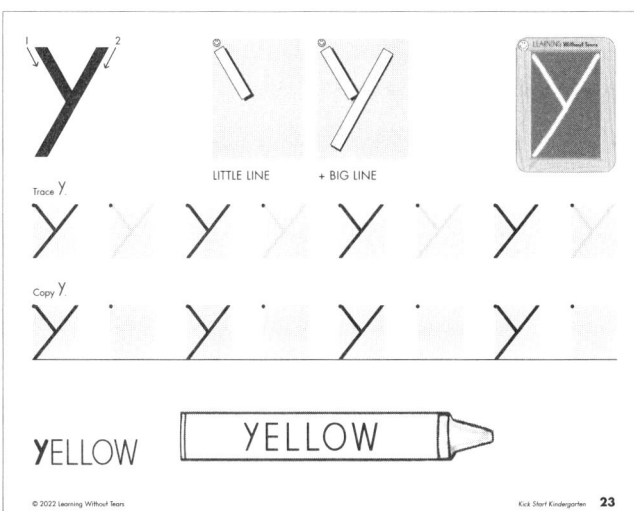

OBJECTIVE
To develop correct habits for writing capital **Y**.

LESSON INTRODUCTION (Warm Up)
Wet-Dry-Try App for Capitals, Numbers & Lowercase (p. 174)

Additional digital resources are available in the Interactive Digital Teaching Tool (IDTT).

LESSON PLAN

1. Direction Instruction (Demo)
Demonstrate **Y** on the Slate Chalkboard or Gray Blocks.
Say the words for each step.

Lesson Y:  Start in the Starting Corner 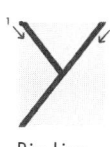 Little Line to the middle Big Line slides down

2. Guided Practice
Children finger trace step-by-step models on the page while saying the words.
Children trace **Y**.
Children copy **Y**.

3. Check Letter
Monitor as children trace and copy letters for correct start and steps.

READ, COLOR & DRAW
Read YELLOW. Say **Y** and make the /y/ sound. Encourage free coloring and drawing. Add another crayon, scribbles, etc.

ENRICHMENT
Have children write **V**, **W**, **X**, and **Y** on Gray Block Paper.

SUPPORT/ELL
Demonstrate diagonals in the air and have children join.

CROSS-CURRICULAR CONNECTIONS
Language Arts: Talk about foods that are yellow (banana, lemon, etc.).

Z

Kick Start Kindergarten – p. 24

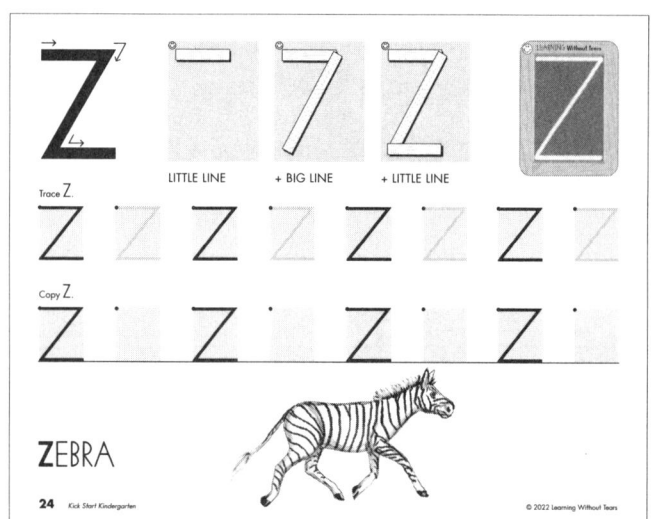

OBJECTIVE

To develop correct habits for writing capital **Z**.

LESSON INTRODUCTION (Warm Up)

Vertical, Horizontal, and Diagonal Positions with Wood Pieces (p. 158)

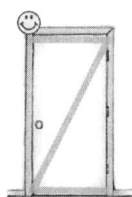

Additional digital resources are available in the Interactive Digital Teaching Tool (IDTT).

LESSON PLAN

1. Direction Instruction (Demo)

Demonstrate **Z** on the Slate Chalkboard or Gray Blocks. Say the words for each step.

Lesson Z:

  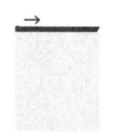  

Start in the Starting Corner | Little Line across the top | Slide down | Little Line across the bottom

2. Guided Practice

Children finger trace step-by-step models on the page while saying the words.
Children trace **Z**.
Children copy **Z**.

3. Check Letter

Monitor as children trace and copy letters for correct start and steps.

READ, COLOR & DRAW

Read ZEBRA. Say **Z** and make the /z/ sound. Encourage free coloring and drawing. Add other animals, grass, dirt, etc.

ENRICHMENT

 Home Link:
Starting Corner Capitals

SUPPORT/ELL

Capital **Z** can be reversed. Use Wet-Dry-Try on the Slate Chalkboard to remediate (p. 164). The Starting Corner prevents the reversal.

CROSS-CURRICULAR CONNECTIONS

Math: Look at the patterns of zebra stripes. Ask children to find and/or make patterns in the classroom.

Starting Corner Capitals Review

p. 25

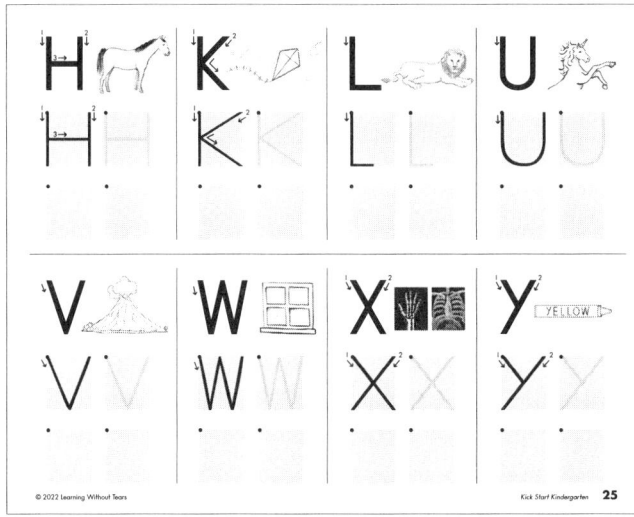

OBJECTIVE
To develop correct habits for writing Starting Corner Capitals.

LESSON INTRODUCTION (Warm Up)
SONG: "Sliding Down to the End of the Alphabet" from *Rock, Rap, Tap & Learn* music album

Additional digital resources are available in the Interactive Digital Teaching Tool (IDTT).

LESSON PLAN

1. Direction Instruction (Demo)
Demonstrate Starting Corner Capitals on the Slate Chalkboard or Gray Blocks. Say the words for each step.

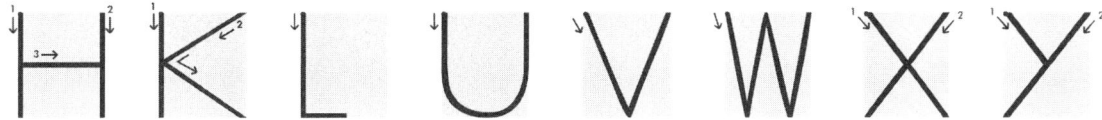

2. Guided Practice
Children trace and copy Starting Corner Capitals.

3. Check Letter
Monitor as children trace and copy letters for correct start and steps.

ENRICHMENT
Randomly call out capitals **H**, **K**, **L**, **U**, **V**, **W**, **X**, and **Y**. Have children take turns describing the letter. For example, Big Line, Big Line, Little Line is **H**.

SUPPORT/ELL
Review and have children build letters using the Mat for Wood Pieces prior to writing (p. 156).

CROSS-CURRICULAR CONNECTIONS
Language Arts: Read an alphabet book of your choice.

Kick Start Kindergarten – p. 26

OBJECTIVE
To develop correct habits for writing capital **C**.

LESSON INTRODUCTION (Warm Up)
Wet-Dry-Try App for Capitals, Numbers & Lowercase (p. 174)

Additional digital resources are available in the Interactive Digital Teaching Tool (IDTT).

LESSON PLAN

1. Direction Instruction (Demo)

Demonstrate **C** on the Slate Chalkboard or Gray Blocks. Say the words for each step.

Lesson C:
Start on the dot   Big Curve

2. Guided Practice

Children finger trace step-by-step models on the page while saying the words.
Children trace **C**.
Children copy **C**.

3. Check Letter

Monitor as children trace and copy letters for correct start and steps.

READ, COLOR & DRAW

Read CAR. Say **C** and make the /c/ sound. Encourage free coloring and drawing. Add a road, another car, passengers, etc.

ENRICHMENT
Call out the letter that makes the /c/ sound and have children write it on Gray Block Paper.

SUPPORT/ELL
 Make a Magic c Bunny napkin puppet using the instructions on A Click Away. Have children use the puppet to form **C** in the air.

CROSS-CURRICULAR CONNECTIONS
Math: Create a pictograph showing different ways children get to school, for example, car, school bus, walk, etc.

p. 27

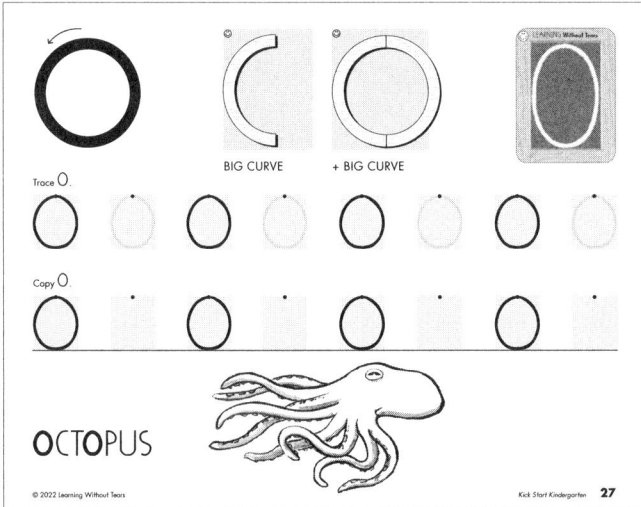

OBJECTIVE
To develop correct habits for writing capital O.

LESSON INTRODUCTION (Warm Up)
Curves and Circles with Wood Pieces (p. 159)

Additional digital resources are available in the Interactive Digital Teaching Tool (IDTT).

LESSON PLAN

1. Direction Instruction (Demo)
Demonstrate O on the Slate Chalkboard or Gray Blocks.
Say the words for each step.

Lesson O:

 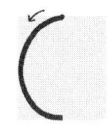  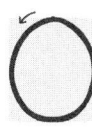

Start on the dot   Big Curve   Keep going   Stop

2. Guided Practice
Children finger trace step-by-step models on the page while saying the words.
Children trace O.
Children copy O.

3. Check Letter
Monitor as children trace and copy letters for correct start and steps.

READ, COLOR & DRAW
Read OCTOPUS. Say O and make the /o/ sound. Encourage free coloring and drawing. Add water, a baby octopus, etc.

ENRICHMENT
Turn off the lights and use a flashlight to trace capital O on the wall. Have children Air Trace O.

SUPPORT/ELL
Help left-handed children begin O with Magic C. Left-handed children are more likely to begin O incorrectly.

CROSS-CURRICULAR CONNECTIONS
Language Arts: Do the syllable activity for OC-TO-PUS. Point out the short /o/ sound in OC and long /o/ in TO (p. 179).

Q

Kick Start Kindergarten – p. 28

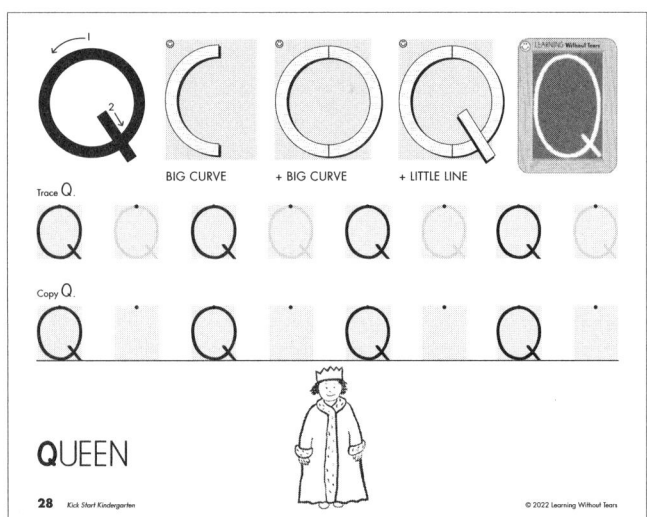

OBJECTIVE
To develop correct habits for writing capital **Q**.

LESSON INTRODUCTION (Warm Up)
Digital Letter and Number Formations (p. 172)

Additional digital resources are available in the Interactive Digital Teaching Tool (IDTT).

LESSON PLAN

1. Direction Instruction (Demo)

Demonstrate **Q** on the Slate Chalkboard or Gray Blocks.
Say the words for each step.

Lesson Q:

 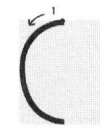   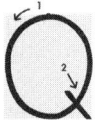

Start on the dot — Big Curve — Keep going — Stop — Little Line slides

2. Guided Practice

Children finger trace step-by-step models on the page while saying the words.
Children trace **Q**.
Children copy **Q**.

3. Check Letter

Monitor as children trace and copy letters for correct start and steps.

READ, COLOR & DRAW

Read QUEEN. Say **Q** and make the /q/ sound. Encourage free coloring and drawing. Add a king, castle, etc.

ENRICHMENT
Have children Air Trace the capital **Q**.

SUPPORT/ELL
Have children use the Slate Chalkboard to trace **Q**. Tell children to move toward the smiley face and say, "hello."

CROSS-CURRICULAR CONNECTIONS
Language Arts: Show pictures of a living queen and a fictional queen. Discuss the difference between real and make-believe.

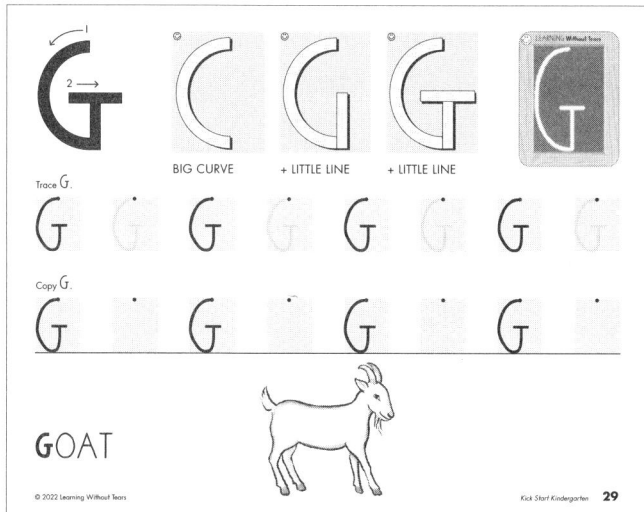

OBJECTIVE
To develop correct habits for writing capital **G**.

LESSON INTRODUCTION (Warm Up)
Capital Letter Cards for Wood Pieces (p. 161)

> Additional digital resources are available in the Interactive Digital Teaching Tool (IDTT).

LESSON PLAN

1. Direction Instruction (Demo)
Demonstrate **G** on the Slate Chalkboard or Gray Blocks.
Say the words for each step.

Lesson G:

   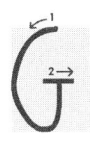

Start on the dot   Big Curve   Little Line up   Little Line across

2. Guided Practice
Children finger trace step-by-step models on the page while saying the words.
Children trace **G**.
Children copy **G**.

3. Check Letter
Monitor as children trace and copy letters for correct start and steps.

READ, COLOR & DRAW
Read GOAT. Say **G** and make the /g/ sound. Encourage free coloring and drawing. Add grass, flowers, etc.

ENRICHMENT
 Alphabet Show and Tell

SUPPORT/ELL
Use the Wood Pieces and build **G** to help children understand the step-by-step directions.

CROSS-CURRICULAR CONNECTIONS
Language Arts: Make a class list of words that rhyme with goat.

S

Kick Start Kindergarten – p. 30

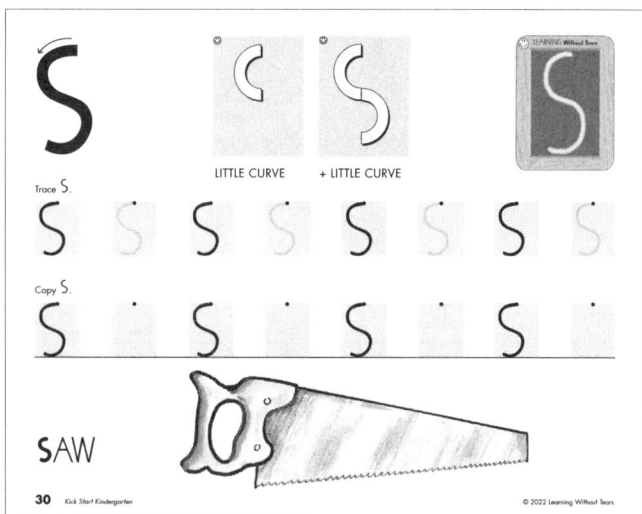

OBJECTIVE
To develop correct habits for writing capital **S**.

LESSON INTRODUCTION (Warm Up)
Curves & Circles with Wood Pieces (p. 159)

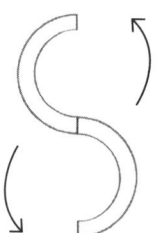

Additional digital resources are available in the Interactive Digital Teaching Tool (IDTT).

LESSON PLAN

1. Direction Instruction (Demo)

Demonstrate **S** on the Slate Chalkboard or Gray Blocks.
Say the words for each step.

Lesson S:

Start on the dot | Little Curve toward the smiley face | Turn | Little Curve toward the bottom

2. Guided Practice

Children finger trace step-by-step models on the page while saying the words.
Children trace **S**.
Children copy **S**.

3. Check Letter

Monitor as children trace and copy letters for correct start and steps.

READ, COLOR & DRAW

Read SAW. Say **S** and make the /s/ sound. Encourage free coloring and drawing. Add a piece of wood, other items, etc.

ENRICHMENT

 Community signs to color and write

SUPPORT/ELL

Capital **S** starts in the center. Show children the center of a door or the Slate Chalkboard and say "center." Tell them to travel toward the smiley face and say "hello."

CROSS-CURRICULAR CONNECTIONS

Language Arts: Describe different tools needed to build a house.

p. 31

OBJECTIVE
To develop correct habits for writing capital **A**.

LESSON INTRODUCTION (Warm Up)
SONG: "Give it a Middle" from *Rock, Rap, Tap & Learn* music album

Additional digital resources are available in the Interactive Digital Teaching Tool (IDTT).

LESSON PLAN

1. Direction Instruction (Demo)

Demonstrate **A** on the Slate Chalkboard or Gray Blocks.
Say the words for each step.

Lesson A:

 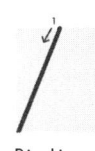 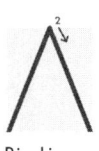 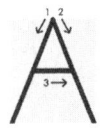

Start on the dot | Big Line slides down | Big Line slides down | Little Line across the middle

2. Guided Practice

Children finger trace step-by-step models on the page while saying the words.
Children trace **A**.
Children copy **A**.

3. Check Letter

Monitor as children trace and copy letters for correct start and steps.

READ, COLOR & DRAW

Read ANT. Say **A** and make the /a/ sound. Encourage free coloring and drawing. Add more ants, grass, dirt, etc.

ENRICHMENT
Look at all the different **A**s in various ABC books.

SUPPORT/ELL
Review with children that **A** starts in the center. Review diagonal strokes.

CROSS-CURRICULAR CONNECTIONS
Math: *Sing The Ants Go Marching*. Count up to 10 as a class.

I

Kick Start Kindergarten – p. 32

OBJECTIVE
To develop correct habits for writing capital **I**.

LESSON INTRODUCTION (Warm Up)
Capital Letter Cards for Wood Pieces (p. 161)

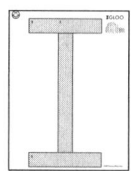

> Additional digital resources are available in the Interactive Digital Teaching Tool (IDTT).

LESSON PLAN

1. Direction Instruction (Demo)

Demonstrate **I** on the Slate Chalkboard or Gray Blocks.
Say the words for each step.

Lesson I:

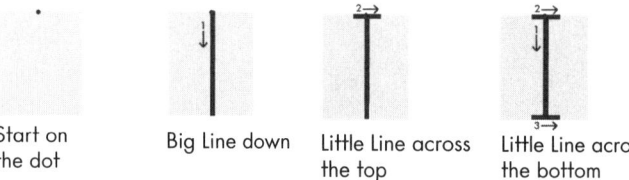

Start on the dot | Big Line down | Little Line across the top | Little Line across the bottom

2. Guided Practice

Children finger trace step-by-step models on the page while saying the words.
Children trace **I**.
Children copy **I**.

3. Check Letter

Monitor as children trace and copy letters for correct start and steps.

READ, COLOR & DRAW

Read ICE CREAM. Say **I** and make the /i/ sound. Encourage free coloring and drawing. Add person, more ice cream, ice cream truck, etc.

ENRICHMENT
Have children write capital **I** on double lines and trace with different colored pencils.

SUPPORT/ELL
Left-handed children can write cross strokes right to left. Review top and bottom position words by building **I** with Wood Pieces.

CROSS-CURRICULAR CONNECTIONS
Language Arts: Read *From Cow to Ice Cream* by Bertram Knight. Have children describe their favorite ice cream.

p. 33

T

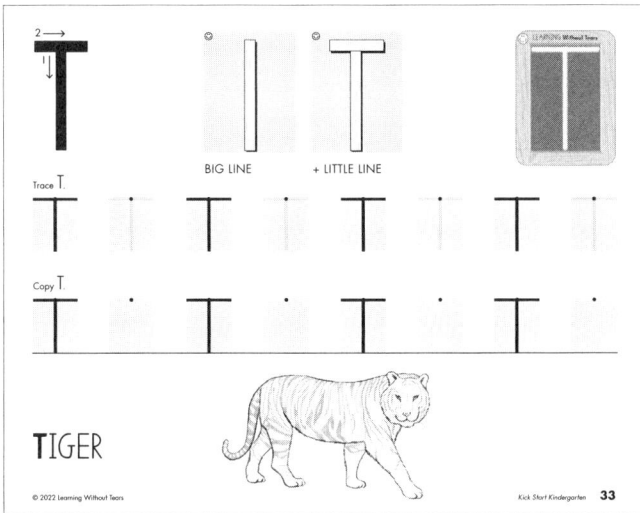

OBJECTIVE
To develop correct habits for writing capital **T**.

LESSON INTRODUCTION (Warm Up)
Vertical, Horizontal, and Diagonal Positions with Wood Pieces (p. 158)

Additional digital resources are available in the Interactive Digital Teaching Tool (IDTT).

LESSON PLAN

1. Direction Instruction (Demo)

Demonstrate **T** on the Slate Chalkboard or Gray Blocks.
Say the words for each step.

Lesson T:

Start on the dot   Big Line down   Little Line across the top

2. Guided Practice

Children finger trace step-by-step models on the page while saying the words.
Children trace **T**.
Children copy **T**.

3. Check Letter

Monitor as children trace and copy letters for correct start and steps.

READ, COLOR & DRAW

Read TIGER. Say **T** and make the /t/ sound. Encourage free coloring and drawing. Add grass, water, sun, etc.

ENRICHMENT
Have children write the word STOP on Gray Block Paper.

SUPPORT/ELL
Capital **T** is for top. Show children how the Little Line is at the top with Wood Pieces.

CROSS-CURRICULAR CONNECTIONS
Social Studies: Get out a world map and identify all the places tigers live.

J

Kick Start Kindergarten – p. 34

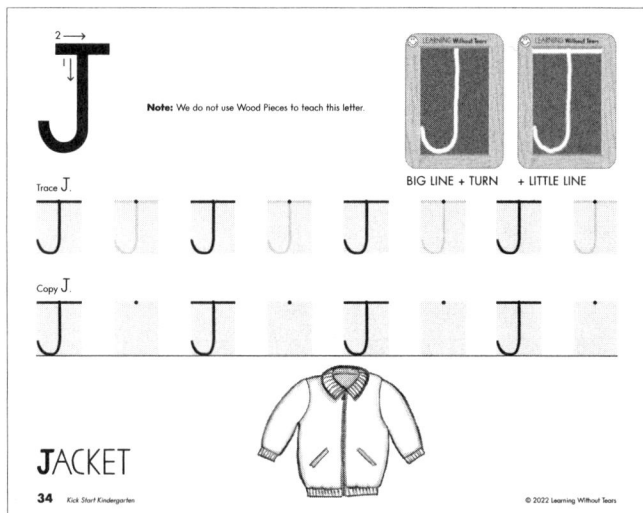

OBJECTIVE
To develop correct habits for writing capital **J**.

LESSON INTRODUCTION (Warm Up)
SONG: "Give it a Top" from *Rock, Rap, Tap & Learn* music album

Additional digital resources are available in the Interactive Digital Teaching Tool (IDTT).

LESSON PLAN

1. Direction Instruction (Demo)

Demonstrate **J** on the Slate Chalkboard or Gray Blocks.
Say the words for each step.

Lesson J:

 Start on the dot

 Big Line down

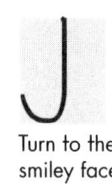 Turn to the smiley face side

Little Line across the top

2. Guided Practice

Children finger trace step-by-step models on the page while saying the words.
Children trace **J**.
Children copy **J**.

3. Check Letter

Monitor as children trace and copy letters for correct start and steps.

READ, COLOR & DRAW

Read JACKET. Say **J** and make the /j/ sound. Encourage free coloring and drawing. Add other clothing, design on jacket, etc.

ENRICHMENT
 Home Link:
Center Starting Capitals

SUPPORT/ELL
Do not make **J** with Wood Pieces because it ends up an odd shape and size. Review the letter using the Slate Chalkboard.

CROSS-CURRICULAR CONNECTIONS
Language Arts: Describe different types of jackets and when you would wear them depending on the weather.

p. 35

Center Starting Capitals Review

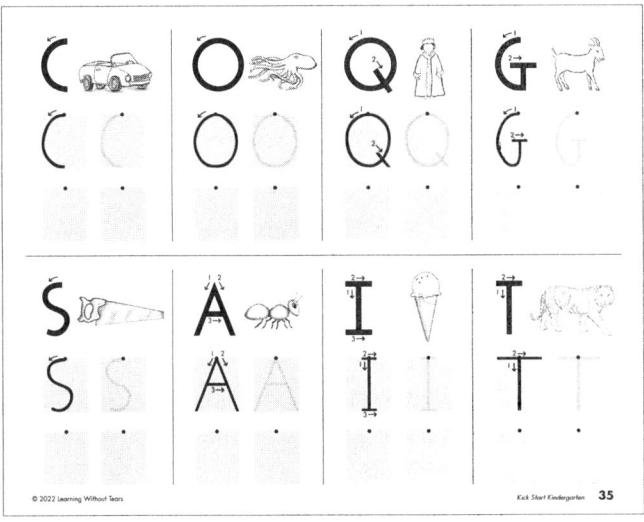

OBJECTIVE
To develop correct habits for writing Center Starting Capitals.

LESSON INTRODUCTION (Warm Up)
Digital Letter and Number Formations (p. 172)

Additional digital resources are available in the Interactive Digital Teaching Tool (IDTT).

LESSON PLAN

1. Direction Instruction (Demo)
Demonstrate Center Starting Capitals on the Slate Chalkboard or Gray Blocks. Say the words for each step.

 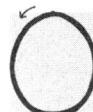 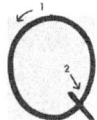   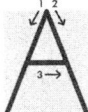 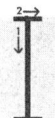 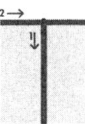

2. Guided Practice
Children trace and copy Center Starting Capitals.

3. Check Letter
Monitor as children trace and copy letters for correct start and steps.

ENRICHMENT
O is for opera. Let children sing and stretch the long vowels O—> A—> I—>. Draw faces with the o shaped singing mouths. Write the vowel in a quote bubble.

SUPPORT/ELL
Review and build letters using the Mat for Wood Pieces prior to writing.

CROSS-CURRICULAR CONNECTIONS
Language Arts: Read an alphabet book of your choice. Encourage children to discuss all the letters they are learning.

Capitals for Me

Kick Start Kindergarten – p. 36

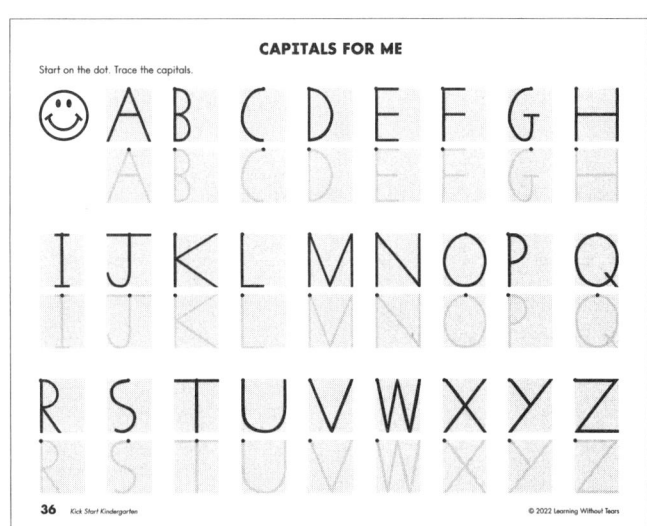

OBJECTIVE

To develop correct habits when tracing all capitals.

LESSON INTRODUCTION (Warm Up)

SONG: "Where Do You Start Your Letters?" from *Rock, Rap, Tap & Learn* music album

Additional digital resources are available in the Interactive Digital Teaching Tool (IDTT).

LESSON PLAN

1. **Direction Instruction (Demo)**

   Demonstrate **A**, **B**, and **C** on the Slate Chalkboard or Gray Blocks.
   Say the words for each step.

   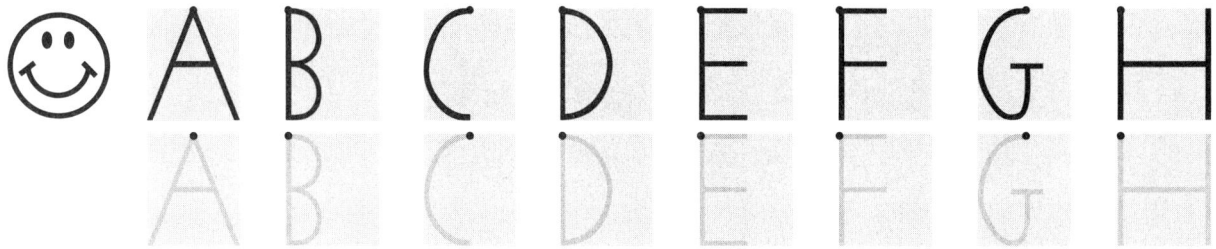

2. **Guided Practice**

   Children trace **A**, **B**, and **C**.
   Children then trace the rest of the alphabet on their own.

3. **Check Letter**

   Monitor as children trace and copy letters for correct start and steps.

ENRICHMENT

Monitor children as they use Gray Block Paper to write capitals on their own.

SUPPORT/ELL

Sing the alphabet as children point and say each letter prior to writing.

CROSS-CURRICULAR CONNECTIONS

Language Arts: Discuss environmental signs, such as STOP and EXIT.

LOWERCASE LETTERS, WORDS & SENTENCES

It's time for all the letters, words, and sentences. The 26 capitals you've taught give your students an excellent start for lowercase letters. Lowercase lessons begin with letters your students already know. We start with **c**, **o**, **s**, **v**, and **w**—five letters that are exactly the same as capitals, just smaller. That's not all. Beginning with those five letters gives another opportunity for you to be sure every child has good habits for **c**, **o**, **s**, **v**, and **w**.

Because only familiar and previously taught letters are used in our word practice, children typically use correct habits for writing every letter. With word practice, those habits become automatic and lead directly to fluency. At first, every new letter takes care and conscious effort, but gradually, more letters are written both correctly and automatically.

In this section, children will:

- Build good habits for lowercase letter formation in a developmentally appropriate sequence

- Be provided with ways to enrich or support each lesson

- Use recently used letters in words to extend their learning

Student Edition Design

LOWERCASE LETTERS, WORDS AND SENTENCES

Children practice newly taught letters in words. These pages model good spacing and review capitals.

As children move to lowercase, our double lines foster handwriting success. The mid line is for size. The base line is for placement. Small letters fit in the middle space. Tall letters go in the top space. Descending letters go in the bottom space. Double lines make it easy for children to place letters and to make them the right size.

The word practice pages contain practice for creating simple words and sentences with an emphasis on correct formation and letter placement. Children will never have to write a letter before they learn how to write it. These writing exercises develop writing skills that will prepare children for success.

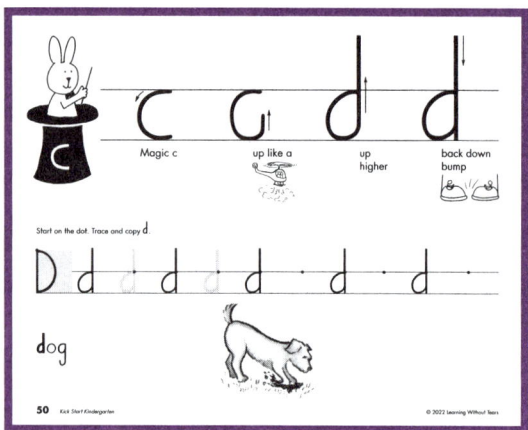

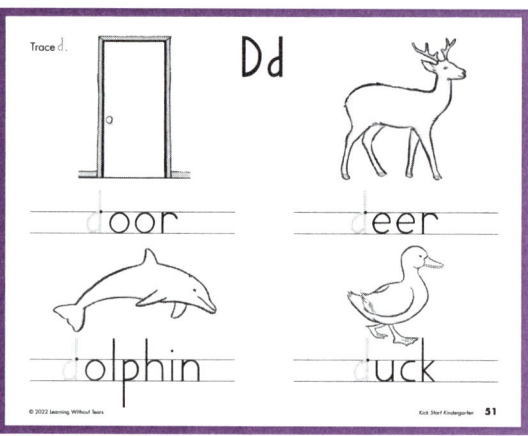

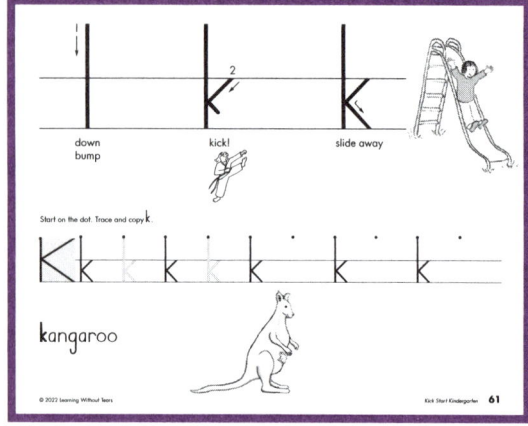

Double Line Success

LINE CONFUSION: DOUBLE LINES ENABLE SUCCESS

For children to become well-rounded in handwriting, they must be able to write efficiently on all types of lined paper. When it comes to choosing a style of paper to stock up on, there are certainly many options: single lines, double lines, triple lines, dotted or straight. But which type is best for students who are new to writing?

Have you seen this in your classroom?

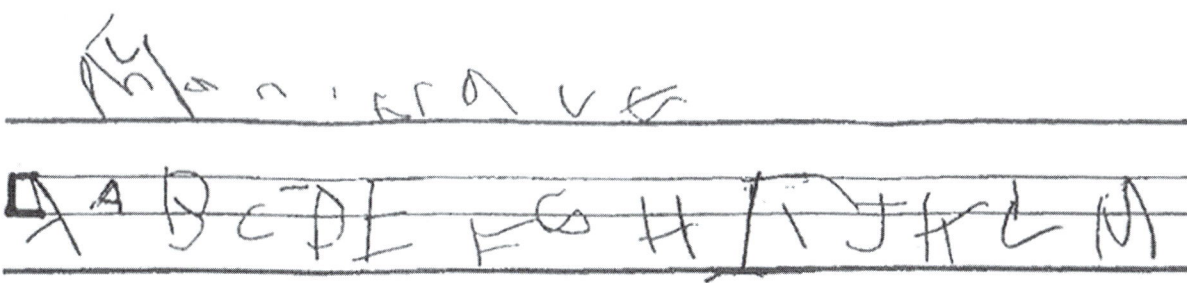

Many children have trouble understanding multiple lines. Giving children a blue line, a dotted line, a red line, and another blue line and then asking them to start at "2 o'clock between the dotted line and the red line" is too confusing.

Become a Line Leader in Double Lines

Our double lines quickly teach children how to place letters: small letters fit in the middle space, tall letters go in the top space, descending letters go in the bottom space. Without having to spend extra time deciding how to orient their letters on the paper, children can launch right into printing their ABCs or putting the poem in their heads onto the paper.

Double lines help children place letters correctly, eliminating line confusion. The base line guides placement, and the mid line controls the size of letters. Students who struggle with start and placement on other styles of paper succeed on double lines.

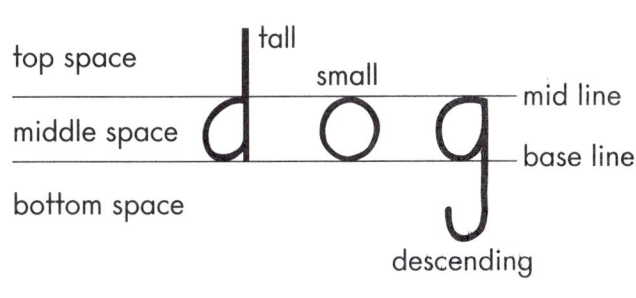

© 2022 Learning Without Tears — Kick Start Kindergarten Teacher's Guide: *Lowercase Letters, Words & Sentences*

Lowercase Teaching Order

LETTER GROUPS

Our lowercase teaching order promotes good habits for letter formation and writing success. This is done by grouping letters to facilitate:

1. Easy start: All lowercase letters (except **d** and **e**) begin at the top.
2. Correct placement: The tall, small, and descending letters are in proportion and placed correctly.
3. Correct orientation: No **b** and **d** confusion, no **g** and **q** confusion, no reversed letters!

LOWERCASE LETTERS ARE TAUGHT IN FIVE GROUPS

Same as Capitals and t

c o s v w   t

The first five letters are exactly like their capitals, just smaller. What an easy start—just bring your good habits from capitals! Lowercase **t** is made like **T**. It's just crossed lower.

Magic c

a d g

These high frequency letters begin with the familiar Magic c. Starting with **c** placed correctly helps children make and place the **d** tall and **g** descending.

Transition Group

u i e l k y j

Here are the rest of the vowels: **u**, **i**, **e**. Letters **u**, **k**, **y**, **j** are familiar from capitals. The focus will be on careful placement and size.

Diver Letters

p r n m h b

These letters all start with the same pattern: they dive down, swim up, swim over! We avoid **b** and **d** confusion by separating the letters and teaching them in different groups based on formation habits.

Final Group

f q x z

Lowercase **f** has a tricky start. Letter **q** is taught here to avoid **g** and **q** confusion. Letters **x** and **z** are familiar, but infrequently used.

p. 37

Lowercase Alphabet

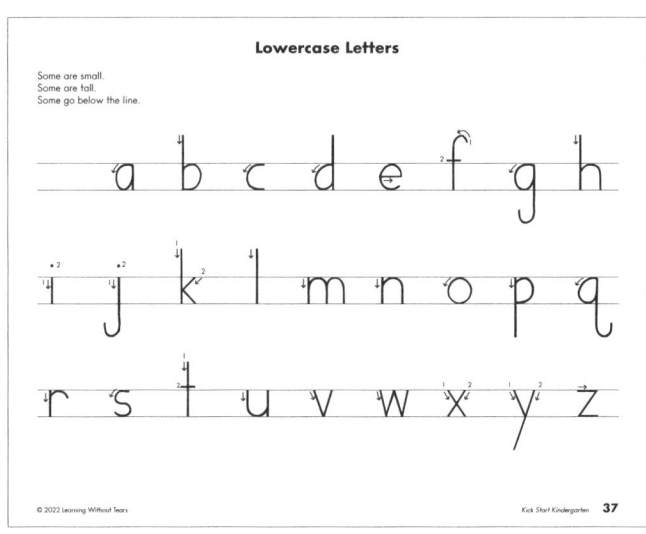

OBJECTIVE
To develop understanding of placement of lowercase letters.

LESSON INTRODUCTION (Warm Up)
Hand Activity (p. 175)

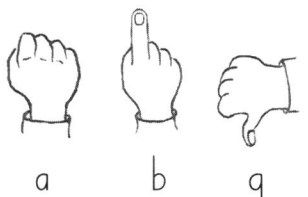

Additional digital resources are available in the Interactive Digital Teaching Tool (IDTT).

LESSON PLAN

1. Direction Instruction (Demo) - Beginning of the Alphabet

Children point and say each letter. Then say if the letter is small, tall, or descending with the hand motion. (Example: **a** - **a** is small, **b** - **b** is tall, etc.)

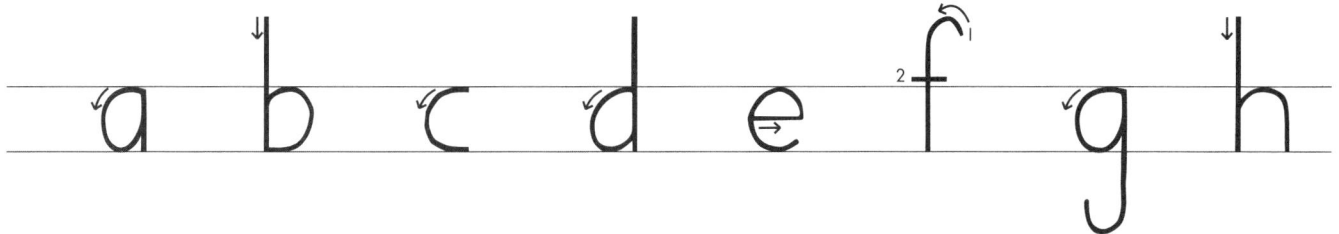

2. Guided Practice

Children name the letters and complete the actions for small, tall, and descending letters.

3. Check Letter

Monitor as children point and name the lowercase letters.
Monitor as they complete the actions for the Hand Activity.

ENRICHMENT
Let pairs of children play "Point & Name Lowercase." One child points, the other child names. Take turns.

SUPPORT/ELL
Point to lowercase letters that are like capitals or familiar to the child's name.

CROSS-CURRICULAR CONNECTIONS
Language Arts: Discuss the beginning, middle, and end of the alphabet.

c

Kick Start Kindergarten – p. 38

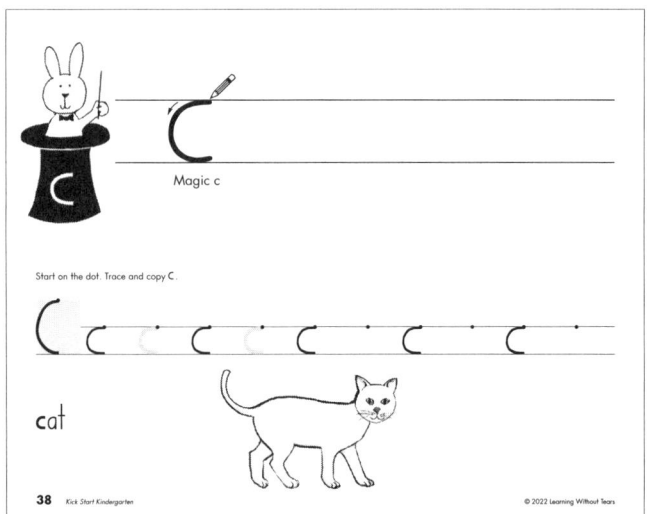

OBJECTIVE
To develop correct habits for writing lowercase **c**.

LESSON INTRODUCTION (Warm Up)
Air Writing (p. 170)

Additional digital resources are available in the Interactive Digital Teaching Tool (IDTT).

LESSON PLAN

1. Direction Instruction (Demo)
Demonstrate **c** on double lines.
Say the words.

Magic c

2. Guided Practice
Children finger trace the large **C** saying the words.
Children trace **c**.
Children copy **c**.

3. Check Letter
Monitor as children trace and copy letters for correct start, steps, and bump.

READ, COLOR & DRAW
Read cat. Say **c** and make the /c/ sound. Encourage free coloring and drawing. Add a mouse, string, a bowl, etc.

ENRICHMENT
Use the Blackboard with Double Lines and have children write capital **C** and lowercase **c** (p. 176).

SUPPORT/ELL
Show children how lowercase **c** is exactly like capital **C**, but half the size.

CROSS-CURRICULAR CONNECTIONS
Language Arts: Make a class list of words that rhyme with cat.

Words C c

OBJECTIVE
To develop correct habits for writing lowercase **c** in a word.

LESSON INTRODUCTION (Warm Up)
Hand Activity (p. 175)

Additional digital resources are available in the Interactive Digital Teaching Tool (IDTT).

LESSON PLAN

1. Direction Instruction (Demo)
Demonstrate writing **c** in words **cow**, **cat**, **city**, and **cloud** on double lines.

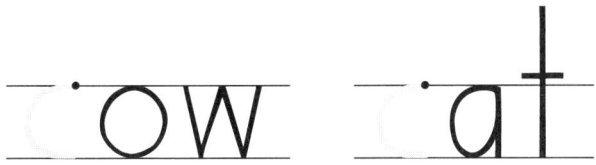

2. Guided Practice
Children trace **c** in words.

3. Check Letters
Monitor as children trace the letters for correct start, steps, and bump.

READ, COLOR & DRAW
Read words. Encourage free coloring and drawing.

ENRICHMENT
Have children look for lowercase **c** in books and on labels in the classroom.

SUPPORT/ELL
Have children finger trace **c** several times before writing.

CROSS-CURRICULAR CONNECTIONS
Social Studies: Compare and contrast cities to small towns.

Kick Start Kindergarten – p. 40

OBJECTIVE
To develop correct habits for writing lowercase **o**.

LESSON INTRODUCTION (Warm Up)
Wet-Dry-Try App for Capitals, Numbers & Lowercase (p. 174)

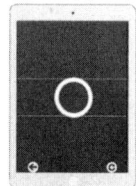

Additional digital resources are available in the Interactive Digital Teaching Tool (IDTT).

LESSON PLAN

1. Direction Instruction (Demo)
Demonstrate **o** on double lines.
Say the words for each step.

2. Guided Practice
Children finger trace the large step-by-step **o** saying the words.
Children trace **o**.
Children copy **o**.

3. Check Letter
Monitor as children trace and copy letters for correct start, steps, and bump.

READ, COLOR & DRAW
Read owl. Say **o** and make the /o/ sound. Encourage free coloring and drawing. Add a tree, branch, nest, etc.

ENRICHMENT
For vowels **a**, **e**, **i**, **o**, and **u**—say the name of the letter, the long /o/ sound. Say the short /o/ sound.

SUPPORT/ELL
Preview lowercase **o** with Wet-Dry-Try on the Blackboard with Double Lines (p. 176).

CROSS-CURRICULAR CONNECTIONS
Science: Show children pictures of owls. Discuss fun facts about owls.

p. 41

Words O o

OBJECTIVE
To develop correct habits for writing lowercase **o** in a word.

LESSON INTRODUCTION (Warm Up)
Hand Activity (p. 175)

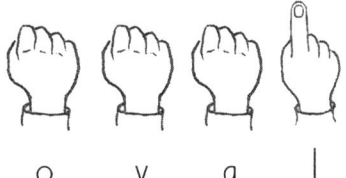

Additional digital resources are available in the Interactive Digital Teaching Tool (IDTT).

LESSON PLAN

1. Direction Instruction (Demo)
Demonstrate writing **o** in words **oval**, **on**, **hop**, and **stop** on double lines.

2. Guided Practice
Children trace **o** in words.

3. Check Letters
Monitor as children trace the letters for correct start, steps, and bump.

READ, COLOR & DRAW
Read words. Say the long /o/ sound in oval. Say the short /o/ in on, hop, stop. Encourage free coloring and drawing.

ENRICHMENT
Compare **C c** and **O o** and have children write on double lines.

SUPPORT/ELL
Encourage children to say the step-by-step directions as they trace over the **o**. Saying the words out loud can help students remember.

CROSS-CURRICULAR CONNECTIONS
Language Arts: Share the nursery rhyme, "Humpty Dumpty sat on a wall." Ask children to say the words that rhyme.

s *Kick Start Kindergarten* – p. 42

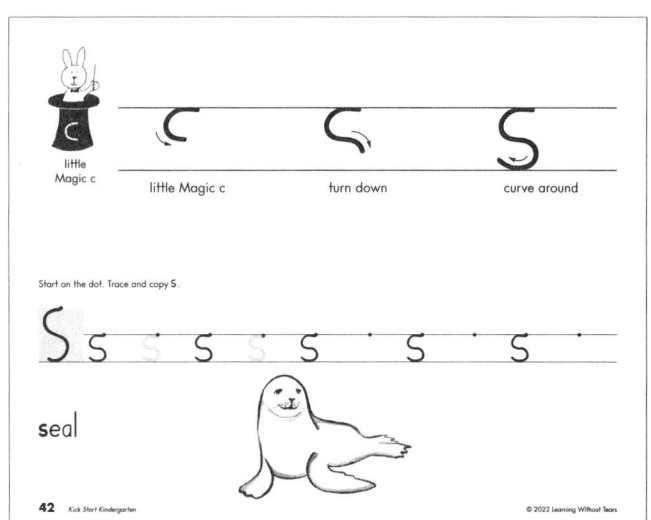

OBJECTIVE
To develop correct habits for writing lowercase **s**.

LESSON INTRODUCTION (Warm Up)
Digital Letter and Number Formations (p. 172)

Additional digital resources are available in the Interactive Digital Teaching Tool (IDTT).

LESSON PLAN

1. Direction Instruction (Demo)

Demonstrate **s** on double lines.
Say the words for each step.

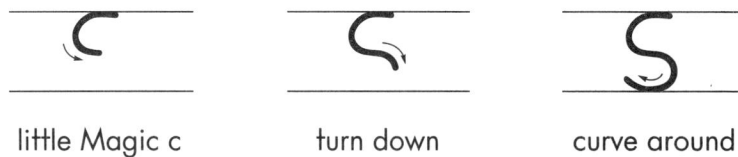

little Magic c   turn down   curve around

2. Guided Practice

Children finger trace the large step-by-step **s** saying the words.
Children trace **s**.
Children copy **s**.

3. Check Letter

Monitor as children trace and copy letters for correct start, steps, and bump.

READ, COLOR & DRAW

Read seal. Say **s** and make the /s/ sound. Encourage free coloring and drawing. Add water, fish, a rock, etc.

ENRICHMENT
Have children write the word **so** on double lines. Model the word before copying.

SUPPORT/ELL
Use Letter Story: *Stop, Drop & Roll with S* to reinforce correct formation of **s** (p. 169).

CROSS-CURRICULAR CONNECTIONS
Science: Show children pictures of seals swimming. Talk about other animals that swim in lakes, rivers, oceans, etc.

p. 43

Sentences

OBJECTIVE
To develop correct habits for tracing letters in a sentence.

LESSON INTRODUCTION (Warm Up)
SONG: "Sentence Song" from *Rock, Rap, Tap & Learn* music album

Additional digital resources are available in the Interactive Digital Teaching Tool (IDTT).

LESSON PLAN

1. Direction Instruction (Demo)

Demonstrate on double lines: **Seals swim.**
Show children that sentences begin with a capital, have space between words, and end with a period.

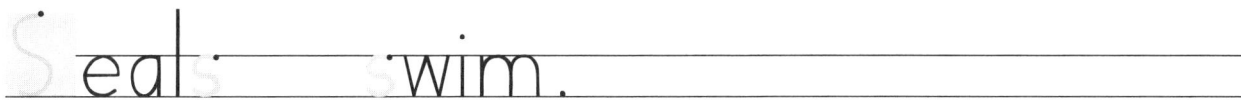

2. Guided Practice

Children trace **S s** in Seals swim.
Children then trace **C c** and **O o** on their own.

3. Check Sentence

Monitor as children trace their letters for correct start, steps, and bump.

Writing

Read words. Encourage free coloring and drawing.

ENRICHMENT
A+ Worksheet Maker: Create a spelling worksheet with a list of singular nouns. Children add an **s** to make them plural.

SUPPORT/ELL
Repeat each sentence two to three times as children place and move their pointer finger under each word.

CROSS-CURRICULAR CONNECTIONS
Language Arts: Ask children questions based on the sentences. Help them respond using complete sentences.

v

Kick Start Kindergarten – p. 44

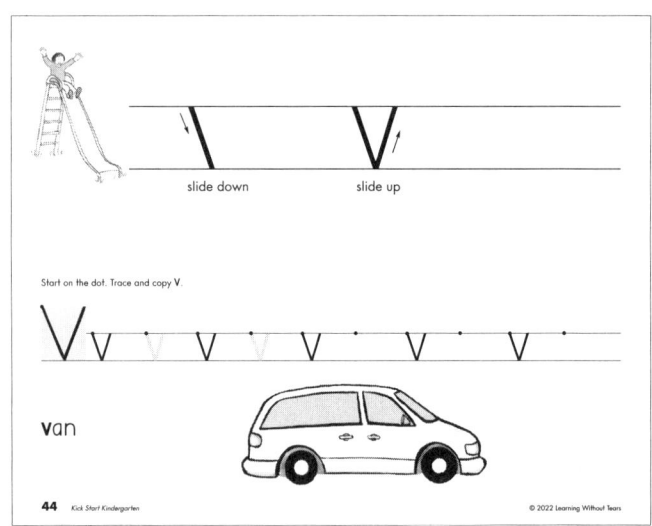

OBJECTIVE
To develop correct habits for writing lowercase **v**.

LESSON INTRODUCTION (Warm Up)
Laser Letters (p.171)

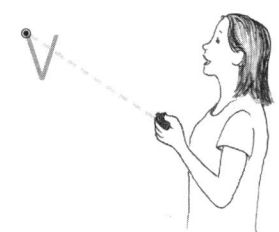

Additional digital resources are available in the Interactive Digital Teaching Tool (IDTT).

LESSON PLAN

1. Direction Instruction (Demo)

Demonstrate **v** on double lines.
Say the words for each step.

slide down   slide up

2. Guided Practice

Children finger trace the large step-by-step **v** saying the words.
Children trace **v**.
Children copy **v**.

3. Check Letter

Monitor as children trace and copy letters for correct start, steps, and bump.

READ, COLOR & DRAW

Read van. Say **v** and make the /v/ sound. Encourage free coloring and drawing. Add people, street, stop sign, etc.

ENRICHMENT
Show children capital **V** with a flashcard. Have children write lowercase **v** on double lines.

SUPPORT/ELL
Practice diagonal positions using the Wood Pieces for **V** before having children write lowercase **v** (p. 158).

CROSS-CURRICULAR CONNECTIONS
Social Studies: Discuss different types of transportation, like vans, buses, trains, and planes.

p. 45

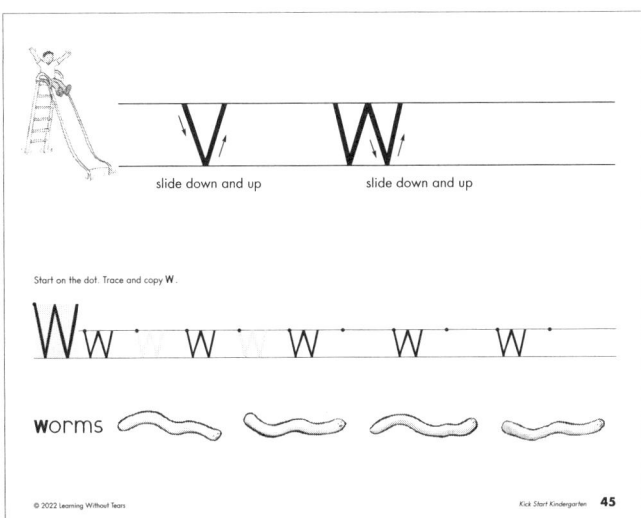

OBJECTIVE
To develop correct habits for writing lowercase **w**.

LESSON INTRODUCTION (Warm Up)
Wet-Dry-Try App for Capitals, Numbers & Lowercase (p. 174)

Additional digital resources are available in the Interactive Digital Teaching Tool (IDTT).

LESSON PLAN

1. Direction Instruction (Demo)

Demonstrate **w** on double lines.
Say the words for each step.

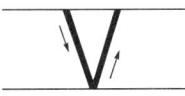
slide down and up

slide down and up

2. Guided Practice

Children finger trace the large step-by-step **w** saying the words.
Children trace **w**.
Children copy **w**.

3. Check Letter

Monitor as children trace and copy letters for correct start, steps, and bump.

READ, COLOR & DRAW

Read worms. Say **w** and make the /w/ sound. Encourage free coloring and drawing. Add dirt, grass, etc.

ENRICHMENT	SUPPORT/ELL	CROSS-CURRICULAR CONNECTIONS
Have children put up two fingers on each hand and talk about how this makes **w**.	Compare capital **W** and lowercase **w**. Review big and little diagonal lines.	Science: Talk about the habitats of worms. Find a spot outside for children to dig up worms.

Kick Start Kindergarten – p. 46

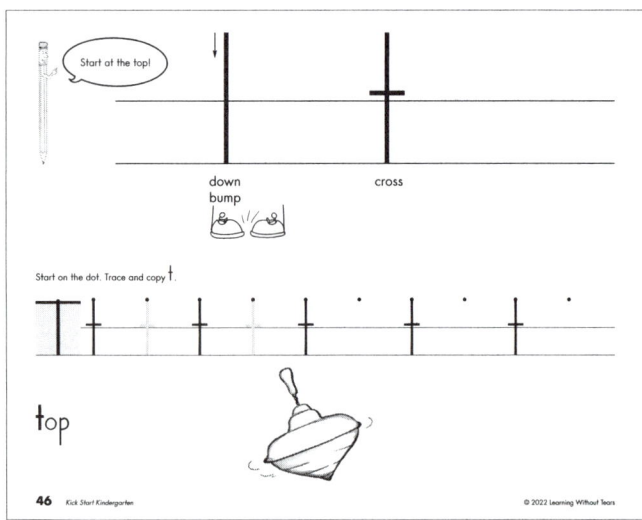

OBJECTIVE
To develop correct habits for writing lowercase t.

LESSON INTRODUCTION (Warm Up)
Wet-Dry-Try on Blackboard with Double Lines (p. 176)

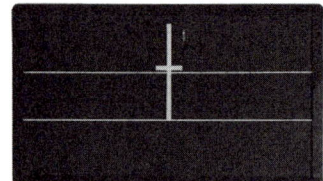

Additional digital resources are available in the Interactive Digital Teaching Tool (IDTT).

LESSON PLAN

1. Direction Instruction (Demo)
Demonstrate t on double lines.
Say the words for each step.

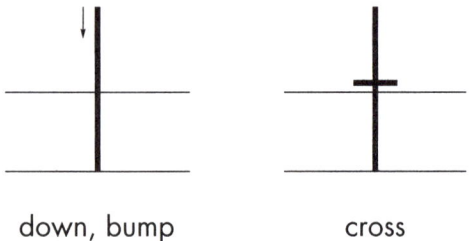

down, bump   cross

2. Guided Practice
Children finger trace the large step-by-step t saying the words.
Children trace t.
Children copy t.

3. Check Letter
Monitor as children trace and copy letters for correct start, steps, and bump.

READ, COLOR & DRAW
Read tops. Say t and make the /t/ sound. Encourage free coloring and drawing. Add other tops.

ENRICHMENT
A+ Worksheet Maker: Create spelling worksheets with simple words that end in t. Have children add the t. For example, ca_, fa_, ma_.

SUPPORT/ELL
Use Letter Story: *Capital T and Lowercase t* to reinforce correct formation of t (p. 169).

CROSS-CURRICULAR CONNECTIONS
Science: Show children a spinning top. Spin to show children how it works and discuss.

p. 47

Sentences

OBJECTIVE
To develop correct habits for tracing letters in a sentence.

LESSON INTRODUCTION (Warm Up)
SONG: "Sentence Song" from *Rock, Rap, Tap & Learn* music album

Additional digital resources are available in the Interactive Digital Teaching Tool (IDTT).

LESSON PLAN

1. Direction Instruction (Demo)

Demonstrate on double lines: **Tops twirl.**
Show children that sentences begin with a capital, have space between words, and end with a period.

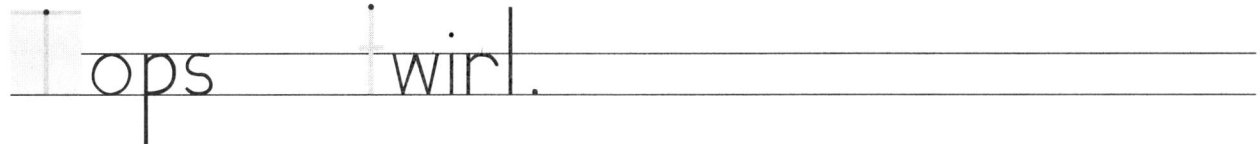

2. Guided Practice

Children trace **T t** in Tops twirl.
Children then trace **V v** and **W w** on their own.

3. Check Sentence

Monitor as children trace their letters for correct start, steps, and bump.

Writing

Read words. Encourage free coloring and drawing.

ENRICHMENT
Draw and/or write a sentence about something you like to see and hear.

SUPPORT/ELL
Point to the words, then have children touch their eyes for "look" and touch their ears for "hear."

CROSS-CURRICULAR CONNECTIONS
Science: How do things move? The tops twirls, spinning around. Wheels spin too. Worms wiggle and stretch.

a

Kick Start Kindergarten – p. 48

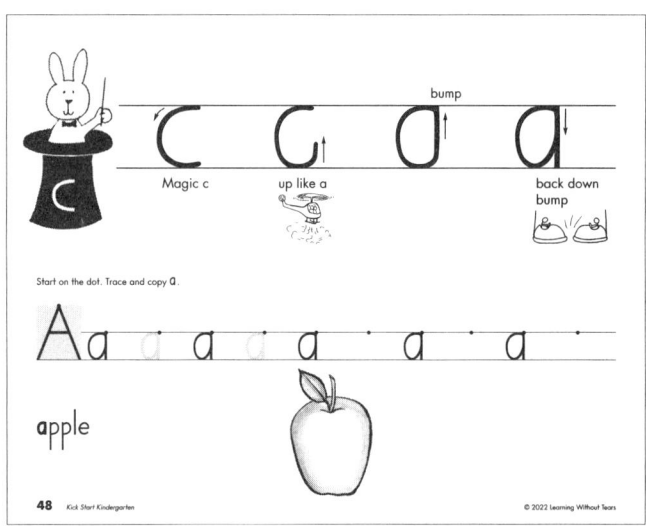

OBJECTIVE

To develop correct habits for writing lowercase **a**.

LESSON INTRODUCTION (Warm Up)

Voices (p. 177)

Additional digital resources are available in the Interactive Digital Teaching Tool (IDTT).

LESSON PLAN

1. Direction Instruction (Demo)

Demonstrate **a** on double lines.
Say the words for each step.

Magic c   up like a helicopter   bump   back down, bump

2. Guided Practice

Children finger trace the large step-by-step **a** saying the words.
Children trace **a**.
Children copy **a**.

3. Check Letter

Monitor as children trace and copy letters for correct start, steps, and bump.

READ, COLOR & DRAW

Read apple. Say **a** and make the /a/ sound. Encourage free coloring and drawing. Add a tree, a pie, a basket, etc.

ENRICHMENT

 Make a Magic C Bunny using a napkin.

SUPPORT/ELL

It's tricky to make lowercase **a** without lifting the pencil. First, have children finger trace lowercase **a** on the Blackboard with Double Lines (p. 176).

CROSS-CURRICULAR CONNECTIONS

Science: Slice apples to share. Discuss taste and different textures.

p. 49

Words A a

OBJECTIVE
To develop correct habits for writing lowercase **a**.

LESSON INTRODUCTION (Warm Up)
Voices (p. 177)

Additional digital resources are available in the Interactive Digital Teaching Tool (IDTT).

LESSON PLAN

1. Direction Instruction (Demo)
Demonstrate writing **a** in words **apron**, **ants**, **pan**, and **cat** on double lines.

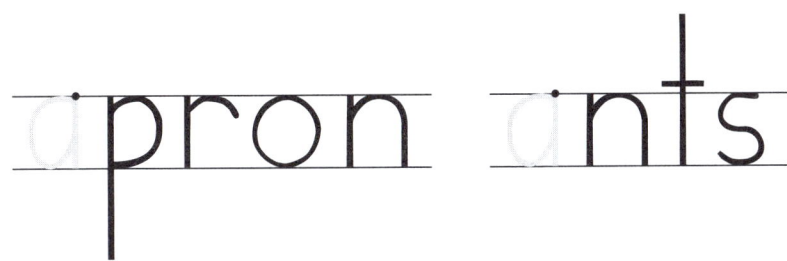

2. Guided Practice
Children trace **a** in words.

3. Check Letters
Monitor as children trace the letters for correct start, steps, and bump.

READ, COLOR & DRAW
Read words. Say the long /a/ sound in apron. Say the short /a/ in ants, pan, cat. Encourage free coloring and drawing.

ENRICHMENT
Review **c**, **o**, and **a** on double lines to help children make the connection to Magic c letters.

SUPPORT/ELL
Preview lowercase **a** with Wet-Dry-Try on the Blackboard with Double Lines (p. 176).

CROSS-CURRICULAR CONNECTIONS
Math: Sing "The Ants Go Marching." Count by twos as a class.

d *Kick Start Kindergarten* – p. 50

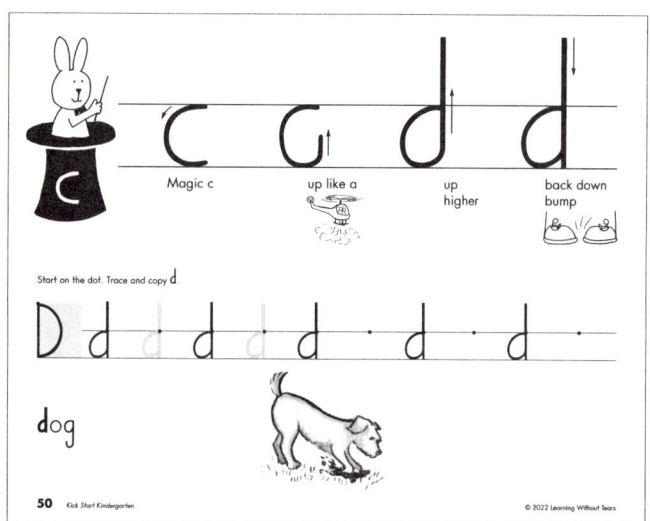

OBJECTIVE
To develop correct habits for writing lowercase **d**.

LESSON INTRODUCTION (Warm Up)
SONG: "Magic c Rap" from *Rock, Rap, Tap & Learn* music album

Additional digital resources are available in the Interactive Digital Teaching Tool (IDTT).

LESSON PLAN

1. Direction Instruction (Demo)

Demonstrate **d** on double lines.
Say the words for each step.

 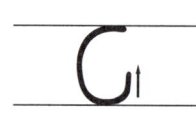 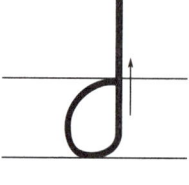 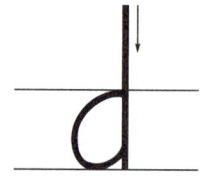

Magic c   up like a helicopter   up higher   back down, bump

2. Guided Practice

Children finger trace the large step-by-step **d** saying the words.
Children trace **d**.
Children copy **d**.

3. Check Letter

Monitor as children trace and copy letters for correct start, steps, and bump.

READ, COLOR & DRAW

Read dog. Say **d** and make the /d/ sound. Encourage free coloring and drawing. Add a ball, a leash, a person, etc.

ENRICHMENT
A+ Worksheet Maker: Create a word list of present tense verbs and have children add lowercase **d** to create past tense verbs. Examples: race, skate, chase, bake.

SUPPORT/ELL
Teach children an alphabet rhyme so they remember how to make **d**. Say, "a-b-c, Magic c turns into d."

CROSS-CURRICULAR CONNECTIONS
Language Arts: Discuss why dogs dig holes. Discuss why people dig holes (fence posts, flower bulbs, etc.).

p. 51

Words D d

OBJECTIVE
To develop correct habits for writing lowercase **d** in a word.

LESSON INTRODUCTION (Warm Up)
Digital Letter and Number Formations (p. 172)

Additional digital resources are available in the Interactive Digital Teaching Tool (IDTT).

LESSON PLAN

1. Direction Instruction (Demo)
Demonstrate writing **d** in words **door**, **deer**, **dolphin**, and **duck** on double lines.

2. Guided Practice
Children trace **d** in words.

3. Check Letters
Monitor as children trace the letters for correct start, steps, and bump.

READ, COLOR & DRAW
Read words. Encourage free coloring and drawing.

ENRICHMENT
Write **c**'s on double line paper. Have children turn **c** into **d**. Say "Magic c turns into d."

SUPPORT/ELL
Slowly read and spell the words together to promote left-right tracking and letter naming.

CROSS-CURRICULAR CONNECTIONS
Math: Take a class poll. What's your favorite animal? Deer, Dolphin or Duck?

Kick Start Kindergarten – p. 52

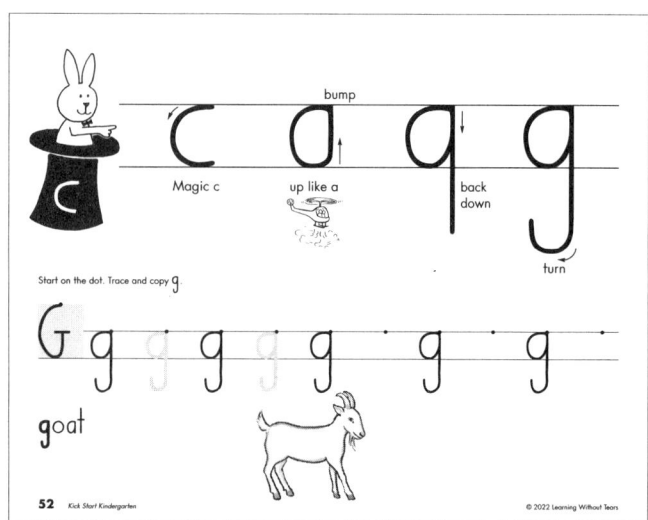

OBJECTIVE
To develop correct habits for writing lowercase **g**.

LESSON INTRODUCTION (Warm Up)
Wet-Dry-Try App for Capitals, Numbers & Lowercase (p. 174)

Additional digital resources are available in the Interactive Digital Teaching Tool (IDTT).

LESSON PLAN

1. Direction Instruction (Demo)

Demonstrate **g** on the Blackboard with Double Lines.
Say the words for each step.

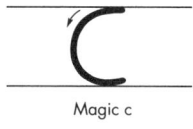
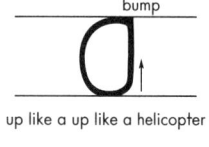
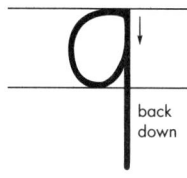
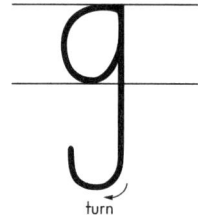

2. Guided Practice

Children finger trace the large step-by-step **g** saying the words.
Children trace **g**.
Children copy **g**.

3. Check Letter

Monitor as children trace and copy letters for correct start, steps, and bump.

READ, COLOR & DRAW

Read goat. Say **g** and make the /g/ sound. Encourage free coloring and drawing. Add grass, rocks, another goat, etc.

ENRICHMENT

 Home Link: Magic c letter group **a**, **d**, and **g**.

SUPPORT/ELL

Model starting lowercase **g** with **c** and focus on the descending part of the letter. This is the first letter that goes below the base line.

CROSS-CURRICULAR CONNECTIONS

Language Arts: Read *The Three Billy Goats Gruff* by Paul Galdone. Ask children to describe the characteristics of each goat.

p. 53

Words G g

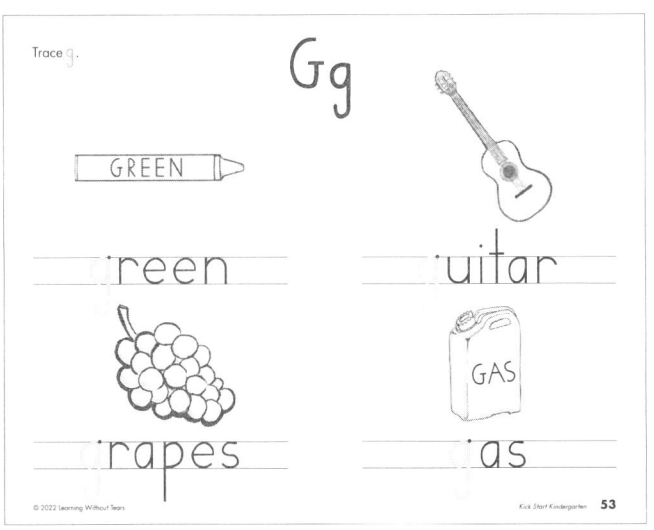

OBJECTIVE
To develop correct habits for writing lowercase **g** in a word.

LESSON INTRODUCTION (Warm Up)
Hand Activity (p. 175)

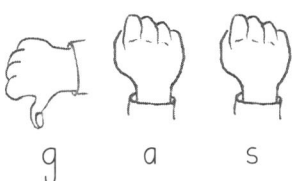

Additional digital resources are available in the Interactive Digital Teaching Tool (IDTT).

LESSON PLAN

1. Direction Instruction (Demo)
Demonstrate writing **g** in words **green**, **guitar**, **grapes**, and **gas** on double lines.

2. Guided Practice
Children trace **g** in words.

3. Check Letters
Monitor as children trace the letters for correct start, steps, and bump.

READ, COLOR & DRAW
Read words. Encourage free coloring and drawing.

ENRICHMENT
Review lowercase **c**, **o**, **a**, and **g** on double lines to help children make the connection to Magic **c** Letters.

SUPPORT/ELL
Use Letter Story: *If George Falls* to reinforce correct formation of **g** (p. 168).

CROSS-CURRICULAR CONNECTIONS
Language Arts: Grapes and green have a /g r/ sound. Make a class list of other words that begin with **gr**.

u *Kick Start Kindergarten* – p. 54

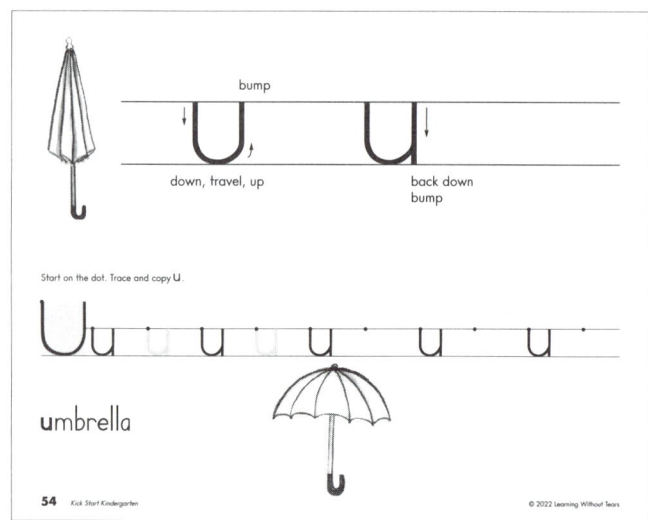

OBJECTIVE
To develop correct habits for writing lowercase **u**.

LESSON INTRODUCTION (Warm Up)
Wet-Dry-Try on Blackboard with Double Lines (p. 176)

Additional digital resources are available in the Interactive Digital Teaching Tool (IDTT).

LESSON PLAN

1. Direction Instruction (Demo)

Demonstrate **u** on the Blackboard with Double Lines.
Say the words for each step.

down, travel, up, bump   back down, bump

2. Guided Practice

Children finger trace the large step-by-step **u** saying the words.
Children trace **u**.
Children copy **u**.

3. Check Letter

Monitor as children trace and copy letters for correct start, steps, and bump.

READ, COLOR & DRAW

Read umbrella. Say **u** and make the /u/ sound. Encourage free coloring and drawing. Add a person, an arrow pointing up, etc.

ENRICHMENT
Show children capital **U** with a flashcard. Have them write lowercase **u** on double line paper.

SUPPORT/ELL
Encourage children to travel on the base line before going up if lowercase **u** is too pointed.

CROSS-CURRICULAR CONNECTIONS
Language Arts: Umbrellas open and close. Discuss other objects that open and close.

p. 55

Words U u

OBJECTIVE
To develop correct habits for writing lowercase **u** in a word.

LESSON INTRODUCTION (Warm Up)
Hand Activity (p. 175)

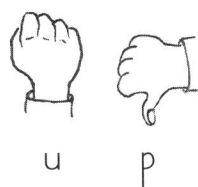

Additional digital resources are available in the Interactive Digital Teaching Tool (IDTT).

LESSON PLAN

1. Direction Instruction (Demo)
Demonstrate writing **u** in words **up**, **under**, **skunk**, and **cut** on double lines.

2. Guided Practice
Children trace **u** in words.

3. Check Letters
Monitor as children trace the letters for correct start, steps, and bump.

READ, COLOR & DRAW
Read words. Say the short /u/ in up, under, skunk, cut. Encourage free coloring and drawing.

ENRICHMENT
Use toy cars to make U-turns and say "Lowercase **u** goes down the street, makes a U-turn, and goes up the street." Have children write lowercase **u** on double line paper.

SUPPORT/ELL
Model the last part of lowercase **u** and explain how that make lowercase **u** different from capital **U**.

CROSS-CURRICULAR CONNECTIONS
Music: Sing "Itsy Bitsy Spider." Do the motions for going "up."

i

Kick Start Kindergarten – p. 56

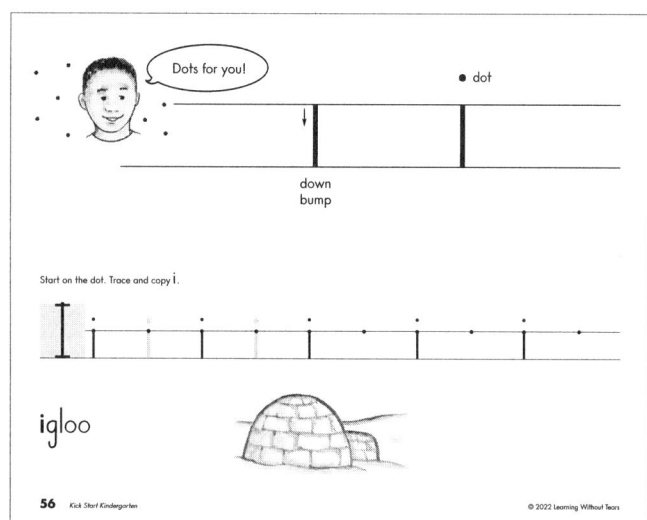

OBJECTIVE
To develop correct habits for writing lowercase **i**.

LESSON INTRODUCTION (Warm Up)
SONG: "Vowels" from *Rock, Rap, Tap & Learn* music album

Additional digital resources are available in the Interactive Digital Teaching Tool (IDTT).

LESSON PLAN

1. Direction Instruction (Demo)
Demonstrate **i** on the Blackboard with Double Lines. Say the words for each step.

2. Guided Practice
Children finger trace the large step-by-step **i** saying the words.
Children trace **i**.
Children copy **i**.

3. Check Letter
Monitor as children trace and copy letters for correct start, steps, and bump.

READ, COLOR & DRAW
Read igloo. Say **i** and make the /i/ sound. Encourage free coloring and drawing. Add a penguin, snowflakes, etc.

ENRICHMENT
Place three starting dots on double lines. Randomly call out letters, **i**, **u**, and **c** and have children write them on double line paper to review.

SUPPORT/ELL
Show children the appropriate size dot when dotting their **i**'s.

CROSS-CURRICULAR CONNECTIONS
Social Studies: Share images of different igloos. Discuss different types of dwellings/homes.

p. 57

Words I i

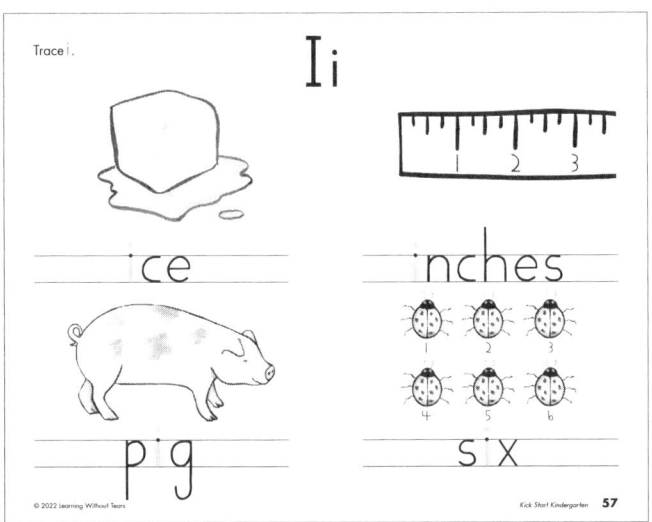

OBJECTIVE
To develop correct habits for writing lowercase **i** in a word.

LESSON INTRODUCTION (Warm Up)
Laser Letters (p.171)

Additional digital resources are available in the Interactive Digital Teaching Tool (IDTT).

LESSON PLAN

1. Direction Instruction (Demo)
Demonstrate writing **i** in words **ice**, **inches**, **pig**, and **six** on double lines.

2. Guided Practice
Children trace **i** in words.

3. Check Letters
Monitor as children trace the letters for correct start, steps, and bump.

READ, COLOR & DRAW
Read words. Encourage free coloring and drawing.

ENRICHMENT
A+ Worksheet Maker: Create a list of simple words where children need to add a lowercase **i**.
For example, s_t, f_t, d_g.

SUPPORT/ELL
Slowly read and spell the words together to promote left-right tracking and letter naming.

CROSS-CURRICULAR CONNECTIONS
Math: Count the six ladybugs on the student edition page. Ask children to find six other things in the classroom.

e

Kick Start Kindergarten – p. 58

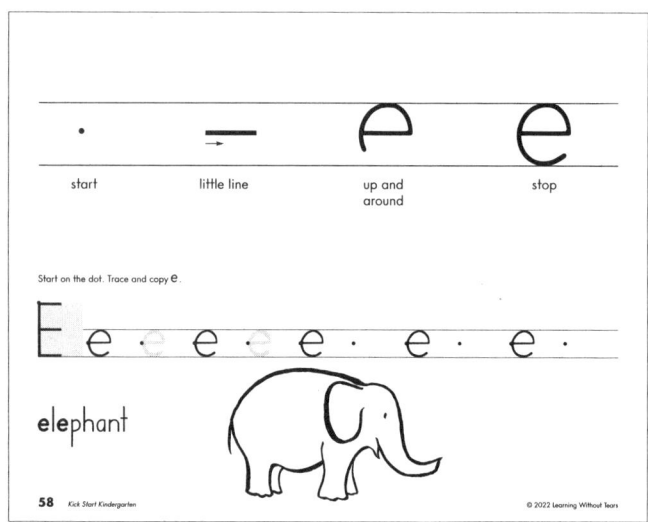

OBJECTIVE
To develop correct habits for writing lowercase **e**.

LESSON INTRODUCTION (Warm Up)
Wet-Dry-Try on Blackboard with Double Lines (p. 176)

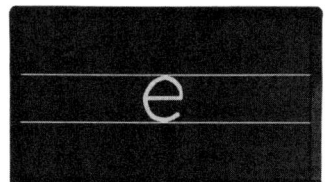

Additional digital resources are available in the Interactive Digital Teaching Tool (IDTT).

LESSON PLAN

1. Direction Instruction (Demo)
Demonstrate **e** on the Blackboard with Double Lines.
Say the words for each step.

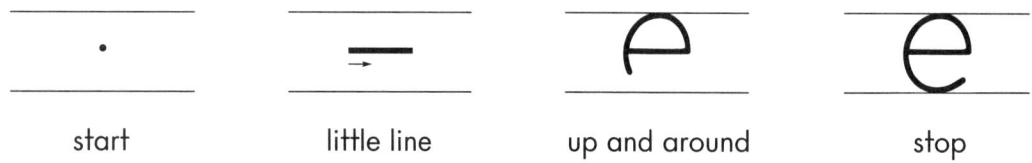

2. Guided Practice
Children finger trace the large step-by-step **e** saying the words.
Children trace **e**.
Children copy **e**.

3. Check Letter
Monitor as children trace and copy letters for correct start, steps, and bump.

READ, COLOR & DRAW
Read elephants. Say **e** and make the /e/ sound. Encourage free coloring and drawing. Add peanuts, water, etc.

ENRICHMENT
A+ Worksheet Maker: Create a list of simple words where children need to add a lowercase **e**.
For example, w_, t_n, g_t.

SUPPORT/ELL
Use the Letter Story: *Run the Bases* to reinforce correct formation of **e** (p. 168).

CROSS-CURRICULAR CONNECTIONS
Science: Compare the size and characteristics of elephants to other animals and people.

Words E e

p. 59

OBJECTIVE
To develop correct habits for writing lowercase **e** in a word.

LESSON INTRODUCTION (Warm Up)
Air Writing (p. 170)

> Additional digital resources are available in the Interactive Digital Teaching Tool (IDTT).

LESSON PLAN

1. Direction Instruction (Demo)
Demonstrate writing **e** in words **exit**, **egg**, **hen**, and **ten** on double lines.

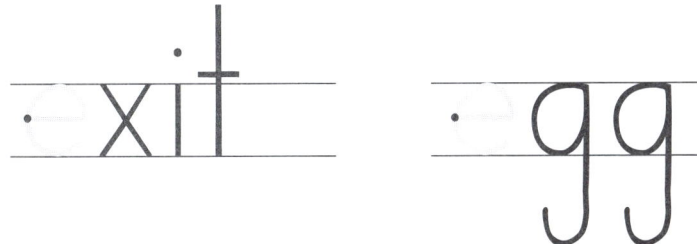

2. Guided Practice
Children trace **e** in words.

3. Check Letters
Monitor as children trace the letters for correct start, steps, and bump.

READ, COLOR & DRAW
Read words. Say the short /e/ sound in exit, egg, hen, ten. Encourage free coloring and drawing.

ENRICHMENT
Have children review vowels **a**, **e**, **i**, **o**, and **u** on double lines.

SUPPORT/ELL
Reinforce lowercase **e** with Wet-Dry-Try on the Blackboard with Double Lines (p. 176).

CROSS-CURRICULAR CONNECTIONS
Language Arts: Make a class list of words that rhyme with **ten** and **hen**.

Kick Start Kindergarten – p. 60

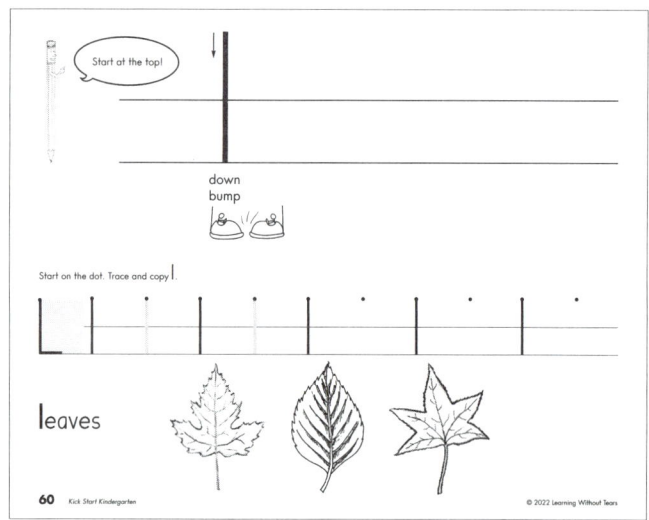

OBJECTIVE
To develop correct habits for writing lowercase l.

LESSON INTRODUCTION (Warm Up)
Laser Letters (p.171)

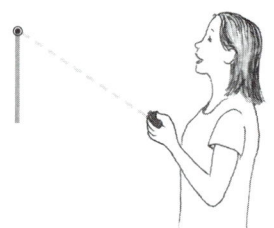

Additional digital resources are available in the Interactive Digital Teaching Tool (IDTT).

LESSON PLAN

1. Direction Instruction (Demo)
Demonstrate l on the Blackboard with Double Lines.
Say the words for each step.

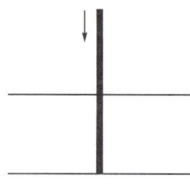

down, bump

2. Guided Practice
Children finger trace the large step-by-step l saying the words.
Children trace l.
Children copy l.

3. Check Letter
Monitor as children trace and copy letters for correct start, steps, and bump.

READ, COLOR & DRAW
Read leaves. Say l and make the /l/ sound. Encourage free coloring and drawing. Add a tree, other leafs, etc.

ENRICHMENT
Have children find a leaf outside and crayon rub on the page. Write capital and lowercase l on page.

SUPPORT/ELL
Finger trace the letter model in the student edition. Show children how l starts in the top space just as capital L does.

CROSS-CURRICULAR CONNECTIONS
Language Arts/Science: Read *The Very Hungry Caterpillar* by Eric Carle. Discuss the stages of a butterfly.

p. 61

k

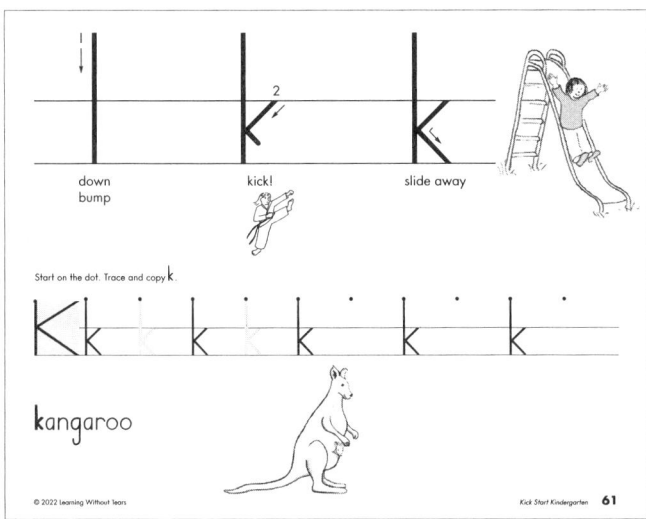

OBJECTIVE
To develop correct habits for writing lowercase **k**.

LESSON INTRODUCTION (Warm Up)
Wet-Dry-Try on Blackboard with Double Lines (p. 176)

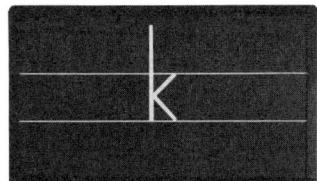

Additional digital resources are available in the Interactive Digital Teaching Tool (IDTT).

LESSON PLAN

1. Direction Instruction (Demo)
Demonstrate **k** on the Blackboard with Double Lines. Say the words for each step.

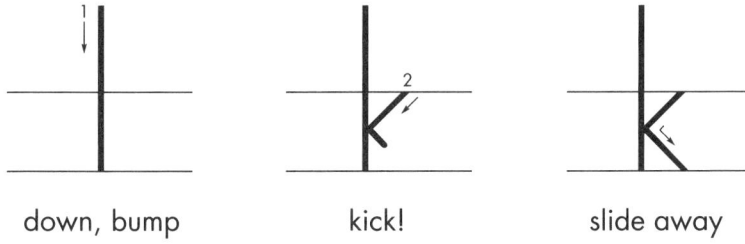

2. Guided Practice
Children finger trace the large step-by-step **k** saying the words.
Children trace **k**.
Children copy **k**.

3. Check Letter
Monitor as children trace and copy letters for correct start, steps, and bump.

READ, COLOR & DRAW
Read kangaroo. Say **k** and make the /k/ sound. Encourage free coloring and drawing. Add grass, a ball to kick, etc.

ENRICHMENT
Turn off the lights and use a flashlight to trace lowercase **k** on the wall. Have children Air Trace **k**.

SUPPORT/ELL
Use the Letter Story: *Karate K* to reinforce correct formation of **k** (p. 168).

CROSS-CURRICULAR CONNECTIONS
Geography: Help children find Australia on a globe. Kangaroos and koalas live there.

y

Kick Start Kindergarten – p. 62

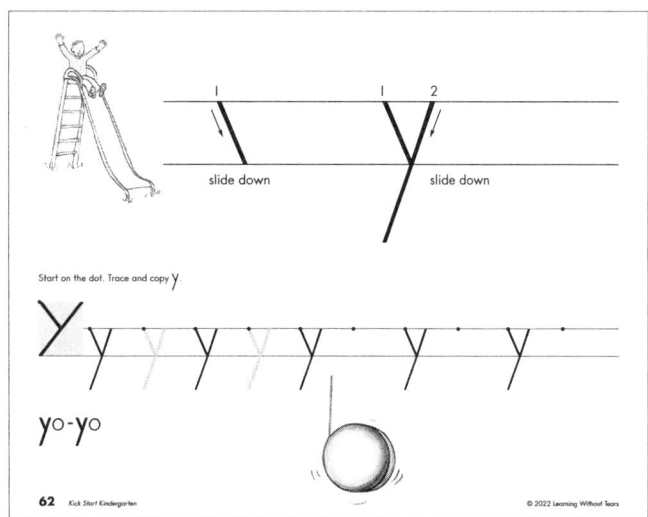

OBJECTIVE
To develop correct habits for writing lowercase **y**.

LESSON INTRODUCTION (Warm Up)
Digital Letter and Number Formations (p. 172)

Additional digital resources are available in the Interactive Digital Teaching Tool (IDTT).

LESSON PLAN

1. Direction Instruction (Demo)

Demonstrate **y** on the Blackboard with Double Lines.
Say the words for each step.

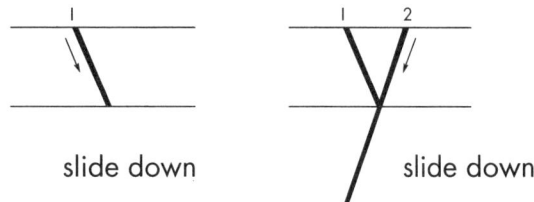

2. Guided Practice

Children finger trace the large step-by-step **y** saying the words.
Children trace **y**.
Children copy **y**.

3. Check Letter

Monitor as children trace and copy letters for correct start, steps, and bump.

READ, COLOR & DRAW

Read yo-yo. Say **y** and make the /y/ sound. Sometimes **y** is a vowel. It makes a long /i/ sound. Encourage free coloring and drawing. Add a person, another yo-yo, etc.

ENRICHMENT
Show children capital **Y** with a flashcard. Have children write lowercase **y** on double lines.

SUPPORT/ELL
Compare capital **Y** and lowercase **y**. Review big and little diagonal lines.

CROSS-CURRICULAR CONNECTIONS
Language Arts: Place a yo-yo in a covered box. Have children reach in and describe physical attributes of the yo-yo.

p. 63 # Sentences

OBJECTIVE
To develop correct habits for tracing letters in a sentence.

LESSON INTRODUCTION (Warm Up)
Syllables (p. 179)

Additional digital resources are available in the Interactive Digital Teaching Tool (IDTT).

LESSON PLAN

1. Direction Instruction (Demo)

Demonstrate on double lines: **Y is for yo-yo.**
Show children that sentences begin with a capital, have space between words, and end with a period.

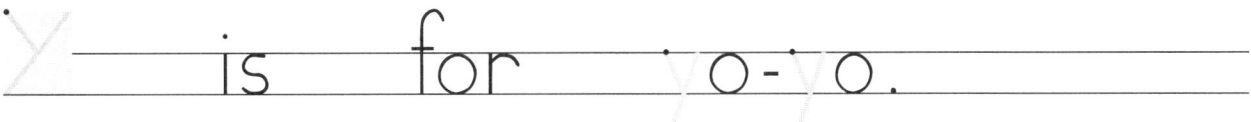

2. Guided Practice

Children trace letters in sentence.

3. Check Sentence

Monitor as children trace their letters for correct start, steps, and bump.

READ, COLOR & DRAW

Read words. Encourage free coloring and drawing.

ENRICHMENT
A+ Worksheet Maker: Create a list of simple words where children need to add a lowercase **y**.
For example, wh_, tr_, sk_, b_.

SUPPORT/ELL
Repeat each sentence two to three times as children place and move their pointer finger under each word.

CROSS-CURRICULAR CONNECTIONS
Science: Bring in different leaves. Describe characteristics as a class. Read a story about how leaves change based on the season.

Kick Start Kindergarten – p. 64

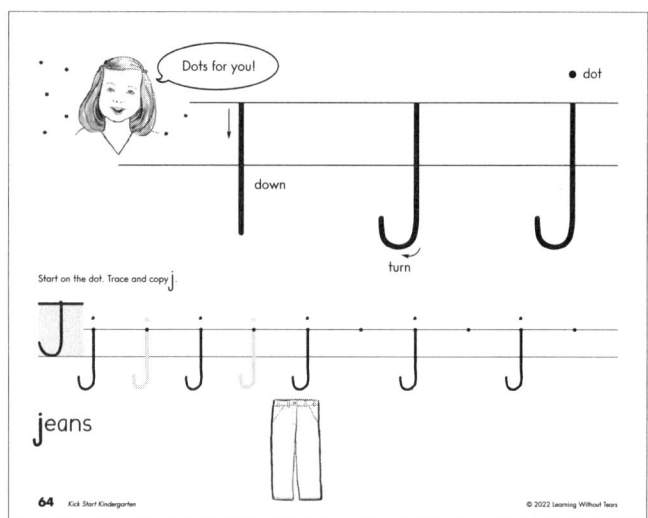

OBJECTIVE
To develop correct habits for writing lowercase **j**.

LESSON INTRODUCTION (Warm Up)
SONG: "Descending Letters" from *Rock, Rap, Tap & Learn* music album

Additional digital resources are available in the Interactive Digital Teaching Tool (IDTT).

LESSON PLAN

1. Direction Instruction (Demo)

Demonstrate **j** on the Blackboard with Double Lines.
Say the words for each step.

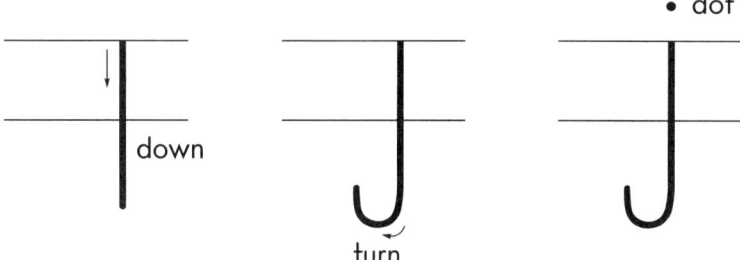

2. Guided Practice

Children finger trace the large step-by-step **j** saying the words.
Children trace **j**.
Children copy **j**.

3. Check Letter

Monitor as children trace and copy letters for correct start, steps, and bump.

READ, COLOR & DRAW

Read jeans. Say **j** and make the /j/ sound. Encourage free coloring and drawing. Add other clothing, feet under jeans, etc.

ENRICHMENT

 Home Link: Transition group **u, i, e, l, k, y,** and **j**.

SUPPORT/ELL

Use Wet-Dry-Try on Blackboard with Double Lines (p. 176) to reinforce **j** is a descending letter.

CROSS-CURRICULAR CONNECTIONS

Social Studies: Discuss clothing students would wear during different seasons.

p. 65   **p**

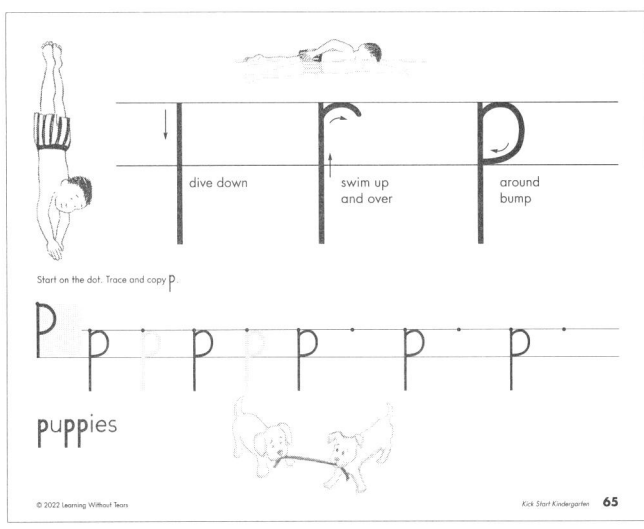

OBJECTIVE
To develop correct habits for writing lowercase **p**.

LESSON INTRODUCTION (Warm Up)
Hand Activity (p. 175)

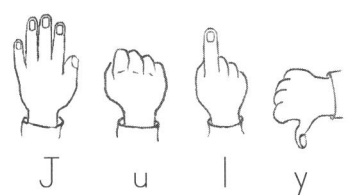

Additional digital resources are available in the Interactive Digital Teaching Tool (IDTT).

LESSON PLAN

1. Direction Instruction (Demo)
Demonstrate **p** on the Blackboard with Double Lines.
Say the words for each step.

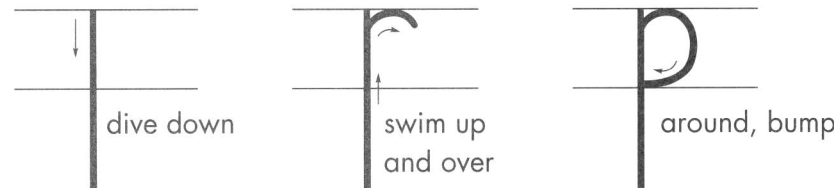

2. Guided Practice
Children finger trace the large step-by-step **p** saying the words.
Children trace **p**.
Children copy **p**.

3. Check Letter
Monitor as children trace and copy letters for correct start, steps, and bump.

READ, COLOR & DRAW
Read puppies. Say **p** and make the /p/ sound. Encourage free coloring and drawing. Add toys, bowl, doghouse, etc.

ENRICHMENT
A+ Worksheet Maker: Create a spelling worksheet with simple words that children have to end by writing **p**. For example, pu_, cu_, li_.

SUPPORT/ELL
If children make lowercase **p** in two strokes, review how to dive down and swim up and over to make this letter in a continuous stroke.

CROSS-CURRICULAR CONNECTIONS
Science: Listen to different animal sounds. Guess the animals from the sounds as a class.

r   Kick Start Kindergarten – p. 66

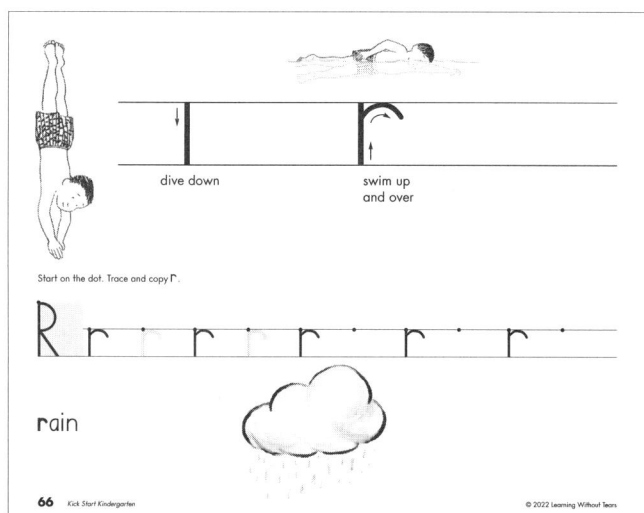

OBJECTIVE
To develop correct habits for writing lowercase **r**.

LESSON INTRODUCTION (Warm Up)
SONG: "Diver Letters School" from *Rock, Rap, Tap & Learn* music album

Additional digital resources are available in the Interactive Digital Teaching Tool (IDTT).

LESSON PLAN

1. Direction Instruction (Demo)

Demonstrate **r** on the Blackboard with Double Lines.
Say the words for each step.

dive down   swim up and over

2. Guided Practice

Children finger trace the large step-by-step **r** saying the words.
Children trace **r**.
Children copy **r**.

3. Check Letter

Monitor as children trace and copy letters for correct start, steps, and bump.

READ, COLOR & DRAW

Read rain. Say **r** and make the /r/ sound. Encourage free coloring and drawing. Add a rainbow, raindrops, etc.

ENRICHMENT
Have children copy words that begin with **r**, such as **ray**, **red**, **rip**, **row**, and **rug**.

SUPPORT/ELL
Making large motions for the Diver Letters before writing will help children with start and sequence.

CROSS-CURRICULAR CONNECTIONS
Science/Language Arts: Read books about rain and discuss why it's important. Write a class story about rain.

p. 67

Sentences

OBJECTIVE
To develop correct habits for tracing letters in a sentence.

LESSON INTRODUCTION (Warm Up)
SONG: "Sentence Song" from *Rock, Rap, Tap & Learn* music album

Additional digital resources are available in the Interactive Digital Teaching Tool (IDTT).

LESSON PLAN

1. Direction Instruction (Demo)

Demonstrate on double lines: **R is for rain.**
Show children that sentences begin with a capital, have space between words, and end with a period.

2. Guided Practice

Children trace letters in sentence.

3. Check Sentence

Monitor as children trace their letters for correct start, steps, and bump.

READ, COLOR & DRAW

Read words. Encourage free coloring and drawing.

ENRICHMENT
Using capital flash cards, show children **R**, **J**, and **P**, and ask them to write the corresponding lowercase letters.

SUPPORT/ELL
Help children clap the number of words in the sentence. Point to the capital, the spaces between words, and the period.

CROSS-CURRICULAR CONNECTIONS
Science: Explore weather. Read a book that describes how rain is formed.

n

Kick Start Kindergarten – p. 68

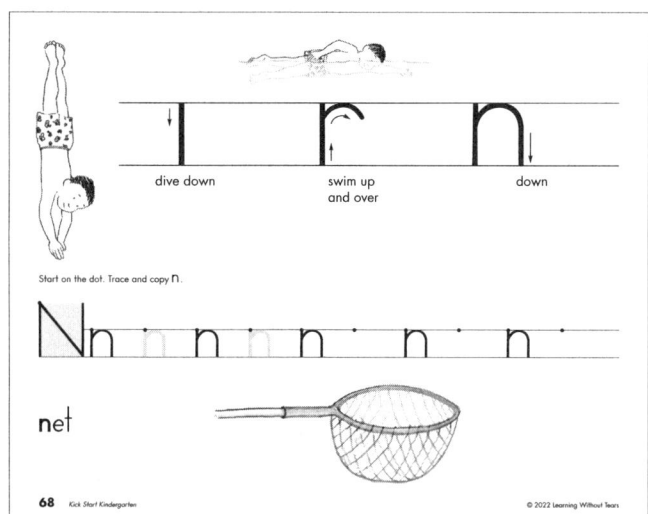

OBJECTIVE
To develop correct habits for writing lowercase **n**.

LESSON INTRODUCTION (Warm Up)
Laser Letters (p.171)

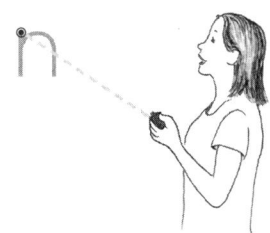

Additional digital resources are available in the Interactive Digital Teaching Tool (IDTT).

LESSON PLAN

1. Direction Instruction (Demo)

Demonstrate **n** on the Blackboard with Double Lines.
Say the words for each step.

dive down   swim up and over   down

2. Guided Practice

Children finger trace the large step-by-step **n** saying the words.
Children trace **n**.
Children copy **n**.

3. Check Letter

Monitor as children trace and copy letters for correct start, steps, and bump.

READ, COLOR & DRAW

Read net. Say **n** and make the /n/ sound. Encourage free coloring and drawing. Add a fish or ball inside net, etc.

ENRICHMENT
Turn off the lights and use a flashlight to trace lowercase **n** on the wall. Have children Air Trace **n**.

SUPPORT/ELL
If children start lowercase **n** from the bottom, show them how to dive down and swim up and over in a continuous stroke.

CROSS-CURRICULAR CONNECTIONS
Science: Have a bucket of water with items floating on top. Let each child use a net to scoop out the items.

p. 69

Words N n

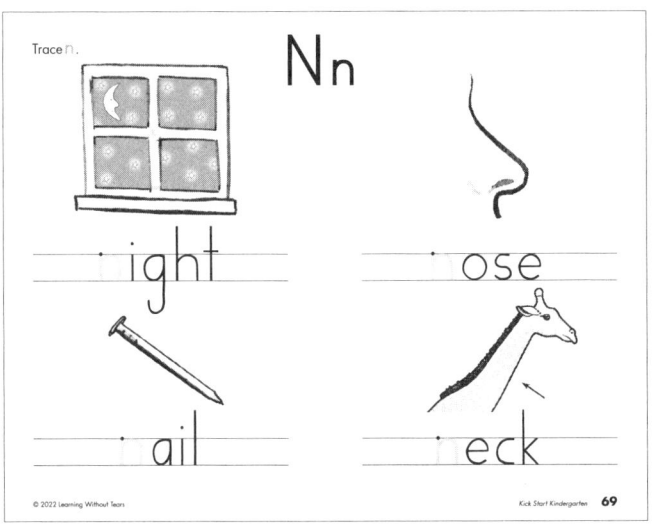

OBJECTIVE
To develop correct habits for writing lowercase **n** in a word.

LESSON INTRODUCTION (Warm Up)
Hand Activity (p. 175)

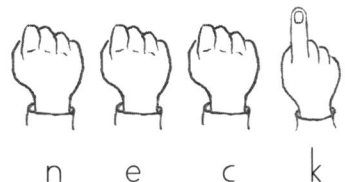

Additional digital resources are available in the Interactive Digital Teaching Tool (IDTT).

LESSON PLAN

1. Direction Instruction (Demo)
Demonstrate writing **n** in words **night**, **nose**, **nail**, and **neck** on double lines.

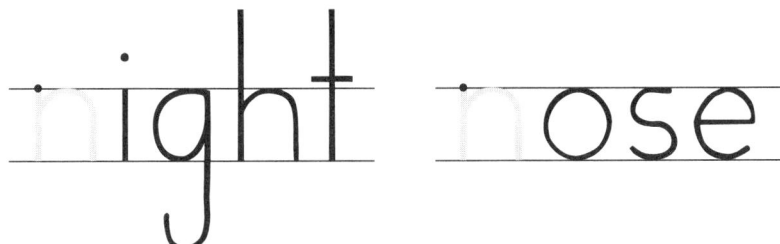

2. Guided Practice
Children trace **n** in words.

3. Check Letters
Monitor as children trace the letters for correct start, steps, and bump.

READ, COLOR & DRAW
Read words. Encourage free coloring and drawing.

ENRICHMENT
A+ Worksheet Maker: Create a spelling worksheet with simple words where children have to add an **n**. For example, o_, te_, wi_.

SUPPORT/ELL
Slowly read and spell the words together to promote left-right tracking and letter naming.

CROSS-CURRICULAR CONNECTIONS
Science: Talk about the senses seeing and smelling. We use our eyes to tell night from day. We use our nose to smell.

Kick Start Kindergarten Teacher's Guide: Lowercase Letters, Words & Sentences

m

Kick Start Kindergarten – p. 70

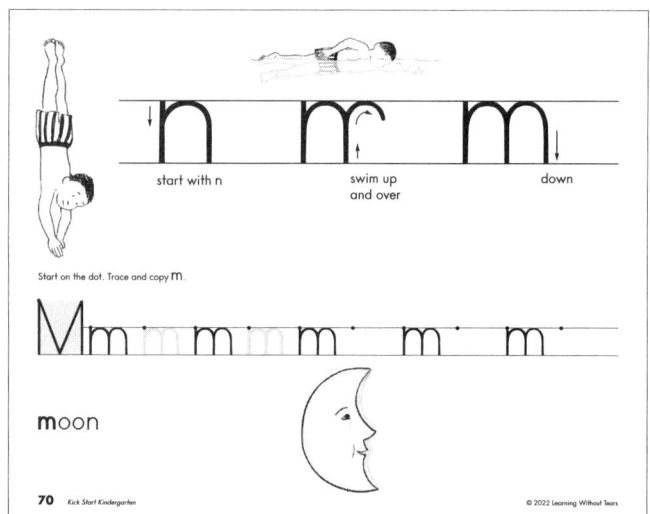

OBJECTIVE
To develop correct habits for writing lowercase **m**.

LESSON INTRODUCTION (Warm Up)
Wet-Dry-Try on Blackboard with Double Lines (p. 176)

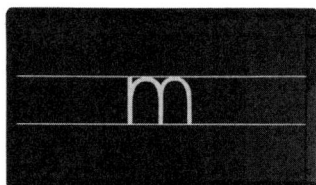

Additional digital resources are available in the Interactive Digital Teaching Tool (IDTT).

LESSON PLAN

1. Direction Instruction (Demo)
Demonstrate **m** on the Blackboard with Double Lines.
Say the words for each step.

start with n

swim up and over

down

2. Guided Practice
Children finger trace the large step-by-step **m** saying the words.
Children trace **m**.
Children copy **m**.

3. Check Letter
Monitor as children trace and copy letters for correct start, steps, and bump.

READ, COLOR & DRAW
Read moon. Say **m** and make the /m/ sound. Encourage free coloring and drawing. Add stars, planets, etc.

ENRICHMENT
Children write **M m** on a blank page. Children cut and paste pictures that begin with **m**.

SUPPORT/ELL
Use Letter Story: *Stinky m* to reinforce correct formation of **m** (p. 169).

CROSS-CURRICULAR CONNECTIONS
Science: Encourage children to look at the moon. Discuss how the moon changes during the month.

p. 71

Words M m

OBJECTIVE
To develop correct habits for writing lowercase **m** in a word.

LESSON INTRODUCTION (Warm Up)
Digital Letter and Number Formations (p. 172)

Additional digital resources are available in the Interactive Digital Teaching Tool (IDTT).

LESSON PLAN

1. Direction Instruction (Demo)
Demonstrate writing **m** in words **mouse**, **moose**, **map**, and **monkey** on double lines.

2. Guided Practice
Children trace **m** in words.

3. Check Letters
Monitor as children trace the letters for correct start, steps, and bump.

READ, COLOR & DRAW
Read words. Encourage free coloring and drawing.

ENRICHMENT
Show capital flash cards **R**, **N**, and **M**, and ask children to write the corresponding lowercase letters.

SUPPORT/ELL
If children start lowercase **m** from the bottom, show them how to dive down and swim up and over and up and over in a continuous stroke.

CROSS-CURRICULAR CONNECTIONS
Social Studies: Compare the habitat of the moose and the monkey. Show Africa and North America on a map.

h

Kick Start Kindergarten – p. 72

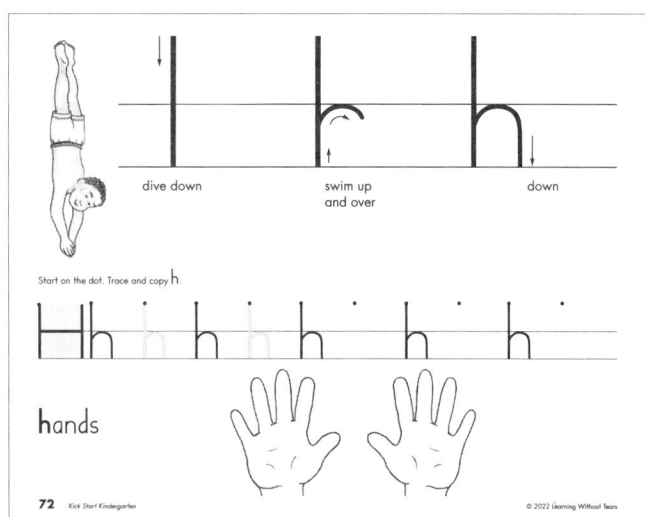

OBJECTIVE
To develop correct habits for writing lowercase **h**.

LESSON INTRODUCTION (Warm Up)
Air Writing (p. 170)

Additional digital resources are available in the Interactive Digital Teaching Tool (IDTT).

LESSON PLAN

1. Direction Instruction (Demo)

Demonstrate **h** on the Blackboard with Double Lines.
Say the words for each step.

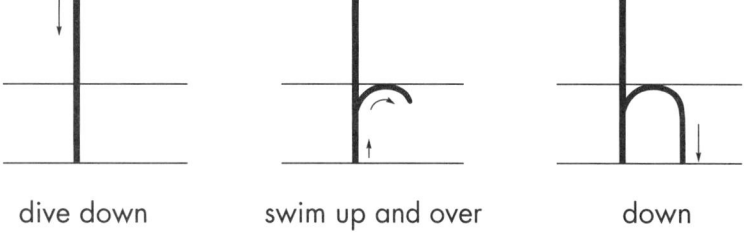

dive down   swim up and over   down

2. Guided Practice

Children finger trace the large step-by-step **h** saying the words.
Children trace **h**.
Children copy **h**.

3. Check Letter

Monitor as children trace and copy letters for correct start, steps, and bump.

READ, COLOR & DRAW

Read hands. Say **h** and make the /h/ sound. Encourage free coloring and drawing. Add different hands, a person, etc.

ENRICHMENT
Have children copy subject-verb sentence: He hops.

SUPPORT/ELL
Pretend to climb up a high ladder for a high dive to show how Diver Letter **h** starts high.

CROSS-CURRICULAR CONNECTIONS
Math: Count fingers to **8**. Show **8** using different fingers. For example, 5+3, 4+4.

p. 73 # Words H h

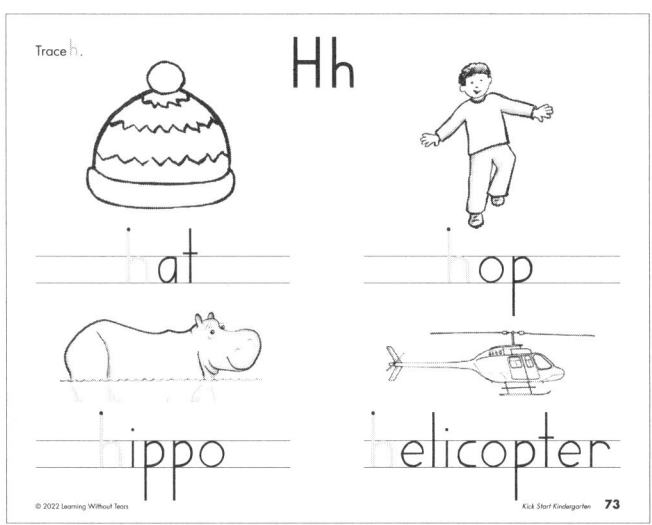

OBJECTIVE
To develop correct habits for writing lowercase **h** in a word.

LESSON INTRODUCTION (Warm Up)
Syllables (p. 179)

Additional digital resources are available in the Interactive Digital Teaching Tool (IDTT).

LESSON PLAN

1. Direction Instruction (Demo)
Demonstrate writing **h** in words **hat**, **hop**, **hippo**, and **helicopter** on double lines.

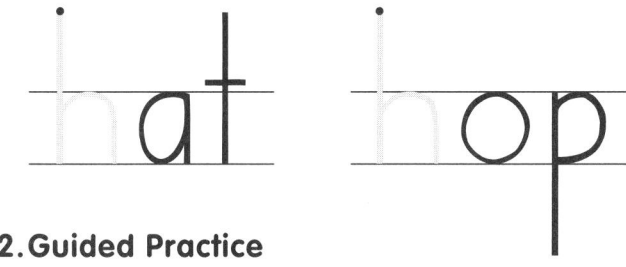

2. Guided Practice
Children trace **h** in words.

3. Check Letters
Monitor as children trace the letters for correct start, steps, and bump.

READ, COLOR & DRAW
Read words. Encourage free coloring and drawing.

ENRICHMENT
Stand up and make the motions for **p, r, n, m, h,** and **b** as a class.

SUPPORT/ELL
Slowly read and spell the words together to promote left-right tracking and letter naming.

CROSS-CURRICULAR CONNECTIONS
Language Arts: **Hop** is a verb. Ask children to identify other verbs by describing what they do on the playground.

b

Kick Start Kindergarten – p. 74

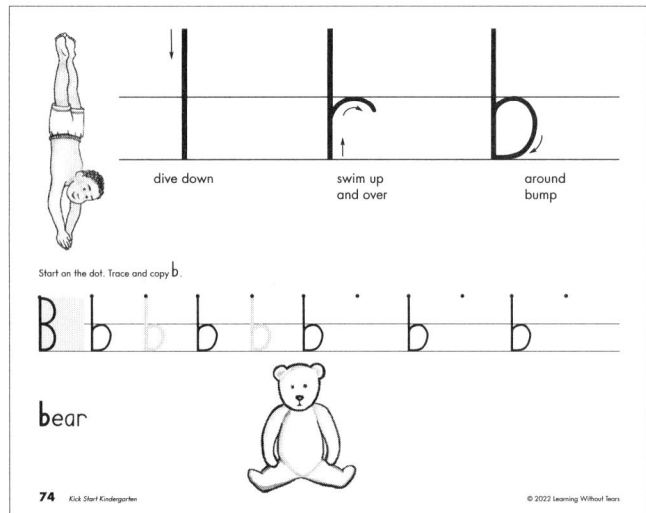

OBJECTIVE
To develop correct habits for writing lowercase **b**.

LESSON INTRODUCTION (Warm Up)
Hand Activity (p. 175)

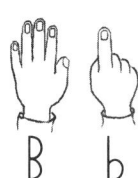

Additional digital resources are available in the Interactive Digital Teaching Tool (IDTT).

LESSON PLAN

1. Direction Instruction (Demo)

Demonstrate **b** on the Blackboard with Double Lines.
Say the words for each step.

dive down   swim up and over   around, bump

2. Guided Practice

Children finger trace the large step-by-step **b** saying the words.
Children trace **b**.
Children copy **b**.

3. Check Letter

Monitor as children trace and copy letters for correct start, steps, and bump.

READ, COLOR & DRAW

Read bear. Say **b** and make the /b/ sound. Encourage free coloring and drawing. Add other bears.

ENRICHMENT

Home Link: Diver letters **p**, **r**, **n**, **m**, **h**, and **b**.

SUPPORT/ELL
Use Letter Story: *Honeybee* to reinforce correct formation of **b** (p. 168).

CROSS-CURRICULAR CONNECTIONS
Language Arts: Read *Brown Bear, Brown Bear, What Do You See?* By Bill Martin Jr. Talk about words that rhyme with bear.

Words B b

OBJECTIVE
To develop correct habits for writing lowercase **b** in a word.

LESSON INTRODUCTION (Warm Up)
Wet-Dry-Try App for Capitals, Numbers & Lowercase (p. 174)

Additional digital resources are available in the Interactive Digital Teaching Tool (IDTT).

LESSON PLAN

1. Direction Instruction (Demo)
Demonstrate writing **b** in words **bugs**, **bat**, **baby**, and **bubbles** on double lines.

2. Guided Practice
Children trace **b** in words.

3. Check Letters
Monitor as children trace the letters for correct start, steps, and bump.

READ, COLOR & DRAW
Read words. Encourage free coloring and drawing.

ENRICHMENT
Children write **B b** on a blank page. Children cut and paste pictures that begin with **b**.

SUPPORT/ELL
Slowly read and spell the words together to promote left-right tracking and letter naming.

CROSS-CURRICULAR CONNECTIONS
Language Arts: Discuss things you do in the summer, for example, blow bubbles, play baseball.

Kick Start Kindergarten – p. 76

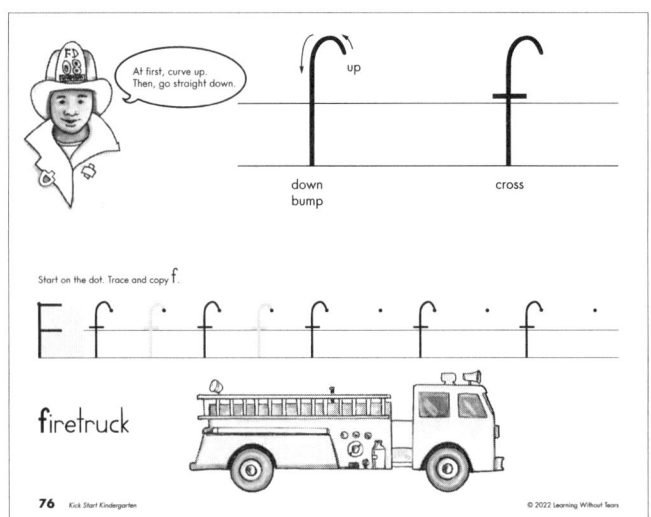

OBJECTIVE
To develop correct habits for writing lowercase **f**.

LESSON INTRODUCTION (Warm Up)
Laser Letters (p.171)

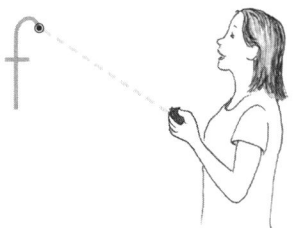

Additional digital resources are available in the Interactive Digital Teaching Tool (IDTT).

LESSON PLAN

1. Direction Instruction (Demo)
Demonstrate **f** on the Blackboard with Double Lines.
Say the words for each step.

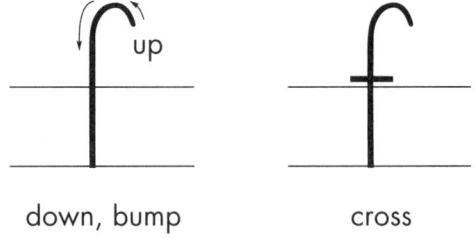

down, bump   cross

2. Guided Practice
Children finger trace the large step-by-step **f** saying the words.
Children trace **f**.
Children copy **f**.

3. Check Letter
Monitor as children trace and copy letters for correct start, steps, and bump.

READ, COLOR & DRAW
Read firetruck. Say **f** and make the /f/ sound. Encourage free coloring and drawing. Add a road, a tree, water hose, etc.

ENRICHMENT
Have children copy the words **sink** and **float** on two cards. Collect objects to drop in water then have children place the object beside the correct card.

SUPPORT/ELL
Use the Letter Story: *Fire Hose Squirt* to reinforce correct formation of **f** (p. 168).

CROSS-CURRICULAR CONNECTIONS
Language Arts: Firetruck is a compound word. Discuss other compound words (cupcake, fishbowl, football, etc.).

p. 77   **Words F f**

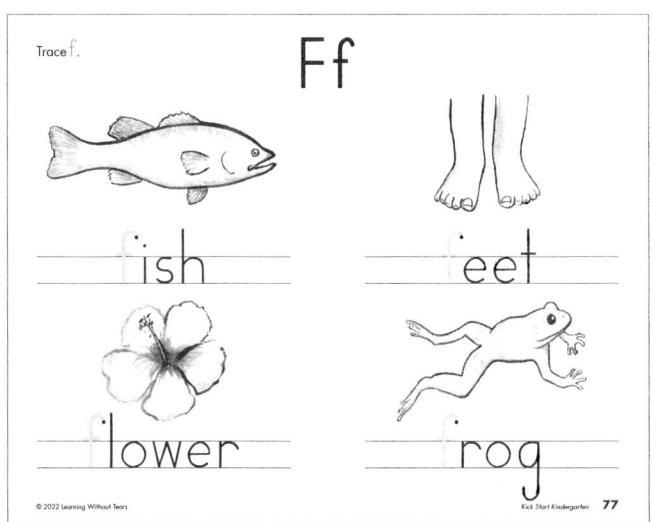

OBJECTIVE
To develop correct habits for writing lowercase **f** in a word.

LESSON INTRODUCTION (Warm Up)
Hand Activity (p. 175)

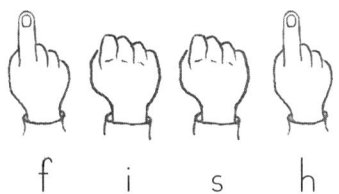

Additional digital resources are available in the Interactive Digital Teaching Tool (IDTT).

LESSON PLAN

1. Direction Instruction (Demo)
Demonstrate writing **f** in words **fish**, **feet**, **flower**, and **frog** on double lines.

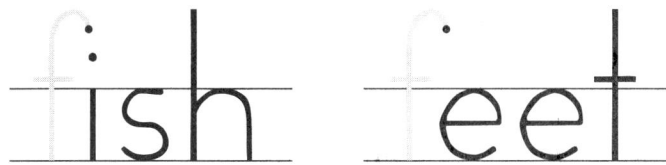

2. Guided Practice
Children trace **f** in words.

3. Check Letters
Monitor as children trace the letters for correct start, steps, and bump.

READ, COLOR & DRAW
Read words. Encourage **free** coloring and drawing.

ENRICHMENT
Show children capital **F** with a flashcard. Have children write **f** on double lines.

SUPPORT/ELL
Review the starting positions for **f** and **e**. They are the only exceptions to the rule to start your letters at the top.

CROSS-CURRICULAR CONNECTIONS
Science: Place flower seeds in a plastic bag by stapling them to a paper towel. Talk about the stages from a seed to a flower.

q   *Kick Start Kindergarten* – p. 78

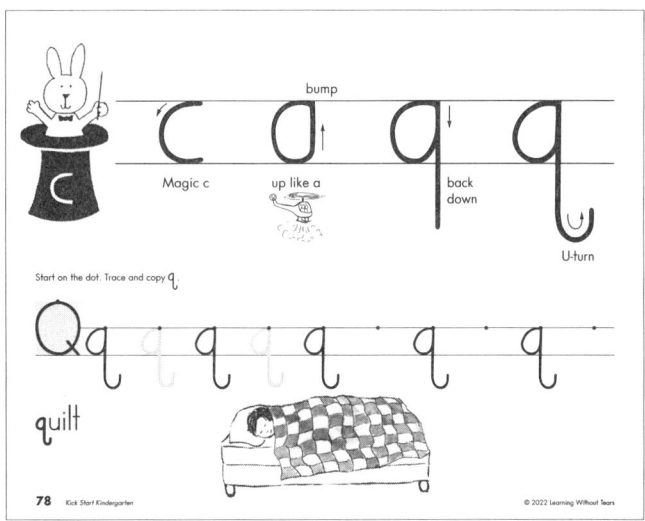

OBJECTIVE
To develop correct habits for writing lowercase q.

LESSON INTRODUCTION (Warm Up)
Voices (p. 177)

Additional digital resources are available in the Interactive Digital Teaching Tool (IDTT).

LESSON PLAN

1. Direction Instruction (Demo)

Demonstrate q on the Blackboard with Double Lines.
Say the words for each step.

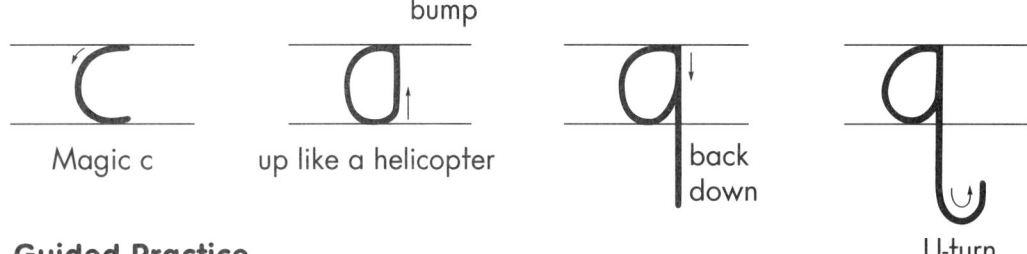

2. Guided Practice

Children finger trace the large step-by-step q saying the words.
Children trace q.
Children copy q.

3. Check Letter

Monitor as children trace and copy letters for correct start, steps, and bump.

READ, COLOR & DRAW

Read quilt. Say q and make letter sound. Encourage free coloring and drawing. Add a design, toys around bed, etc.

ENRICHMENT
Have children make lowercase q with pipe cleaners or wick sticks.

SUPPORT/ELL
Use Letter Story: *U-turn* to reinforce correct formation of q (p. 169).

CROSS-CURRICULAR CONNECTIONS
Language Arts/Arts: Create a class quilt with children's drawings. Describe the different patterns on the quilt.

p. 79

X

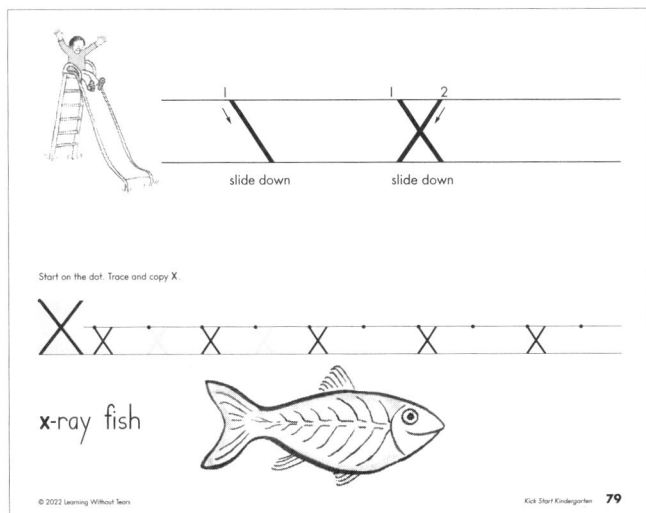

OBJECTIVE
To develop correct habits for writing lowercase **x**.

LESSON INTRODUCTION (Warm Up)
Laser Letters (p.171)

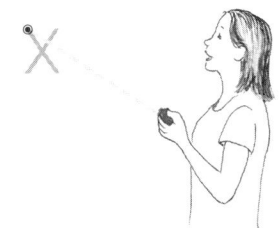

Additional digital resources are available in the Interactive Digital Teaching Tool (IDTT).

LESSON PLAN

1. Direction Instruction (Demo)

Demonstrate **x** on the Blackboard with Double Lines.
Say the words for each step.

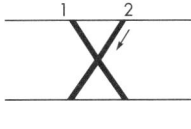

2. Guided Practice

Children finger trace the large step-by-step **x** saying the words.
Children trace **x**.
Children copy **x**.

3. Check Letter

Monitor as children trace and copy letters for correct start, steps, and bump.

READ, COLOR & DRAW

Read x-ray. Say **x** and make the /x/ sound. Encourage free coloring and drawing. Add other X-ray fish, water, etc.

ENRICHMENT
Teach children how to play Tic-Tac-Toe activity.

SUPPORT/ELL
Left-handed children often need support to begin **x** at the top left. Highlight the first slide down stroke so children can trace.

CROSS-CURRICULAR CONNECTIONS
Science: Talk about the meaning and use of an X-ray. Share images of an X-ray fish or an X-ray to help children make a connection.

z

Kick Start Kindergarten – p. 80

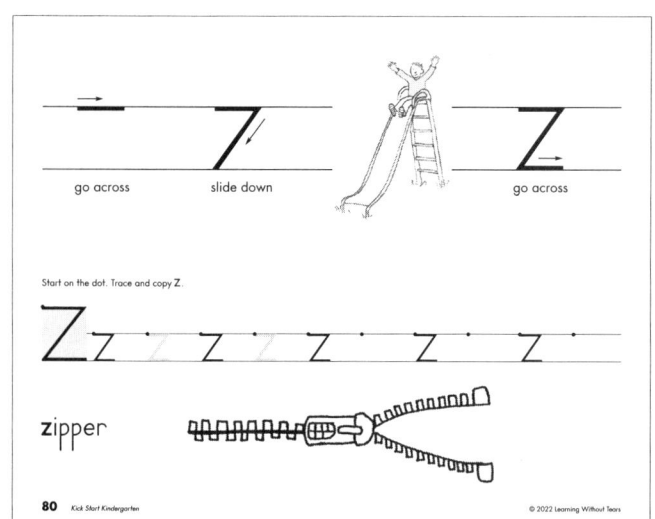

OBJECTIVE
To develop correct habits for writing lowercase **z**.

LESSON INTRODUCTION (Warm Up)
Wet-Dry-Try on Blackboard with Double Lines (p. 176)

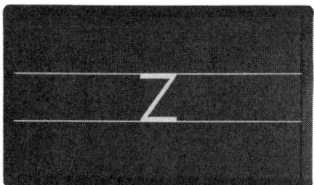

Additional digital resources are available in the Interactive Digital Teaching Tool (IDTT).

LESSON PLAN

1. Direction Instruction (Demo)

Demonstrate **z** on the Blackboard with Double Lines.
Say the words for each step.

go across   slide down   go across

2. Guided Practice

Children finger trace the large step-by-step **z** saying the words.
Children trace **z**.
Children copy **z**.

3. Check Letter

Monitor as children trace and copy letters for correct start, steps, and bump.

READ, COLOR & DRAW

Read zipper. Say **z** and make the /z/ sound. Encourage free coloring and drawing. Add clothes, etc.

ENRICHMENT

Home Link: Final Group **f**, **q**, **x**, and **z**.

SUPPORT/ELL
Use Letter Story: *Z Chase* to reinforce correct formation of **z** (p. 169).

CROSS-CURRICULAR CONNECTIONS
Language Arts: Pass around items with a zipper. Compare zippers and plastic bags. Real zippers have teeth.

p. 81

Sentences

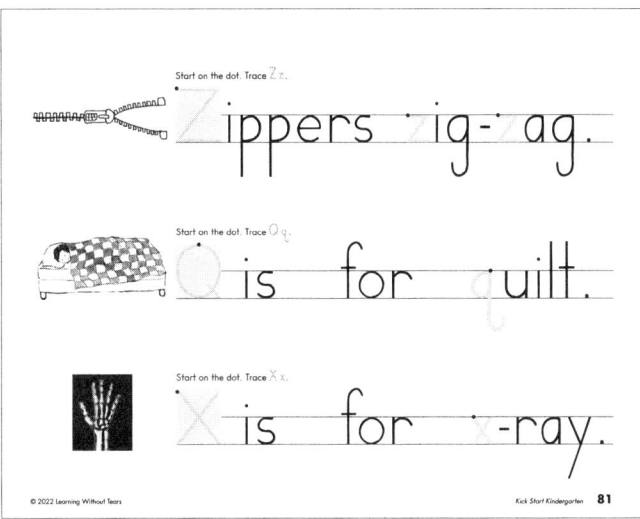

OBJECTIVE

To develop correct habits for tracing letters in a sentence.

LESSON INTRODUCTION (Warm Up)

SONG: "Sentence Song" from *Rock, Rap, Tap & Learn* music album

Additional digital resources are available in the Interactive Digital Teaching Tool (IDTT).

LESSON PLAN

1. Direction Instruction (Demo)

Demonstrate on double lines: **Zippers zig-zag.**
Show children that sentences begin with a capital, have space between words, and end with a period.

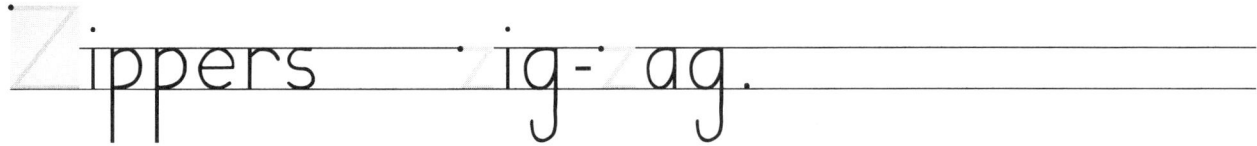

2. Guided Practice

Children trace letters in the sentence.

3. Check Sentence

Monitor as children trace their letters for correct start, steps, and bump.

READ, COLOR & DRAW

Read words. Encourage free coloring and drawing.

ENRICHMENT

Z is for zero. Have children write the word zero on double line paper.

SUPPORT/ELL

Repeat each sentence two to three times as children place and move their pointer finger under each word.

CROSS-CURRICULAR CONNECTIONS

Math: Show children pictures of quilts and discuss the different patterns.

Name

Kick Start Kindergarten – p. 94

OBJECTIVE
To develop correct habits for writing name in title case.

LESSON INTRODUCTION (Warm Up)
Sign In, Please (p. 151)

Additional digital resources are available in the Interactive Digital Teaching Tool (IDTT).

LESSON PLAN

1. Direction Instruction (Demo)

Demonstrate child's name on double lines.
Say the step-by-step formations for each letter. Model one letter at a time.

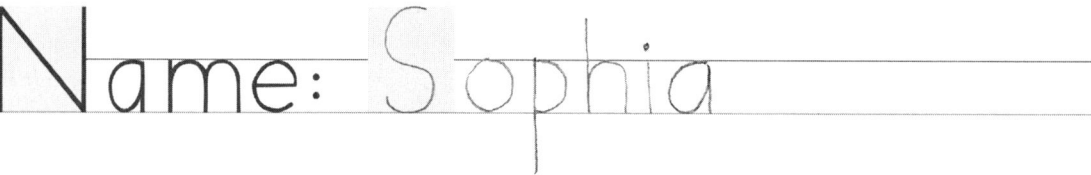

2. Guided Practice

Children copy their names, one letter at a time.

3. Check Name

Check to see if children write their names with correct size, placement, and closeness.

READ, COLOR & DRAW

Read words. Encourage free coloring and drawing.

ENRICHMENT	SUPPORT/ELL	CROSS-CURRICULAR CONNECTIONS
Help Me Write My Name. Remind families to model one letter at a time.	Highlight each letter for children who need extra guidance.	Language Arts: Have children identify the beginning, middle, and end of the alphabet.

NUMBERS

Let's talk about numbers. If you're new to Handwriting Without Tears®, you are in for a surprise. You can joyfully and efficiently teach your students to write numbers correctly. That means numbers that start at the top, use the right strokes, and face correctly.

Teach numbers at the beginning of the year, along with capitals. We use the same methods to teach capitals and numbers. Teach numbers during your math lessons.

Don't forget about using multisensory instruction first, such as Wet-Dry-Try on the Slate, Air Writing, Laser Letters, and music. These hands-on activities are for teaching letters and numbers.

What about reversals? Not a problem. Our materials and strategies work to prevent letter and number reversal problems. A smiley face in the top left corner of the Slate Chalkboard or Gray Block does the trick. The smiley face orients children. That's something to smile about!

In this section, children will:

- Build correct habits for number formation

- Get extra practice in math skills

- Discover ways to enrich or support each lesson

Numbers on the Slate Chalkboard *Kick Start Kindergarten – p. 82*

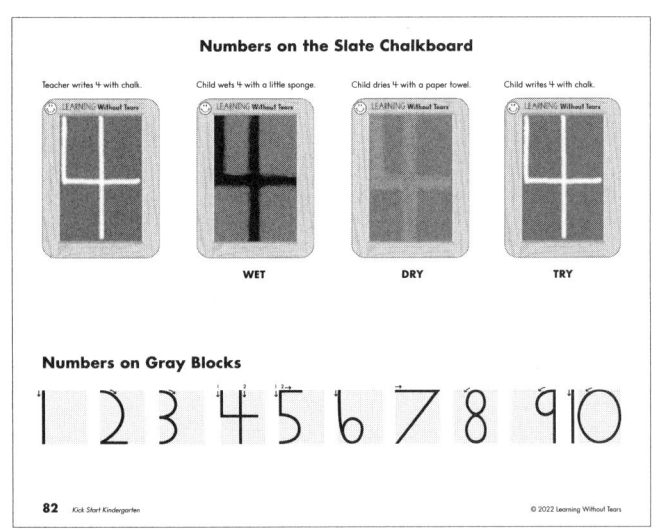

OBJECTIVE
To write numbers **1–10** correctly.

LESSON INTRODUCTION (Warm Up)
SONG: "Where Do You Start Your Letters?" from *Rock, Rap, Tap & Learn* music album (Substitute letters for numbers when singing.)

Additional digital resources are available in the Interactive Digital Teaching Tool (IDTT).

LESSON PLAN

Note: This is the direction for completing Wet-Dry-Try for all numbers. Number 4 is used as an example.

Prepare Slate Chalkboards: Write number with chalk as a model to trace.

1. Direction Instruction (Demo)

Demonstrate a number on your own Slate Chalkboard.
Say the words for each step.

 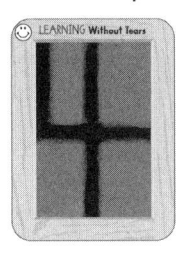 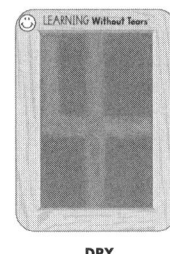 

WET   DRY   TRY

2. Guided Practice

Use the Wet-Dry-Try method. Children say the words for each step.
Wet: Child uses a Little Sponge Cube to trace the number.
Dry: Child uses a little piece of a paper towel to dry the number.
Try: Child uses a Little Chalk Bit to write the number.

3. Check Numbers

Monitor as children complete the steps of Wet-Dry-Try for correct start and steps.

ENRICHMENT
Progress from the Slate Chalkboard to pencil by asking children to write numbers on Gray Block Paper.

SUPPORT/ELL
Say the words for each step slowly. Children join when they can. Encourage children to repeat after you.

CROSS-CURRICULAR CONNECTIONS
Math: Have children count body parts. For example, **1** head, **2** hands, **10** fingers.

Number Stories

Fun stories help children remember numbers. Beyond our simple verbal cues, we made up stories that are fun to share and help make these numbers memorable.

1 starts in the Starting Corner.
1 makes a Big Line down.
1 stops in the corner.

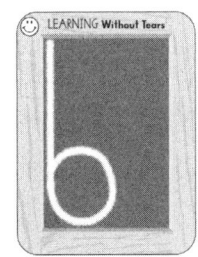

6 starts in the Starting Corner.
6 is a baby bear.
6 goes down to curl up in the corner.
6 is hibernating.

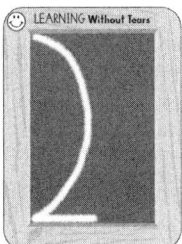

2 starts in the Starting Corner.
2 makes a Big Curve.
2 stops in the corner.
2 walks away on the bottom.

7 starts in the Starting Corner.
7 makes a Little Line across the top.
7 says, "I better slide down."

3 starts in the Starting Corner.
3 makes a Little Curve to the middle.
3 makes another Little Curve to the bottom corner.

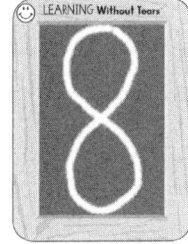

8 is different.
8 doesn't like corners.
8 starts at the top center.
8 begins with S and then goes home.

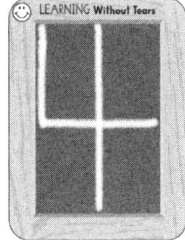

4 starts in the Starting Corner.
4 makes a Little Line down to the middle.
4 walks across the dark night.
4 jumps to the top and says, "I did it." (Big Line down)

9 is so special.
9 has its own corner.
9 makes a Little Curve and goes up to the corner.
9 makes a Big Line down.

5 starts in the Starting Corner.
5 makes a Little Line down to the middle. It starts to rain.
5 makes a Little Curve around.
5 puts a Little Line on top to stop the rain.

10 uses two places.
1 comes first.
0 is next.
0 starts at the top center.
10 is finished.

Kick Start Kindergarten – p. 83

OBJECTIVE
To develop correct habits for writing number 1.

LESSON INTRODUCTION (Warm Up)
SONG: "My Teachers Writes" from *Rock, Rap, Tap & Learn* music album

Additional digital resources are available in the Interactive Digital Teaching Tool (IDTT).

LESSON PLAN

1. Direction Instruction (Demo)
Demonstrate 1 on the Slate Chalkboard or Gray Block. Say the words for each step.

Lesson 1:

Start in the Starting Corner   Big Line down

2. Guided Practice
Children finger trace the step-by-step models on the Slate Chalkboard while saying the words.
Children trace 1.
Children copy 1.

3. Check Number
Monitor as children trace and copy numbers for correct start and steps.

READ, COLOR & DRAW
Read the word: one and 1 flamingo. Encourage free drawing and coloring.

ENRICHMENT
Children take turns writing 1 on a vertical surface. For example, whiteboard, flipchart, etc.

SUPPORT/ELL
Use Number Story 1 to reinforce correct formation (p. 133). Reinforce starting at the top by singing, "Where do you start your numbers… at the top."

CROSS-CURRICULAR CONNECTIONS
Math: Show children how everything down the middle of their body is one: one head, one nose, one mouth, one belly button.

p. 84

OBJECTIVE
To develop correct habits for writing number 2.

LESSON INTRODUCTION (Warm Up)
Wet-Dry-Try on Slate Chalkboard (p. 164)

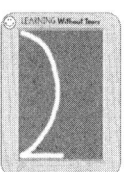

Additional digital resources are available in the Interactive Digital Teaching Tool (IDTT).

LESSON PLAN

1. Direction Instruction (Demo)
Demonstrate 2 on the Slate Chalkboard or Gray Block. Say the words for each step.

Lesson 2:

 Start in the Starting Corner

 Big Curve to the bottom

 Little Line across

2. Guided Practice
Children finger trace the step-by-step models on the Slate Chalkboard while saying the words.
Children trace 2.
Children copy 2.

3. Check Number
Monitor as children trace and copy numbers for correct start and steps.

READ, COLOR & DRAW
Read the word: two and 2 chicks. Encourage free drawing and coloring.

ENRICHMENT
Make 2 with sand or shaving cream in a tray with a smiley face in left corner to guide start and sequence.

SUPPORT/ELL
Use Number Story 2 to reinforce correct formation (p. 133). Help children associate the Big Curve and Little Curve of number 2 by using Wood Pieces.

CROSS-CURRICULAR CONNECTIONS
Math: Create simple AB patterns using two objects or colors.

Kick Start Kindergarten – p. 85

OBJECTIVE
To develop correct habits for writing number 3.

LESSON INTRODUCTION (Warm Up)
Wet-Dry-Try on Slate Chalkboard (p. 164)

Additional digital resources are available in the Interactive Digital Teaching Tool (IDTT).

LESSON PLAN

1. Direction Instruction (Demo)

Demonstrate 3 on the Slate Chalkboard or Gray Block. Say the words for each step.

Lesson 3:

Start in the Starting Corner   Little Curve to the middle   Little Curve to the bottom

2. Guided Practice

Children finger trace the step-by-step models on the Slate Chalkboard while saying the words.
Children trace 3.
Children copy 3.

3. Check Number

Monitor as children trace and copy numbers for correct start and steps.

READ, COLOR & DRAW

Read the word: three and 3 pigs. Encourage free drawing and coloring.

ENRICHMENT
Have children write numbers 1, 2, and 3 on Gray Block Paper.

SUPPORT/ELL
Use Number Story 3 to reinforce correct formation (p. 133). Build 3 on the Mat for Wood Pieces. Use two Little Curves (p. 162).

CROSS-CURRICULAR CONNECTIONS
Language Arts: Read the story of the *Three Little Pigs*. Count items in the book to develop number sense.

p. 86

OBJECTIVE
To develop correct habits for writing number 4.

LESSON INTRODUCTION (Warm Up)
SONG: "Number Song" from *Rock, Rap, Tap & Learn* music album

Additional digital resources are available in the Interactive Digital Teaching Tool (IDTT).

LESSON PLAN

1. Direction Instruction (Demo)
Demonstrate 4 on the Slate Chalkboard or Gray Block. Say the words for each step.

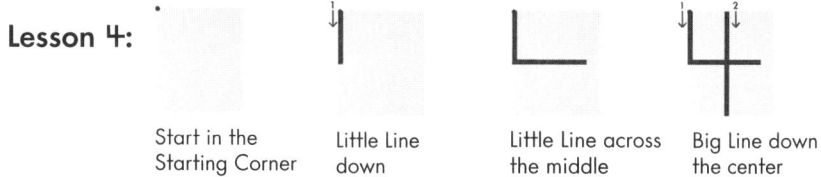

Lesson 4: Start in the Starting Corner | Little Line down | Little Line across the middle | Big Line down the center

2. Guided Practice
Children finger trace the step-by-step models on the Slate Chalkboard while saying the words.
Children trace 4.
Children copy 4.

3. Check Number
Monitor as children trace and copy numbers for correct start and steps.

READ, COLOR & DRAW
Read the word: four and 4 cars. Encourage free drawing and coloring.

ENRICHMENT
Make 4 with sand or shaving cream in a tray with the smiley face in left corner to guide start and sequence.

SUPPORT/ELL
Use Number Story 4 to reinforce correct formation (p. 133). Have children slowly trace and say the directions for 4 before they trace it.

CROSS-CURRICULAR CONNECTIONS
Math: Place the Wood Pieces around the Mat to build a rectangle. Ask children to look for other rectangles in the classroom.

© 2022 Learning Without Tears   Kick Start Kindergarten Teacher's Guide: **Numbers**   **137**

5

Kick Start Kindergarten – p. 87

OBJECTIVE
To develop correct habits for writing number **5**.

LESSON INTRODUCTION (Warm Up)
Wet-Dry-Try on Slate Chalkboard (p. 164)

Additional digital resources are available in the Interactive Digital Teaching Tool (IDTT).

LESSON PLAN

1. Direction Instruction (Demo)

Demonstrate **5** on the Slate Chalkboard or Gray Block.
Say the words for each step.

Lesson 5:

 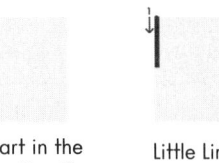  

Start in the Starting Corner   Little Line down to the middle   Little Curve to the bottom   Little Line across the top

2. Guided Practice

Children finger trace the step-by-step models on the Slate Chalkboard while saying the words.
Children trace **5**.
Children copy **5**.

3. Check Number

Monitor as children trace and copy numbers for correct start and steps.

READ, COLOR & DRAW

Read the word: five and **5** fingers. Encourage free drawing and coloring.

ENRICHMENT
Count five fingers in front of the class and have children write **5** on Gray Block Paper.

SUPPORT/ELL
Use Number Story **5** to reinforce correct formation (p. 133). Teach the number in two steps, starting at the smiley face of the Slate Chalkboard.

CROSS-CURRICULAR CONNECTIONS
Math: Have children trace their hand and then count five fingers.

p. 88

OBJECTIVE
To develop correct habits for writing number 6.

LESSON INTRODUCTION (Warm Up)
Wet-Dry-Try on Slate Chalkboard (p. 164)

Additional digital resources are available in the Interactive Digital Teaching Tool (IDTT).

LESSON PLAN

1. Direction Instruction (Demo)
Demonstrate 6 on the Slate Chalkboard or Gray Block.
Say the words for each step.

Lesson 6: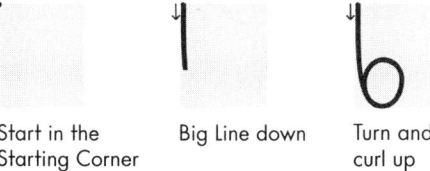

Start in the Starting Corner   Big Line down   Turn and curl up

2. Guided Practice
Children finger trace the step-by-step models on the Slate Chalkboard while saying the words.
Children trace 6.
Children copy 6.

3. Check Number
Monitor as children trace and copy numbers for correct start and steps.

READ, COLOR & DRAW
Read the word: six and 6 bears. Encourage free drawing and coloring.

ENRICHMENT
Count 2, 4, and 6 as a class and have children write 6 on Gray Block Paper.

SUPPORT/ELL
Use Number Story 6 to reinforce correct formation (p. 133). With use, 6 will curve nicely and won't be reversed.

CROSS-CURRICULAR CONNECTIONS
Language Arts: Play "I Spy 6." Ask children to find the numeral 6 on books, the classroom wall, etc.

7

Kick Start Kindergarten – p. 89

OBJECTIVE
To develop correct habits for writing number **7**.

LESSON INTRODUCTION (Warm Up)
Door Tracing (p. 163)

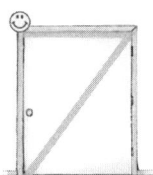

Additional digital resources are available in the Interactive Digital Teaching Tool (IDTT).

LESSON PLAN

1. Direction Instruction (Demo)

Demonstrate **7** on the Slate Chalkboard or Gray Block.
Say the words for each step.

Lesson 7: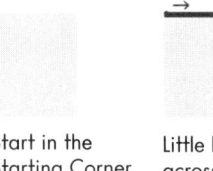

Start in the Starting Corner

Little Line across the top

Big Line slides down

2. Guided Practice

Children finger trace the step-by-step models on the Slate Chalkboard while saying the words.
Children trace **7**.
Children copy **7**.

3. Check Number

Monitor as children trace and copy numbers for correct start and steps.

READ, COLOR & DRAW

Read the word: seven and **7** ducklings. Encourage free drawing and coloring.

ENRICHMENT	SUPPORT/ELL	CROSS-CURRICULAR CONNECTIONS
Have children make **7** using pipe cleaners.	Use Number Story **7** to reinforce correct formation (p. 133).	Language Arts/Math: Name the **7** days of the week. Tuesday has **7** letters. Count the letters.

140 *Kick Start Kindergarten Teacher's Guide: Numbers* © 2022 Learning Without Tears

p. 90

OBJECTIVE
To develop correct habits for writing number 8.

LESSON INTRODUCTION (Warm Up)
Wet-Dry-Try App for Capitals, Numbers & Lowercase (p. 174)

Additional digital resources are available in the Interactive Digital Teaching Tool (IDTT).

LESSON PLAN

1. Direction Instruction (Demo)
Demonstrate **8** on the Slate Chalkboard or Gray Block. Say the words for each step.

Lesson 8:

Start on the dot   Begin with S   Up to the top

2. Guided Practice
Children finger trace the step-by-step models on the Slate Chalkboard while saying the words.
Children trace **8**.
Children copy **8**.

3. Check Number
Monitor as children trace and copy numbers for correct start and steps.

READ, COLOR & DRAW
Read the word: eight and **8** octopus legs. Encourage free drawing and coloring.

ENRICHMENT
Read left-hand page numbers 2, 4, 6, 8, etc.

SUPPORT/ELL
Use Number Story **8** to reinforce correct formation (p. 133). Writing **8** requires changing direction. Highlight **8** for children to pencil trace.

CROSS-CURRICULAR CONNECTIONS
Language Arts: Share "Little Miss Muffet" and "The Itsy Bitsy Spider" with the class. Discuss what the spider does in each rhyme.

9

Kick Start Kindergarten – p. 91

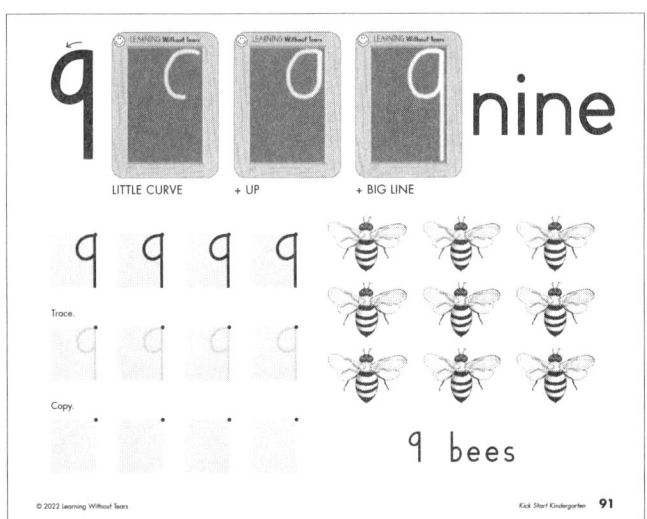

OBJECTIVE
To develop correct habits for writing number 9.

LESSON INTRODUCTION (Warm Up)
Wet-Dry-Try on Slate Chalkboard (p. 164)

Additional digital resources are available in the Interactive Digital Teaching Tool (IDTT).

LESSON PLAN

1. Direction Instruction (Demo)

Demonstrate 9 on the Slate Chalkboard or Gray Block. Say the words for each step.

Lesson 9:

9 has its own corner   Little Curve up   Big Line down

2. Guided Practice

Children finger trace the step-by-step models on the Slate Chalkboard while saying the words.
Children trace 9.
Children copy 9.

3. Check Number

Monitor as children trace and copy numbers for correct start and steps.

READ, COLOR & DRAW

Read the word: nine and 9 bees. Encourage free drawing and coloring.

ENRICHMENT
Count 9 items in the classroom and have children write 9 on Gray Block Paper.

SUPPORT/ELL
Use Number Story 9 to reinforce correct formation (p. 133). Have children write 9 in a continuous stroke with the Little Curve first.

CROSS-CURRICULAR CONNECTIONS
Math: Show how 9 objects always equal 9, even if they are positioned in different ways.

p. 92

10

OBJECTIVE
To develop correct habits for writing number **10**.

LESSON INTRODUCTION (Warm Up)
SONG: "10 Fingers Rock" from *Rock, Rap, Tap & Learn* music album

Additional digital resources are available in the Interactive Digital Teaching Tool (IDTT).

LESSON PLAN

1. Direction Instruction (Demo)
Demonstrate **10** on the Slate Chalkboard or Gray Block.
Say the words for each step.

Lesson 10:

 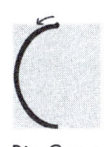  

Big Line down   Big Curve   Keep going   Stop

2. Guided Practice
Children finger trace the step-by-step models on the Slate Chalkboard while saying the words.
Children trace **10**.
Children copy **10**.

3. Check Number
Monitor as children trace and copy numbers for correct start and steps.

READ, COLOR & DRAW
Read the word: ten and **10** balloons. Encourage free drawing and coloring.

ENRICHMENT
Count **10** fingers as a class and have children write **10** on Gray Block Paper.

SUPPORT/ELL
Use Number Story **10** to reinforce correct formation (p. 133).

CROSS-CURRICULAR CONNECTIONS
Math: Make a pyramid with **10** cups. Count each one as a class.

Numbers Review

Kick Start Kindergarten – p. 93

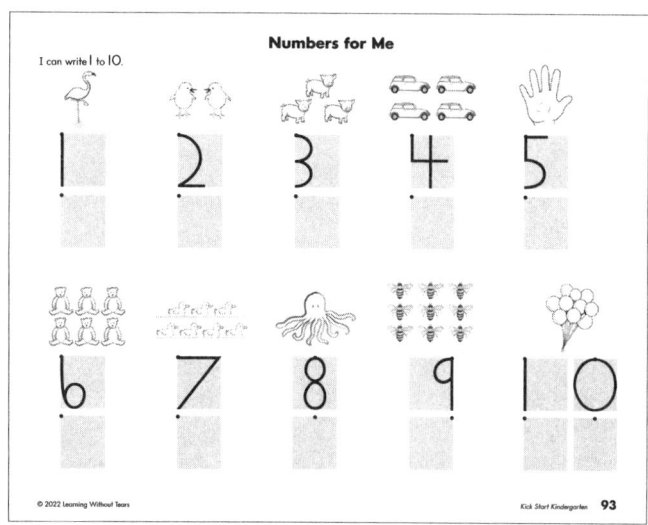

OBJECTIVE
To develop correct habits when writing numbers 1–10.

LESSON INTRODUCTION (Warm Up)
SONG: "Number Song" from *Rock, Rap, Tap & Learn* music album

Additional digital resources are available in the Interactive Digital Teaching Tool (IDTT).

LESSON PLAN

1. Direction Instruction (Demo)
Demonstrate 1, 2, 3, 4, and 5 on the Slate Chalkboard or Gray Block. Say the words for each step.

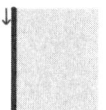   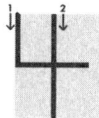 

2. Guided Practice
Children copy numbers 1–10.

3. Check Numbers
Monitor as children copy numbers for correct start and steps.

ENRICHMENT
Have children write numbers 1–10 on Gray Block Paper.

SUPPORT/ELL
If children are still having difficulty with numbers, review with Wet-Dry-Try on the Slate Chalkboard (p. 164).

CROSS-CURRICULAR CONNECTIONS
Math: Countdown from 10–0. Blast off! Pretend children are in a spaceship.

About Reversals

Understanding & Preventing Reversals

Do you wonder why children reverse numbers? It's simply because they're transitioning into symbols. They're applying what they know about the real world to symbols. In the real world, position doesn't change identity. A boy is a boy no matter which way he faces. But symbols are different. Position matters.

Unlike a boy, letter **b** is not **b** if it faces a different way (**d**). Welcome to the world of symbols and reversals.

In the past, teachers and families thought of reversals as inevitable and something children had to outgrow. But reversals are not inevitable. They go away when you orient children spatially and teach directionality with the Slate Chalkboard, Gray Blocks, and Number Stories. Children especially enjoy the Wet-Dry-Try activity and you will enjoy the results. That multisensory activity carries over to the Gray Blocks in *Kick Start Kindergarten*. Gray Blocks work the same way the Slate Chalkboard does to orient children spatially, to help them place numbers correctly.

Correcting Reversals

Even with your good teaching, and even if children write numbers correctly in *Kick Start Kindergarten*, reversals may still occur on math worksheets. Children are thinking about the answer, not how to write the number.

They may just revert back to old ways. You may be tempted to ignore those reversals, or you may be tempted to correct them all. We suggest a happier, more efficient strategy that works.

1. Check math papers for reversals.

2. Mark only one number reversal per paper. Always mark the lowest number that is reversed. Ignore all other reversals.

3. Help the child with that one number. Re-teach the number with the Slate Chalkboard or Gray Blocks.

Because you always help with the lowest number, that number takes priority and gets all the teaching it needs. Gradually and systematically, children stop reversing, and all reversals are eliminated.

MULTISENSORY ACTIVITIES

You know the importance of self-directed play and multisensory, active learning. Research is on your side. It supports multisensory teaching to address children's diverse learning styles: visual, tactile, auditory, and kinesthetic.

Activities with hands-on materials address different senses to teach correct formation, spacing, and sequencing. We help children develop their writing skills through explicit, multisensory, play-based instruction.

Each letter lesson begins with a multisensory introduction. There are many fun activities that rotate to add variety and appeal.

Multisensory activities can be hands-on. For example, Wet-Dry-Try on the slate. There may also be a digital version of the activity on the Interactive Digital Teaching Tool and Digital Student App.

In this section, children will:

- Move, touch, feel, and manipulate real objects as they learn the habits and skills essential for writing
- Learn songs that make learning fun and memorable
- Engage with technology in a developmentally appropriate manner
- Develop social-emotional skills

Multisensory Cues

This guide has cues throughout the book to indicate that there is a correlating multisensory activity you can do with children in that section. Multisensory activities address children's different senses and bring your teaching to life. Many of these activities, such as music, the Slate, Laser Letters, and Air Writing are perfect to use for numbers, too!

Readiness

 Stomp Your Feet
 Pencil Grip
 Music
 Shake Hands With Me
 Build Mat Man®

CAPITALS

 Bodies & Positions
 Capital Letter Cards for Wood Pieces
 Show Me Magnetic Pieces
 Mat for Wood Pieces
 Capitals on the Door
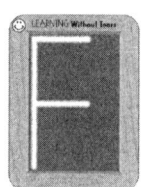 Slate

CAPITALS and Lowercase Letters

 Music
 Letter Stories
 Air Writing
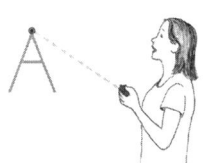 Laser Writing

 Digital Letter and Number Formations
  Wet-Dry-Try App
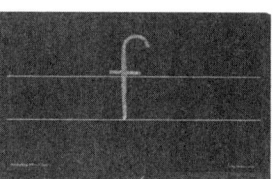 Blackboard with Double Lines
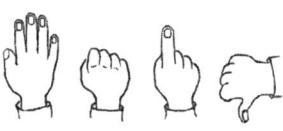 Hand Activity

 Voices
 "Sentence Song"
 Syllables

Songs for Readiness

Music makes learning memorable and joyful. Start by playing the album in the background during free play. This builds familiarity. Then, when you sing during activities, children happily remember and are ready to participate.

Materials
- *Rock, Rap, Tap & Learn* music album

Activity

Choose a song and an activity to go with it.

"Hey, Hey Big Line"
This song teaches positions, (front, back, up, down, Etc.). While singing and dancing. Use the wood pieces and give each child a big line before the beginning of the song.

"Big Line March"
This song builds attention and responsiveness.
Children follow along to learn high/low, up/down, loud/soft. Etc.

"Tapping to the ABC's"
This song teaches the alphabet while having children tap along. Give each child two wood pieces to tap.

"Diagonals"
This song teaches the diagonal movement. Children can stand up and use their bodies to move to the song.

Shake Hands With Me

Use shaking hands to teach another important skill: directionality. Children can learn to tell left from right easily with this activity. How does it work? We teach only the right hand and associate it with shaking hands. When children learn just the right hand, they're never confused. They know the right, and what's left is left.

Materials
- Lotion
- Rubber stamp
- Scent
- Cup of water

Activity

1. Greeting—Shake hands with each child. Smile and make eye contact.

2. Say, **Hello. This is your right hand. I'm going to do something to your right hand.**
   - Lotion—Put a dab on the right thumb. **Rub your fingers together.**
   - Rubber Stamp—Stamp the right hand. **Look at your right hand now.**
   - Scent—Dab a scent on the right hand to smell.
   - Water—Dip child's right fingertips in a cup. Have them shake fingers.

3. Direct students to raise their right hands and say with you, **This is my right hand. I shake hands with my right hand.**

Sign In, Please

This activity is a crowd pleaser. Children enjoy the suspense (What letter will it be?) and the affirmation (I knew it would be **D**.). Keep the name of each new letter a secret until you finish writing it. Children will be excited to repeat this activity. What are children learning? They're learning alphabetical order, letter recognition, associating capitals with their friend's names, start at the top, and stop on a line.

Materials
- Whiteboard or blackboard with wide stop line near bottom
- Erasable crayon, marker, or chalk

Activity

1. Write **A**, describing each step: **Big Line, Big Line, Little Line.**

2. Ask, **Whose name begins with A?** Wait for children to respond. **Adam's name begins with A.**

3. Introduce Adam. Pause to let children finish your sentences.
   This is . . . Adam. Adam starts with letter . . . A.
   The first sound in Adam is . . . /a/.

4. Adam signs in with a Big Line down from **A**. He stops on the line. Continue to write letters so that children can sign in alphabetically.

Where Do You Start Your Letters?

Children never forget where to start their letters with this fun song. Not only are they moving and having fun, they are learning prepositions, too!

Materials
- "Where Do You Start Your Letters?" from *Rock, Rap, Tap & Learn* music album

Activity

1. Play "Where Do You Start Your Letters?" in the background as children play so they will become familiar with the lyrics. They'll know the tune from "If You're Happy and You Know It."

2. Sing the song with children. Make a questioning gesture with hands for "Where?" and point high for "At the top!"

3. End by writing a letter on the board.

Note: For numbers, change the word "letters" to "numbers."

Top to Bottom

English is a top-to-bottom, left-to-right language. Teaching a top-to-bottom habit is the secret to handwriting success. Children who start letters at the top develop speed and neatness. Those who start from the bottom generally struggle with handwriting.

Often, we judge a young child's writing only by how the letters look. Do not be misled by the appearance of children's letters and numbers. Children's fluency and, ultimately, their neatness depends on their habits for letter and number formation. This is particularly true when writing demands increase. Try this experiment:

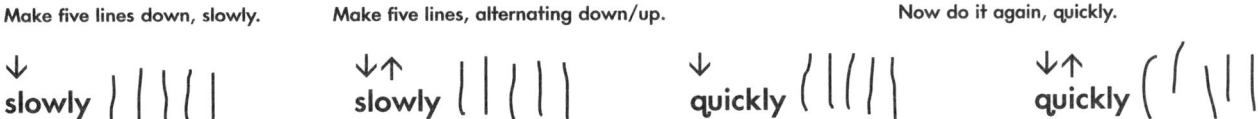

Notice that when you make lines slowly, it doesn't really matter where you start. But, when you add speed, it does matter where you start. Children who start at the top can be fast and neat! Tell families about this. Send children home singing this song to remind families to help children start at the top.

Where Do You Start Your Letters?
Tune: "If You're Happy and You Know It"

Build Mat Man®

Young children are often asked to draw pictures of themselves or of other people. Mat Man teaches drawing with building and singing. First you build him, piece by piece, and then give him away piece by piece. Children sing as they put him together. They learn about body parts, where they go, and what they do. This activity will set children up for drawing him in the same way.

Materials
- Mat for Wood Pieces
- Wood Pieces Set for Capital Letters
- Mat Man accessories

Activity
1. Children sit on the floor in a circle.
2. You build Mat Man on the floor.
3. You give Mat Man's parts to children.
4. Children build Mat Man while singing the "Mat Man" song.
5. Extra accessories (belly button, hair, clothing, seasonal items) make Mat Man more interesting or change him into a different Mat person.

Mat Man Song
Tune: "The Bear Went Over the Mountain"

Mat Man has
1 head, 1 head, 1 head,
Mat Man has 1 head!
So that he can…*think!*

Mat Man has
2 eyes, 2 eyes, 2 eyes
Mat Man has 2 eyes
So that he can…*see!*

Mat Man has
1 nose, 1 nose, 1 nose,
Mat Man has 1 nose
So that he can…*smell!*
Mat Man has
1 mouth, 1 mouth, 1 mouth,
Mat Man has 1 mouth
So that he can…*eat!*

Mat Man has
2 ears, 2 ears, 2 ears,
Mat Man has 2 ears
So that he can…*hear!*

Draw Mat Man®

You will see improvement in children's same-day drawings. Weeks later, you will see that the improvement remains. Children's drawings will be consistently more complex (number of body parts) and accurate (parts placed correctly) than before. What changes over time is the personality of the drawings.

Materials
- Blank paper (1 per child)
- Crayons
- Easel
- Markers

Activity

1. Children sit at tables/desks facing you. You draw a large Mat Man at the board or easel.

2. Draw each part in order. Sing/say, **Mat Man has one head. Watch me draw the head. Now it's your turn!**

3. Continue to draw eyes, nose, mouth, ears, body, arms, hands, legs, and feet.

4. Encourage children to add other details to their drawings.

Before / After
4-Year-Old: Same Day

Before / After
4-Year-Old: Same Day

Before / After
4-Year-Old: Same Day

Wood Pieces Set

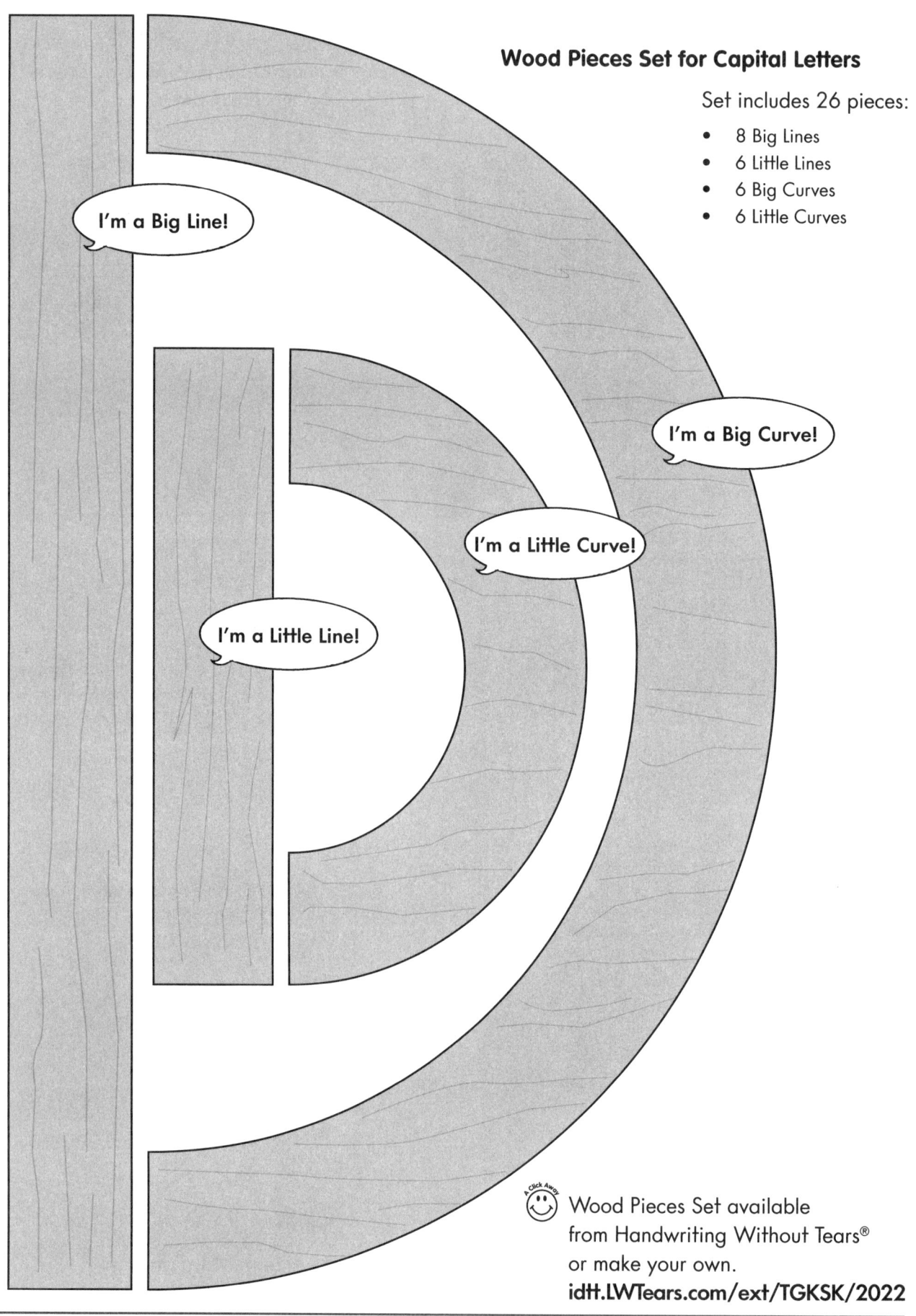

Wood Pieces Set for Capital Letters

Set includes 26 pieces:
- 8 Big Lines
- 6 Little Lines
- 6 Big Curves
- 6 Little Curves

Wood Pieces Set available from Handwriting Without Tears® or make your own.
idtt.LWTears.com/ext/TGKSK/2022

Trade, Polish & Sort Wood Pieces

Children learn the Wood Piece names: **Big Lines, Little Lines, Big Curves, Little Curves**. They will understand your words when you teach them how to make capitals with Wood Pieces.

Materials
- Wood Pieces Set for Capital Letters
- Old socks or paper towels

Activity

1. Introduce and talk about the Wood Pieces. Gradually, children will pick up the important words (Big Line, Little Line, Big Curve, Little Curve) along with the pieces. You can say:

   You have a Big Curve. I have a Big Curve. We picked the same pieces. You have a Big Line. I have a Big Curve. Do you want to trade?

2. Polish the Wood Pieces. You can say:
   Let's polish lines. Do you want to polish a Big Line or a Little Line? It's time to collect the Wood Pieces. Who has a Big Line?

Positions & Body Parts with Wood Pieces

Children need to know words to communicate and follow directions. They need to feel a sense of belonging and participating. It's fun for them to follow you. Big Line up in the air, under your chair, etc. Have fun! As children follow you, they learn not just words but how to imitate, pay attention, and respond quickly.

Materials
- Wood Pieces Set for Capital Letters

Activity

1. Give each child one Big Line.
2. Say the position words as you demonstrate. Children imitate and say them, too.
3. Say body parts as you touch them with a Big Line. Children imitate and say them, too.

Hold the Big Line **up** in the air. Move it **up** and **down**.

Hold the Big Line **under** your chair. Move it **under** your arm, and **over** your arm.

Hold the Big Line **out** to one side. Move it **around** in a circle.

Hold the Big Line in **front** of you. Move it **behind** your back, **between** your fingers. Hold it at the **bottom**, it's **vertical**.

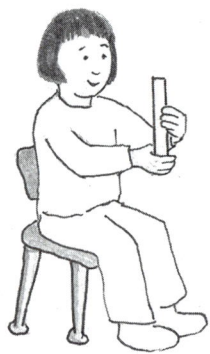

Climb **up** and **down** the Big Line. Hold it at the **top**, **middle**, and **bottom**.

Hold the Big Line **horizontal**. Move it **side** to **side**.

Curves & Circles

By imitating you, children learn position concepts. They need awareness of curves and circles for capitals **B, C, D, G, O, P, Q, R, S, U**. Children learn that O can be a circle, a number zero, or a letter **O**. In art, encourage children to rotate their arms and wrists to draw anything with a circular shape: snowmen, wheels, faces.

Materials
- Wood Pieces Set for Capital Letters

Activity

1. Give each child two Big Curves or two Little Curves.

2. Say the name of each position as you demonstrate. Have children say it, too.

3. Teach **O** as a letter, a number, and a shape.

Rainbow
Hold **up** a Big Curve. Hold the Big Curve, and then trace **over** the rainbow with the other hand.

Smile
Hold up a Big Curve to make a happy face. Turn it **down** to make a sad face.

Apart
Hold the Big Curves **apart**.

Together
Bring them **together**.

O or zero
Say "**O**" or "**Zeeeero.**" Hold up two Big Curves to your face. Look at a friend's **O**. Make circles in the air now.

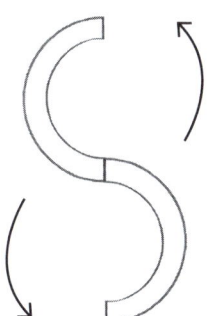

Squiggle-Wiggle
Hold up two Big Curves with just one end touching. Move them alternately **up** or **down**.

Vertical Horizontal & Diagonal

By imitating you, children learn position concepts. They need awareness of vertical and horizontal for capitals **E**, **F**, **H**, **I**, **L**, and **T**. They need diagonals for **A**, **K**, **M**, **N**, **R**, **V**, **W**, **X**, **Y**, and **Z**.

Materials
- Wood Pieces Set for Capital Letters

Activity

1. Give each child two Big Lines.

2. Use the position words **vertical**, **horizontal**, and **diagonal**, and have children say the words as they imitate you.

3. Introduce the capitals **V**, **T**, **A**, and **X** as they make them with you.

Make a Big Line stand **up**. It's **vertical**. Make it walk **on** your arm.

Now it's tired. Make it lie **down**. It's **horizontal**.

Hold two Big Lines **end** to **end** diagonally. Move and say, **diagonal**, **diagonal**.

Put them **together** at the **top**. Looks like a teepee or start of **A**.

One Big Line is standing **up**. One Little Line **across** the **top**. It's capital **T**.

Hold two Big Lines **together** in one hand.

Open them! Hold them **out**. Say, Voilà! It's a **V**. Help children finger trace **V**.

Together at the **middle**— It's **X**! **X** marks the spot.

Capital Letter Cards for Wood Pieces

Capital Letter Cards show a capital made with Wood Pieces. Children put real Wood Pieces on the card. This is a great first letter play activity, especially for children who are just learning to turn and place pieces. They build the letters piece by piece. It's also a beginning activity for observation and organization.

Materials
- Capital Letter Cards for Wood Pieces
- Wood Pieces Set for Capital Letters

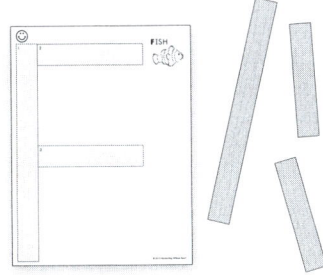

Activity

1. Place a different Capital Letter Card in front of each child. Have them point to the ☺. This shows that the letter is right side up.

2. Point to each child's Letter Card. Say, **This is capital _____. What pieces do you need for _____? That's right. Collect the pieces. Put them near your card. Then wait until everyone is ready.**

3. Place the pieces as a group, like this:
   **Pick up the first piece for your letter. Wait for everybody.
   Put it in place. Pick up the second piece. Wait… everyone ready?
   Put it in place. Pick up the third piece. Wait… everyone ready?
   Put it in place. You made _____.**

Note: This activity also works well with numbers.

Show Me Magnetic Pieces for Capitals

This activity teaches correct letter formation as you demonstrate for the entire class using a vertical surface. Children can all see you as they build letters with their own Wood Pieces and Mat.

Materials
- Show Me Magnetic Pieces for Capitals
- Wood Pieces Set for Capital Letters
- Mat for Wood Pieces

Activity

1. Scatter the Wood Pieces on the floor in front of children.

2. Give each child a Mat to place right side up. The smiley face will be at the top.

3. Use the Show Me Magnetic Pieces to build a letter piece by piece for children to imitate. To see the order for any letter, refer to the letter page in this teacher's guide.

4. Describe each step as you build the letter: **I put the Big Line here, under the ☺. Your turn. I put a Little Curve at the top. Your turn. It's letter _____!**

Note: This activity also works well with numbers.

Capitals on the Mat for Wood Pieces

The Mat for Wood Pieces is blue with a yellow smiley face in the top left corner. That's the Starting Corner for **B, D, E, F, H, K, L, M, N, P, R, U, V, W, X, Y,** and **Z**. Many of them (**B, D, E, F, H, K, L, M, N, P, R**) start with a Big Line on the left side. When the Big Line is on the left, the next part of the letter is always on the right side of the Big Line.

Materials
- Wood Pieces Set for Capital Letters
- Mat for Wood Pieces
- ☺ Wood Pieces Letter Chart

Activity

1. Scatter the Wood Pieces on the floor in front of children.
2. Give each child a Mat to place right side up. The smiley face will be at the top left. Make sure your Mat is in the same orientation as theirs.
3. Build a letter piece by piece for children to imitate. To see the sequence for any letter, refer to the Wood Pieces Letter Chart.
4. Describe each step as you build the letter:
   I put the Big Line here, under the ☺. Your turn.
   I put a Little Line at the top. Your turn.
   I put another Little Line at the middle. It's letter _____!

Demonstrate

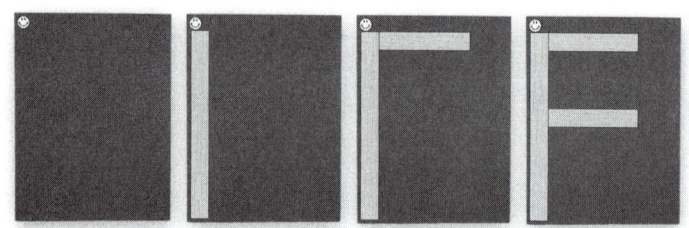

Digital Version

 Interactive Digital Teaching Tool: Share via your interactive whiteboard or smartboard

 Digital Student App: Integrated in lessons and on "My Tools" for additional practice

Capitals on the Door

Doors can do more than open and close. They can also help you teach lessons and end reversals. Just put a smiley face in the top left corner, and the door is ready to help. The smiley face brings a child's eye to the top and to the Starting Corner.

Materials
- Bright yellow smiley face mounted on top left corner of door
- Small laser pointer

Note: In place of a laser pointer, you may also use a flashlight or other small pointer.

Activity

1. Air Write a laser letter on the door for all to see. What letter will it be? Choose a familiar Starting Corner letter, perhaps **B**, **D**, **E**, **F**, **H**, **K**, **L**, **P**, **R**, **V**, **X**, or **Z** (hide laser beam when jumping to start another stroke).

2. Have children hold their pencils correctly in the air. Everyone checks pencil grips.

3. Children pretend to write on the door by following the laser beam.

4. Children name the letter after you finish writing.

Note: This activity also works well with numbers.

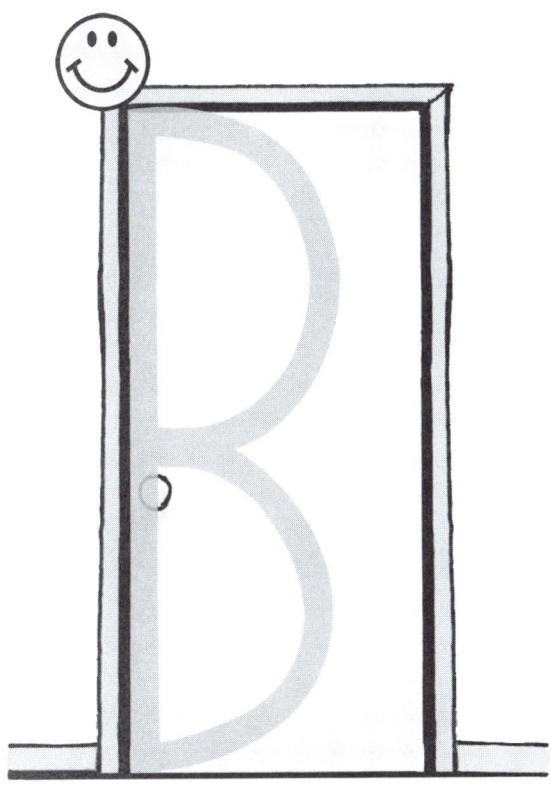

Wet-Dry-Try for Capitals

This is a favorite activity. You write a chalk letter and teach each step. Children wet the letter, dry it, and then try it with chalk. The Little Sponge Cubes and Little Chalk Bits reinforce correct grip. Repetition reinforces correct letter formation. Place Little Chalk Bits and Little Sponge Cubes in small cups so children can reach them. This is the physical version. The digital version is available on the Interactive Digital Teaching Tool and Digital Student App.

Materials
- Slate Chalkboard (1 per child)
- Little Chalk Bits (1")
- Little Sponge Cubes (1/2")
- Little cups of water
- Paper towel pieces
- 😊 Capital Formation Chart

Activity

1. **Prepare Slate Chalkboards**
   Write letter with chalk as a model to trace.

2. **Teacher's Part**
   Demonstrate letter on your own Slate Chalkboard. Say the words for each step.

3. **Child's Part - Use the Wet-Dry-Try method**
   (Child says the words for each step)
   Wet: Child uses a Little Sponge Cube to trace the letter.
   Dry: Child uses a Little Piece of paper towel to dry the letter.
   Try: Child uses a Little Chalk Bit to write the letter.

Start in the Starting Corner,
Big Line down,
Frog Jump to 😊,
Little Line across the top,
Little Line across the middle

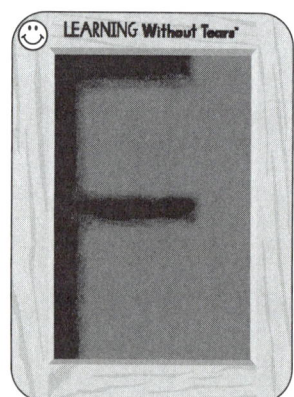
WET:
Wet **F** with sponge,
Wet **F** with wet finger,
Say the words

DRY:
Dry **F** with towel,
Dry **F** with gentle blow,
Say the words

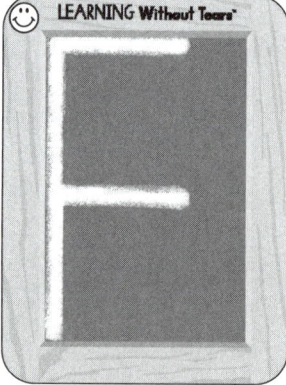
TRY:
Try **F** with chalk,
Say the words

Digital Version

 Interactive Digital Teaching Tool: Share via your interactive whiteboard or smartboard

 Digital Student App: Integrated in lessons and on "My Tools" for additional practice

Mystery Letters on the Slate Chalkboard

You can play Mystery Letters with children as a fun way to develop good habits. Mystery Letter activities teach correct letter formation. The secret is to make the first stroke correctly before telling children the name of the letter they're going to make. This ensures they start the letter correctly.

Materials
- Slate Chalkboard (1 per child)
- Little Chalk Bits (1")
- Paper towel pieces
- Gray Block Paper

Activity

1. Gather the Slate Chalkboards, Little Chalk Bits, and paper towels for erasing.
2. Say the directions for a capital letter, leaving the last part a mystery (see directions below). Have children practice Wet-Dry-Try after completing the letter.

Note: Play the Mystery Letter games to reinforce correct habits for Starting Corner and Center Starting Capitals. You can play these games on Gray Block Paper.

Starting Corner Capitals

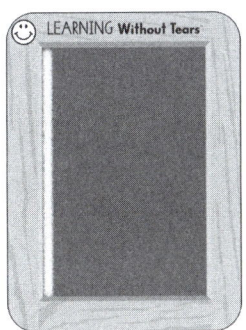

For **F, E, D, P, B, R, N, M**,
Start in the Starting Corner,
Big Line down,
Frog Jump to the Starting Corner,
Now make ____

For **H, K, L**,
Start in the Starting Corner,
Big Line down,
Now make ____

For **U, V, W, X, Y, Z**
Start in the Starting Corner,
Now make ____

Center Starting Capitals

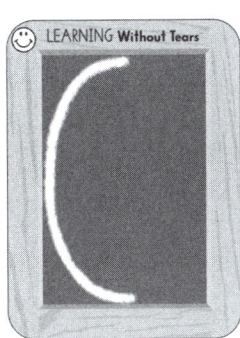

For **C, O, Q, G**
Start at the top center,
Make a Magic C,
Now make ____

For **S, A, I, T, J**,
Start at the top center,
Now make ____

Songs for Capitals

Music makes learning memorable and joyful. Start by playing the album in the background during free play. This builds familiarity. Then, when you sing during activities, children happily remember and are ready to participate.

Materials
- *Rock, Rap, Tap & Learn* music album

Activity

Choose a song and an activity to go with it.

"Frog Jump Letters"
Children stand up and finger trace the Frog Jump Capitals (p. 46) in the air. Let children jump around between the letter exercises.

"Give It A Middle"
This song helps children learn the middle position in letter formation as they finger trace or watch as you model letters on the board.

"Give It A Top"
Children learn about letters that have a top and can follow you as you model these letters on the board or in the air.

Songs for Lowercase

We also use music for lowercase letters. We even have a song to help children remember to leaves spaces when they write sentences. Try them all. Children will soon let you know their favorite.

Materials
- *Rock, Rap, Tap & Learn* music album

Activity

Choose a song and an activity to go with it.

"Sentence Song"
Children learn to start with a capital, write a word, and leave a space. Sung with the "Yankee Doodle" tune, sentences are such fun.

"CAPITALS & lowercase"
This song teaches capital/lowercase letters: **C c**, **O o**, **S s**, **V v**, and **W w**.

"Magic C Rap"
Magic c starts **a**, **d**, and **g**. This song teaches letters with the Magic c.

"Descending Letters"
Singing about **g**, **j**, **y**, **p**, and **q** is fun: **g** and **j** go down and turn, **y** goes sliding down, **p** goes straight down, and **q** goes down with a U-turn.

Letter Stories

Fun stories help children remember letters that are a bit tricky. Beyond our simple verbal cues, we made up some stories that are fun to share and help make these letters memorable. Many of these stories have a Live Teaching Video located in the Resource section of the Interactive Digital Teaching Tool.

Honeybee

Say, "Let's make letter **h**. Now let's make another **h**. I have a surprise. This is an **h** for a honeybee." Turn **h** into **b**.

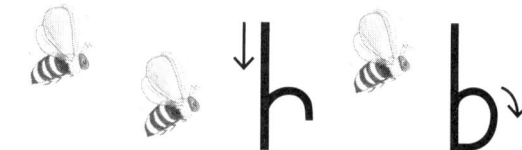

Run the Bases

Place the pencil on the dot. Say, "Batter up to bat. Here comes the pitch. Hit the ball, wait, then run the bases: first, second, third, stop! It's not a home run."

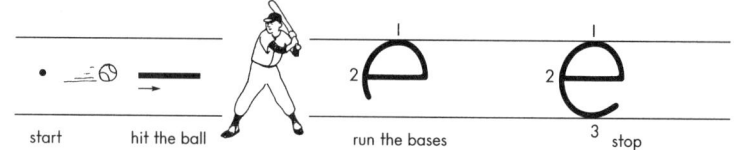

Fire Hose Squirts

Say, "**f** is like water squirting out of a fire hose. It goes up and then falls down."

If George Falls

Say, "Inside **g** lives a little man named George (draw a little face in **g**). He says, 'Ohhhh, if I fall, will you catch me?' Sure, I will catch you (turn the **g** to catch George) if you fall."

Karate K

Say, "The Big Line is Mr. Kaye, your karate teacher. He wants you to show him your kick.

K: Put your chalk in the corner. That's you. Now kick Mr. Kaye. Hiiii-ya. That's the karate **K**.

k: Put the pencil on the line. That's you. Now kick Mr. Kaye. Hiiii-ya. That's the karate **k**."

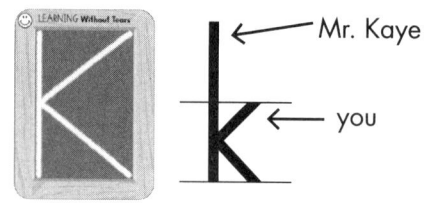

Letter Stories

Stinky m

m

Say, "If **m** has a big gap, people will throw trash in the gap. Don't make a big gap. Make the gap so little, there is only room for an upside down chocolate kiss."

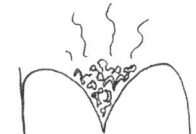 

U-Turn

q

Say, "The letter **q** is followed by **u**.
Think of quiet, quit, quibble, quaint, etc.
At the bottom of **q**, stop and make a U-turn."

Stop, Drop & Roll with S

s

Start **s** with a little **c**. Go over and say hello to the smiley face. Say, "What do you do if your clothes catch on fire? You stop, drop, and roll!"

 Say hello to the smiley face.  Stop, drop, and roll.

T Is Tall, t Is Tall But…

Tt

Say, "Look at me. I can make capital **T**.
Look at me. I can make lowercase **t**.
Capital **T** is tall.
Lowercase **t** is tall, but it's crossed lower.
Capital **T** and lowercase **t** are both tall."

Z Chase

z

Say, "Left hand says, 'I'm going to chase you.' Right hand picks up the pencil and runs across the page.

Left hand says, 'I'm kidding! Come back.'
Right hand slides back down toward the left hand.

Left hand says, 'Ha! I'm going to chase you.'
Right hand runs back across."

(This story is for right-handers with z reversal problems, but can be adapted for lefties.)

Air Writing

Air Writing is a kinesthetic strategy with visual and auditory components. Picking up and holding pencils adds a tactile component. This strategy allows you to watch the entire class and ensures that all students form their letters correctly.

Materials
- "Air Writing" from *Rock, Rap, Tap & Learn* music album (optional)
- Brightly colored ball

Activity

1. Sing "Air Writing" to prepare the class for participation.
2. Choose a letter. Use a brightly colored ball to trace the letter in the air in front of your class.
3. Have students hold a pencil correctly in the air. Everyone checks pencil grips.
4. Retrace the letter again with your students.

Note: If you are facing your students, make the letter backwards in relation to you so that the letter will be correct from your students' perspective. This activity also works well with numbers.

Laser Letters

Children are always amazed by this activity. You can easily catch their attention when you use a small laser. By using a laser, you provide a nice visual to follow while tracing letters in the air.

Materials
- Small laser pointer
- Chalk or markers
- Large board or easel

Note: In place of a laser pointer, you may also use a flashlight or other small pointer.

Activity

1. Students hold pencils ready to point to laser dot.

2. Teacher points to start of letter and slowly writes a laser letter saying its step-by-step directions.

3. Students follow the laser with their pencils, saying the directions with the teacher.

Digital Letter & Number Formations

Introducing simple technology into your daily classroom experiences can make learning letters and numbers engaging and fun. This process also exposes young children to the world of technology at an early age.

How to locate:
- Go to +Live Insights, pli.lwtears.com
- Interactive Digital Teaching Tool: These formations are integrated in your letter and number lessons for you to share via your Interactive Whiteboard for in-class learning. They are also located on the Digital Formation Tools for additional practice outside of lessons.
- Student Digital App: Students can access the Letter & Number Formations on "My Tools" for additional practice.

Materials
- Computer or interactive whiteboard (IWB)

Activity

1. Go to the Interactive Digital Teaching Tool. Select Digital Formation Tools. Select Letter & Number Formations.
2. Select a letter or number. Prepare to demonstrate.
3. Children point their pointer fingers at the screen.
4. As children trace the letter, say the parts of the letter.
   **We are going to trace F in the air.
   Big line down. Frog Jump, Little line across the top. Little line across the bottom.
   We made an F.**
5. Children can take turns coming to the whiteboard to trace and write the letter or number.

A+ Worksheet Maker

The A+ Worksheet Maker includes customizable worksheets. These customizable worksheets can be used for extra practice on double lines. Worksheets include spelling, vocabulary, sentence writing, and more. You can use these worksheets in different subject areas throughout the classroom day.

How to locate:
- Go to +Live Insights, pli.lwtears.com
- Interactive Digital Teaching Tool: Select the A+ Worksheet Maker to create customizable worksheets that can be used for additional practice using the HWT font and double lines outside of handwriting lessons. Worksheets include spelling, vocabulary, sentence writing and more. You can use these worksheets in different subject areas throughout the classroom day.

Activity

1. Select the Interactive Digital Teaching Tool. The A+ Worksheet Maker has its own tab.

2. Select your grade and size of double lines.

3. Choose a worksheet.

4. Customize the worksheet and print.

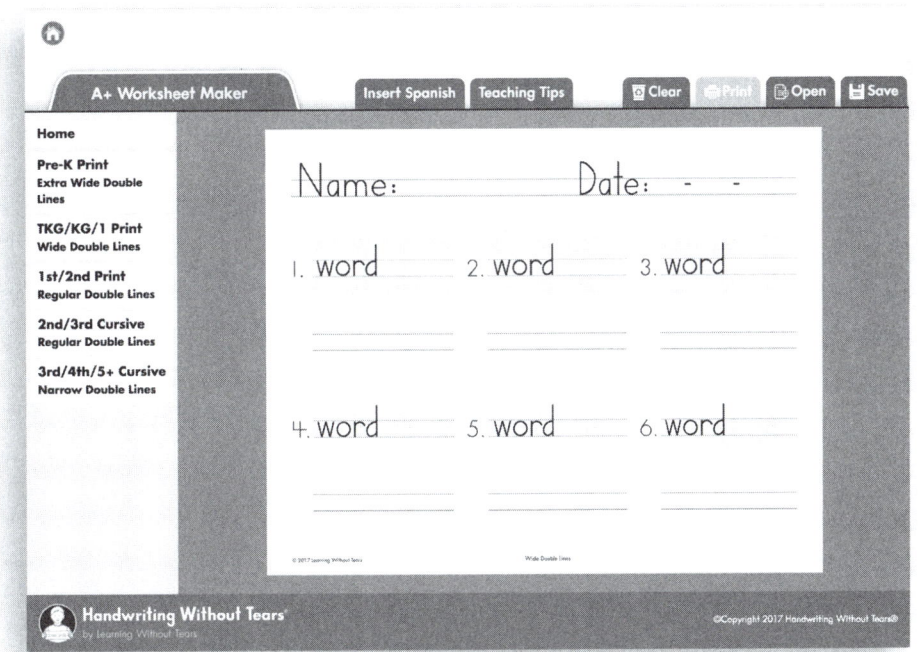

A+ Worksheet Maker

Wet-Dry-Try App

Children love using a tablet and participating in the Wet-Dry-Try App. They will listen to the personal handwriting coach to practice forming letters accurately in a fun way. There are three star levels with Level 1 having full letter formation guidance with audio and permanent visual cues. Level 2 has only flashed visual cues. Level 3 has no visual cues.

Materials
- Tablet with Wet-Dry-Try App installed

Activity

1. Confirm that the app is on each tablet in the classroom.

2. Children will begin by opening the Wet-Dry-Try App.

3. Children will put in their passcode. (This can be found in the teacher's account on Wet-Dry-Try +Live Insights.)

4. You can have children start in a particular section (i.e., capitals, lowercase, or numbers) or you can have them select or specific letter or number to work on.

Wet

Dry

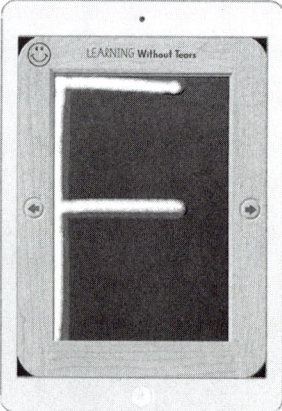

Try

Hand Activity

Children move their hands to show capitals and small, tall and descending lowercase letters. Share the digital animation of this activity located on the resource section of the Interactive Digital Teaching Tool.

Note: Avoid using the Hand Activity if there are children in your class who use sign language.

Activity

Capital & Lowercase Activity

1. Make left hand flat. Say **Capital C**.
2. Make right hand into a fist. Say **Lowercase c**.
3. Continue with **O o, S s, V v, W w**.

Small Lowercase Letters
14 lowercase letters are small: **c, o, s, v, w**, and **a, u, i, e, r, n, m, x, z**.

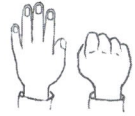   

tall small

C   c   o   s   v   w

Tall Lowercase Letters
7 lowercase letters are just as tall as a capital. Lowercase **t** is as tall as capital, but it's a lowercase letter.

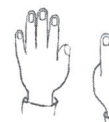    

tall tall

T t   d   l   k   h   b   f

Descending Lowercase Letters
5 lowercase letters are descending letters. They go below the line.

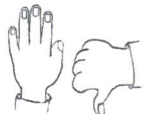

tall descending

G   g   j   y   p   q

Digital Version

 Interactive Digital Teaching Tool: Share via your interactive whiteboard or smartboard

 Digital Student App: Integrated in lessons

Wet-Dry-Try for Lowercase Letters

Wet-Dry-Try is an innovative teaching strategy. We use a slate chalkboard for capitals and numbers. For lowercase letters and words we use the Blackboard with Double Lines. This is the physical version. The digital version is available on the Interactive Digital Teaching Tool and Digital Student App. The latest research on brain development supports this activity. This research calls for fewer elements (just two lines), modeling, sensory engagement, and immediate feedback (Sousa 2011).

Materials
- Blackboard with Double Lines* (1 per child)
- Little Chalk Bits (1")
- Little Sponge Cubes (1/2")
- Little cups of water
- Paper towel pieces

Activity

1. **Prepare Blackboards**
   Write letter with chalk as a model to trace.

2. **Teacher's Part – Write f with Chalk**
   Use chalk to write a letter on double lines.
   Say the step-by-step directions.

3. **Child's Part – Wet-Dry-Try**
   As the child does each part, say the step-by-step directions to guide the child. The child is encouraged to join in, saying the words.
   Wet: The child uses a Little Sponge Cube to trace the letter.
   Dry: The child uses a little piece of paper towel to trace the letter.
   Try: The child uses a Little Chalk Bit to write the letter.

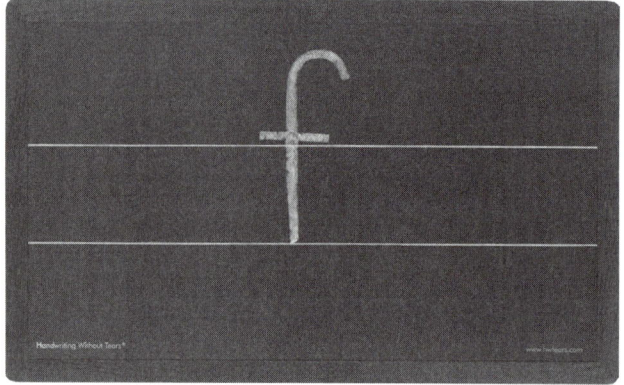

*If you don't have a Blackboard with Double Lines, consider using our Double Line Writer on your whiteboard. This product is available at LWTears.com.

Digital Version

 Interactive Digital Teaching Tool: Share via your interactive whiteboard or smartboard

 Digital Student App: Integrated in lessons and on "My Tools" for additional practice

Voices

Children should learn to write letters in the correct sequence. If you demonstrate with different voices, your students will quickly learn and memorize all the steps. This activity is filled with the repetition children need, but it is so much fun that the repetition is never boring.

Materials
- Large board, prepared with double lines
- Magic C Bunny puppet (optional)

Activity

1. Help children find the step-by-step words in their student editions. Read the words together as children point. Demonstrate the letter, saying the steps with the children.

2. Let the Magic C Bunny whisper a request for a different voice. Slowly demonstrate the letter again using a new voice. Children join in by saying the steps and modeling your voice. Repeat.

3. Write the letter. Children put their pencils on the dot. They use their voices together to say the steps as they write.

4. Repeat the activity with different voices: high, low, loud, soft, slow, fast.

Sentence Song

Why do some children runwordstogether? Speech doesn't use spaces between words. Children may naturally write like they talk, without spaces. Bad worksheets can also force children to squeeze words together. By teaching with "Sentence Song" and generous spaces, you boost sentence skills.

Materials
- "Sentence Song" from *Rock, Rap, Tap & Learn* music album

Activity

1. Teach sentence skills as you write on double lines: "We can write."

2. Teach each sentence part as you write:
   W = I start the sentence with a capital letter.
   We = I write a word and leave a space. (Be generous!)
   We can = I write a word and leave a space.
   We can write. = I write the last word. This is the end. I make a period.

3. Play "Sentence Song." Play it again and sing along while you point to the capitalization, spacing, and punctuation with your students.

Syllables

A small word part with one vowel sound is called a syllable. Children move their bodies using different motions for each syllable. Breaking (segmenting) words into syllables helps with reading and spelling.

Activity

1. Say the word for the children: for example, hippopotamus.
2. Have children stand up and complete the syllable activity together while saying the word. For each syllable, move hands to a different part of the body starting at head and moving to shoulders, waist, knees, and feet.
3. Repeat for other words.

hip - po - pot - a - mus

RESOURCES

School-to-Home Connections p. 182

Sentence School p. 183

Remediation Tips pp. 184–190

Strategies for English Language Learners pp. 191–193

Strategies for Children with Special Needs pp. 194–196

Handwriting Standards for Written Production pp. 197–199

References p. 200

Index pp. 201–205

School-to-Home Connections

Research consistently shows that a strong school-to-home connection helps children build self-esteem, curiosity, and motivation to learn new things. Home and school are the two most important places for young children. When teachers and families work together, everyone wins. Here are 10 ways to make a strong school-to-home connection:

1. Reinforce learning at home. We developed ☺ A Click Away and Home Links so you can share important handwriting information along the way. The icon above is featured throughout this teacher's guide. It will remind you when it's time to send something home.

2. Find opportunities to communicate during planned school events like family-teacher meetings, conferences, and school visits. Take a few extra steps to communicate through letters, email, and even podcasts. Download our "Welcome Letter" from A Click Away resources at **idtt.LWTears.com/ext/TGKSK/2022**.

3. Share important assessment information about your students' progress. Consider using our Screener of Handwriting Proficiency to monitor progress throughout the year at **myLWTears.com**.

4. Share this curriculum with families. Let them play with some of our hands-on products. Tell them about our website, **LWTears.com**, so that they can explore the many resources available.

5. Share music with families. Send children home singing songs from our *Rock, Rap, Tap & Learn* music album. If there is a fun song that families sing at home, ask them to share it with you.

6. Model language and thinking skills out loud. Children benefit from hearing adults talk and solving problems. Send home letter charts so families can use the same language you use in school when talking about letters.

7. Encourage families to read to children as much as possible and to look for letters in the books. Reading is fun and helps build comprehension and language skills. Hunting for letters builds alphabet knowledge.

8. Share the *Kick Start Kindergarten* student edition with families. Send it home when children have completed it. Encourage families to review it with their children and share it with other family members.

9. Help families prepare children to write. Encourage them to learn proper grip and encourage their children to hold a pencil correctly. Teach families how to help children write their names (see next page). These educational articles, along with others, are available for download on ☺ A Click Away resources at **idtt.LWTears.com/ext/TGKSK/2022**.

10. Encourage families to help their children to recognize letters and notice letters all around them. Point out signs, logos, and letters wherever you go.

Sentence School

The Sentence School program works alongside the Handwriting Without Tears® curriculum to teach the skills kindergarten children need to build sentences and become confident, skillful writers. Although *Sentence School* is not included in our teaching guidelines, you may want to add it as a language arts activity for Mondays, Wednesdays, and Fridays.

The Sentence School Curriculum

Supports your teaching:
- Integrates with your existing curricula
- Engages students and reinforces concepts through movement, touch, sight, and sound
- Fits into your language arts time block
- Takes only 10–15 minutes a day

Children will:
- Increase vocabulary—Learn words and their meanings, and use words in sentences
- Develop conceptual understanding—Understand the relationship among words and reinforce their meanings
- Build grammar skills—Speak in complete sentences and learn correct grammar through example and practice
- Cultivate writing skills—Follow the basic rules: begin with a capital, leave space between words, and end with punctuation

For more information about *Sentence School* and to download a sample lesson, visit **LWTears.com**

Monday – Action Sentences

Wednesday – Describing Sentences

Friday – Question and Answers

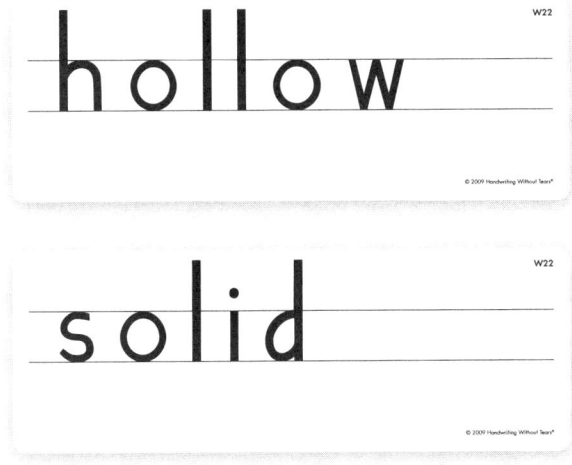

Remediation Tips

HANDWRITING ASSESSMENTS

Handwriting Without Tears and Get Set for School have three types of assessments. You can find more information about each assessment at **LWTears.com**. You will also find information about webinars and workshops related to each assessment.

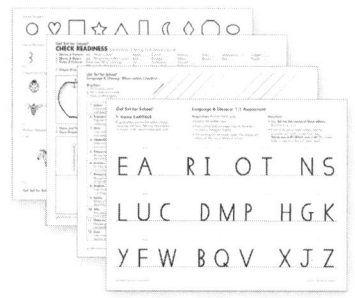

Pre-K Assessments: 1:1 assessments
1. Readiness & Writing
2. Language & Literacy
3. Numbers & Math

Use the Readiness & Writing Assessment to check pre-writing skills: fill-in coloring, grip and hand preference, copying shapes, drawing a person, naming 10 capitals and numbers, and writing name in capitals. To check naming/recognizing all capitals and lowercase letters, see the Language & Literacy Assessment. For shape and number naming, use the Numbers & Math Assessment. See **LWTears.com** for more information.

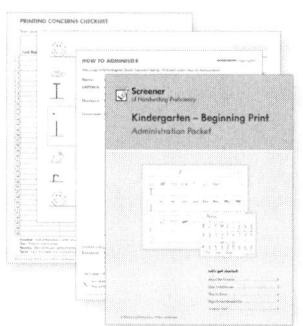

Screener of Handwriting Proficiency
(Printing: Grades K–3+)

Administer the class screener to check handwriting progress three times during the year. Use online scoring for these printing skills: letter/number memory, orientation, placement, and sentence writing. The results show progress for each child and the class. Use the results to plan class instruction and quickly identify children who need further evaluation with The Print Tool.

The Print Tool: 1:1 evaluation
(Printing: Grades K–3+)

The Print Tool is a complete evaluation that includes student and school information, a review of school papers, and careful observation of the child's physical approach and fine motor skills. Administered individually, The Print Tool evaluates capitals, numbers, lowercase letters, and seven specific handwriting components: memory, orientation, placement, size, start, sequence, and word spacing.

When scored, the Evaluate form shows exactly which letters/numbers and components are causing difficulty. Based on this information, remediation is targeted and specific. Children get precisely the materials and strategies they need to remediate their specific difficulties.

Remediation Tips

PHYSICAL APPROACH

Handedness
Switching hands does not allow one hand to become the skilled hand. Observe the child eating, cutting, tapping, etc. The child will usually begin with the skilled hand first. Work with families to promote the use of the dominant, skilled hand.

Pencil Grip
Teaching grip is essential as children begin formal handwriting instruction, but sometimes children will come to you with awkward grips. Start by using golf-size pencils. They are the perfect pencil size for young children and help promote an appropriate grip. We also suggest this strategy:

Remediate in 3 stages:
1. Pick-Up – Make circles in the air with a correct grip. Drop and do it again. Repeat five times a day for a couple of weeks.
2. Scribble & Wiggle with Pencil Pick-Ups – Complete pencil pick-ups daily at home and at school using a correct grip. Access Pencil-Pickups on ☺A Click Away.
3. Write – Have children write their names with a correct grip. Once they consistently write their name with a correct grip, give them permission to use it for all of their writing.

Adaptive Devices
Experiment with adaptive devices and use them only if they make it easier for the child to hold a pencil. With young children, physical devices should not be used as a substitute for physical demonstration.

Rubber Band Trick
If the pencil is pointing straight up in the air, it will be difficult to write. Loop two rubber bands or ponytail holders together. One goes around the child's writing hand, the other around the pencil.

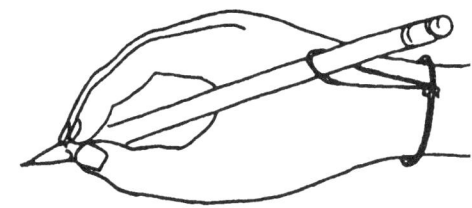

Remediation Tips

Reward Good Grip

 Try using the reward activity to motivate a good grip.

Pencil Pressure
Too Hard: Try a mechanical pencil or placing paper over a mouse pad to provide feedback.
Too Soft: Have children pencil in small shapes until they are black. Use pencils with softer lead.

Name the Helper Hand
A helper hand that twirls hair or props up a forehead will not support the paper. Try naming the helping hand, children find it funny. For example, John's helping hand is called Jacob. You talk to "Jacob" about how it's his job to hold the paper. You are not reprimanding the child, but just the name of their helping hand.

The Eraser Challenge

 Some children spend a lot of time erasing. We suggest giving children a pencil without an eraser and telling them to cross out the mistake. They are less likely to stop and do this. You can also try the Eraser Challenge. This activity is designed for children to be accountable. The goal is that all the erasers are left at the end of the day.

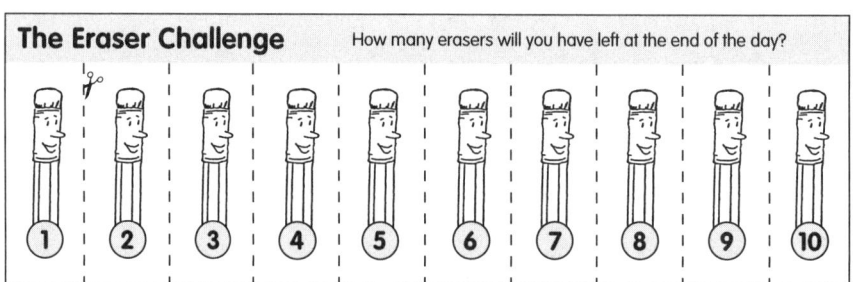

Remediation Tips

CAPITALS

Memory
Memory is being able to picture the letter in your mind. Use consistent language to help children picture the capitals: for example: B has a Big Line and two Little Curves, D has a Big Line and a Big Curve, etc. Active demonstration is the first step. We also suggest these activities:

 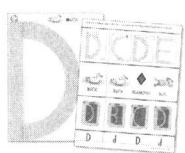  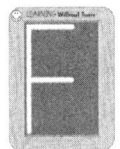 

"Frog Jump Capitals" | Capital Letter Cards for Wood Pieces | Mat for Wood Pieces | Wet-Dry-Try Slate | Digital Letter and Number Formations

Orientation
There are several capitals that can be reversed. Use the smiley face to orient children to starting their capitals at the top. Most capitals start in the top left corner. We also suggest these activities:

Mat for Wood Pieces | Gray Block Paper | Wet-Dry-Try Slate | Capitals on the Door | Digital Letter and Number Formations

Placement & Size
All capitals are tall. They sit on the base line. Having children make tally marks and playing tic-tac-toe will help them learn to stop on a line, which is essential for placement. We also suggest these activities:

Gray Block Paper | Digital Letter and Number Formations | A+ Worksheet Maker

Start & Sequence
All capitals will start at the top. Most will start in the top left corner. Some start in the center. Remediate in the three groups: Frog Jump Capitals, Starting Corner Capitals and Center Starting Capitals to help children use correct start and sequence. We also suggest these activities:

"Where Do You Start Your Letters?"
"Frog Jump Letters"
"Sliding Down to the End of the Alphabet" | Wet-Dry-Try Slate | Gray Block Paper | A+ Worksheet Maker

Remediation Tips

LOWERCASE

Memory
Quick and automatic recall of letters is important. Memory is essential for independent handwriting. Always spend time comparing capital letters to their lowercase partners so children can quickly and automatically write the correct letter. Demonstration and direct instruction are essential. We also suggest these activities:

"CAPITALS & Lowercase"

Blackboard with Double Lines

Wet-Dry-Try App

Digital Letter and Number Formations

Orientation
Facing letters in the correct direction is important for reading and spelling. Orientation errors are distracting because children stop and think about which way the letters go. The most common lowercase reversals are the **b** and **d**. Use the Honey Bee Story (p. 168) to fix. We also suggest these activities:

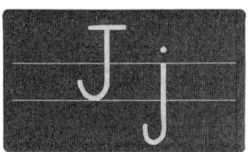
Blackboard with Double Lines

Wet-Dry-Try App

 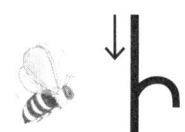 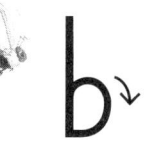
Honey Bee Story

Placement & Size
Placing letters on a line makes writing easier to read. Children need to be able to control their size so their writing isn't too big for their grade. Using the appropriate size double lines is the best way to help children place and write their letters a correct size. Our student editions also promote line generalization, as children will need to write on different lines for success in the classroom. We also suggest these activities:

"Capitals & Lowercase"
"Descending Letters"
"Vowels"

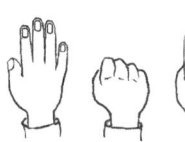
Hand Activity

Double Line Paper

A+ Worksheet Maker

Start and Sequence
Correct start and sequence are essential for quick and automatic printing skills. The ability to write letters correctly is acquired through direct teaching and correct practice. We also suggest these activities:

"Where Do You Start Your Letters?"
"Magic c Rap"

Teach in groups:
Magic c
Diver Letters

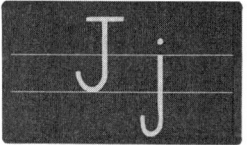
Blackboard with Double Lines

Double Line Paper

A+ Worksheet Maker

Remediation Tips

NUMBERS

Memory
Quick recall of numbers will allow children to focus on math. Active demonstration is the first step. We also suggest these activities:

"My Teacher Writes"　　　Wet-Dry-Try Slate　　　Wet-Dry-Try App　　　Digital Letter and Number Formations

Orientation
There are several numbers that can be reversed. Use the smiley face to orient children to start their numbers at the top. Most capitals start in the top left corner. We also suggest these activities:

 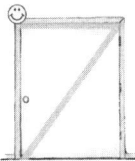 

Wet-Dry-Try Slate　　　Door Tracing　　　Gray Block Paper

Placement & Size
Numbers are the same size as capitals. Having children make tally marks and playing tic-tac-toe will help them learn to stop on a line, which is essential for placement. We also suggest these activities:

Gray Block Paper　　　Digital Letter and Number Formations

Start & Sequence
All numbers will start at the top: numbers 1–7 will start in the top left corner, number 8 starts in the center, number 9 has its own corner. Remediate numbers in chronological order, starting with number 1. We also suggest these activities:

  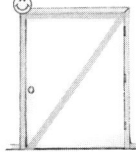  

"Number Song" "10 Fingers"　　　Wet-Dry-Try Slate　　　Wet-Dry-Try App　　　Door Tracing　　　Gray Block Paper　　　Digital Letter and Number Formations

Remediation Tips

SPACING

Having appropriate spacing after words is essential for reading the content. We recommend playing the "Sentence Song" prior to teaching sentence skills to help children remember to leave a space. Direct instruction along with leaving plenty of room after each word is also key for children to understand and see what a space is. We also suggest these activities:

"Sentence Song"

Touching Fingers
Teach your students to put letters in a word close to each other. Have them put their index fingers up and bring them close together, without touching. Say, "In a word, the letters are close, but don't touch." Draw fingers for them on their paper as a reminder.

Sick Sentence Clinic
Write a sentence with the letters too far apart. Circle each word in the sentence. Now, copy the sentence over, putting the letters closer. For example:

    I a m b i g.   I am big.

Now, write a sentence with the letters too close. Children underline each word in the sentence. Now, copy the sentence over with spaces between the words.

    Icanrun.   I can run.

The Nothing Bottle
If students run their words together: Say that you will give them what they need to create spaces. Have them hold out their hands to catch it. Take a huge empty bottle (or any container) and make a big show of pouring into their hands. Ask, "What did you get?" Nothing! Tell them to put nothing after every word they write.

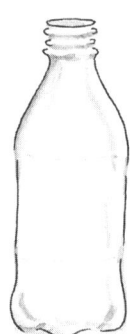

Strategies for English Language Learners

Our program and research-based teaching strategies help diverse learners master handwriting and were developed to meet the needs of all learners, including English language learners (ELLs). Our strategies provide simple best practices you can seamlessly integrate into a classroom setting, benefitting all children. Use the following strategies to help your ELL children succeed in your classroom:

Prior Knowledge Activation

Research tells us that children learn more effectively when they already know something about a content area and when concepts in that area mean something to them and to their particular background or culture. When you link new information to a student's prior knowledge, you activate the child's interest and curiosity and infuse instruction with a sense of purpose. Prior knowledge has a large influence on student performance (Dochy, Segers, & Buehl, 1999). English language learners need opportunities to practice previously learned knowledge and what they are presently learning. Hill and Bjork (2008) acknowledge the importance of practice to prevent ELLs from learning incorrectly.

We use child friendly, consistent language with clear, direct instruction that uses simple verbal cues paired with fun stories for children to make connections and activate prior knowledge. When teaching particular groups of letters, you may ask children what they already know about the letter group like shape, size, and starting position.

Conducive Learning Environment

Research indicates that the prevention of failure among English language learners involves two critical elements: the creation of educational environments that are conducive to their academic success and the use of instructional strategies known to be effective with these students (Ortiz, 1997; Ortiz & Wilkinson, 1991).

To maximize a child's ability to master handwriting, prepare your classroom or teaching space so children can see and hear what you are modeling. You should also ensure that children have the proper materials including the correct size chairs and desks. Children's feet should be flat on the floor with their arms resting comfortably at the desk. While instructing, you should have children arrange their desks in rows or in a V shape. During guided instruction, you should be strategic in grouping ELLs, rotating them to allow interaction with a variety of English speaking peers.

Strategies for English Language Learners

Cooperative Learning Strategies

According to research, cooperative learning is particularly beneficial for any child learning a second language. Cooperative learning activities promote peer interaction, which helps language development and concept and content learning. It is important to assign ELLs to different teams so that they can benefit from English language role models. ELLs learn to express themselves with greater confidence when working in small teams and pick up vocabulary by observing how their peers learn and solve problems.

"Having students work together cooperatively is a powerful way for them to learn and has positive effects on the classroom climate" (David Johnson and Roger Johnson, 2001). Skill grouping reduces anxiety among ELLs, thus, making it an effective format for teaching skills that are difficult to comprehend (MacIntyre and Gardner, 1994). Our program and multisensory activities offer many opportunities for children to be move around and work together in diverse groups to reinforce letter formation.

Multisensory Instruction

Numerous individuals report the importance of using visual, auditory, and tactile aids to make content more understandable to ELLs (Carey, 2007; Herrell & Jordan, 2008; Samway & Taylor, 2008). Our multisensory instruction and interactive activities include strategies to address the diverse learning styles of all children. We have methods to meet the needs of auditory, visual, tactile, and kinesthetic learners. For auditory learners, we use consistent, child friendly language that helps children learn and remember easily. To meet the needs of visual learners, we provide step-by-step illustrations of letter formation and give clear visual direction. Our clean, uncluttered, and black and white pages also support a visually simple format to support the learning style of visual learners. Our student editions have step-by-step models that are big enough for finger tracing to meet the needs of tactile letters, and we use music and movement to engage kinesthetic learners. Additional strategies include using dough to form letters and playing visual memory games.

Thematic Instruction

Research reports that themes help children understand new concepts. Themes provide mental organizing schemes for students to approach new ideas (Caine & Caine, 1997; Kovalik, 1994). Our teaching order helps children learn handwriting skills in the easiest, most efficient way. Specifically, we teach letter formation in groups that have similar strokes. These thematic groups allow children to repeat important vocabulary words that are common to letter groups and promote good writing habits.

Repeated Lesson/Concept/Vocabulary

Recent research (Rydland & Aukrust, 2005) states the importance of second language learners' use of repetition for conversational participation and language learning. Research also indicates that word repetition is a favorable condition in vocabulary learning (Nation, 2001). We use consistent, child friendly terminology for teaching letter formation and specifically repeat the same vocabulary through the lessons and grade levels. We do not make assumptions about what a child knows and our direct instruction only uses words that children are familiar with and uses as few words as possible. As children practice writing letters and words, have them repeat the letter formation steps as they form letters and words. Ensure that

Strategies for English Language Learners

they use the same vocabulary. You can also have children create flash cards with the letters on one side and vocabulary/pictures on the other side (review the cards repeatedly). Alternate the side of the card that is used as the prompt and have children work in pairs to quiz one another.

Immediate Feedback

Research shows that "immediate feedback motivates students to make necessary adjustments, encourages cooperation with and support of others, increases student response, and promotes activity and harmony within the group" (Weissglass 1996). Research also shows that learning improves with consistent feedback (Linnenbrink & Pintrich, 2002; Pintrich & Schunk, 2002; Heath & Glen, 2005). In addition, when children work cooperatively, you should strive to provide immediate feedback.

We provide ample opportunities to assess skill mastery within the student editions, enabling you to quickly determine if you need to re-teach or give specific support. We also provide additional resources online for additional skill assessment.

Think-Aloud Modeling/Metacognition (Show and Tell)

According to research, modeling thought processes helps students become more aware of their own thinking (Simons 1995; Resnick and Klopfer 1989, Paris and Winograd 1990). As you model letter formation, we provide simple step-by-step instructions to help children learn the correct steps for forming letters. After you model thinking aloud, children can work in pairs and model to one another.

Differentiated Instruction

Research indicates that a student's learning profile includes learning style (i.e., visual, auditory, tactile, or kinesthetic), grouping preferences (i.e., individual, small group, or large group), and environmental preferences (i.e., lots of space or a quiet area to work). You may differentiate instruction based on any one of these factors or any combination of factors (Tomlinson, 1999). Research also indicates that although some of the techniques may remain the same, it is necessary that you differentiate instruction for ELLs to accommodate the different levels of language development (Genesee, Lindholm-Leary, Saunders, & Christian, 2006).

We provide many opportunities to differentiate instruction for diverse learners. By recognizing a child's prior knowledge, readiness, language, learning styles, and interests, you are able to meet the needs of all learners. You can group children according to different learning styles or you can also group them by level of mastery (i.e., advanced children may be grouped with and can support struggling children).

Strategies for Children with Special Needs

Handwriting Without Tears can be used easily and effectively for children with disabilities. Here are some suggestions:

Fine Motor Activities

To help children with fine motor delays, use the first 10–15 minutes of a session doing fine motor work. If children are delayed in their fine motor skills, they will likely need extra help with handwriting. Spend the last 10 minutes of a session forming letters.

Autism Spectrum Disorder (ASD)

Often, concentration and compliance are challenging for children with autism, so they may struggle with handwriting, fine motor skills, or perceptual delays. Children on the autism spectrum who are high functioning, such as those with Asperger's Syndrome, tend to relate well to tangible, hands-on materials. Children who do not respond well to verbal cues (language) usually do well with the Handwriting Without Tears program. You can demonstrate many of the teaching techniques with few or no verbal cues as the child attends visually to the task. Teacher demonstration and child imitation are the keys to successful handwriting. Keep these tips in mind when teaching children with ASD:

- Use as many multisensory experiences as possible
- Use the Magic C Bunny to incorporate socialization and interaction
- Be very consistent with the child
- Be careful when using abstract teaching strategies; children with ASD tend to take things literally.

Down Syndrome

Use several multisensory activities and repetitions. If the child has a classroom assistant (IEP aide), allow extra time for the child to practice handwriting. Because the child may be easily distracted, you may want to schedule extra time for breaks. Here are some tips for working with children who have low muscle tone (hypotonia) due to Down Syndrome:

- If the child struggles with writing because of low muscle tone, have them write in all capital letters
- Assess the child's comfortable size of writing
- Use a modified pencil grasp
- Adapt seating in the classroom and at home
- Work on extra fine motor activities to strengthen the hands.

Strategies for Children with Special Needs

Poor Vision

If a child has poor vision, modify teaching materials appropriately. Here are some ideas to increase the visibility of teaching materials:

- Use brightly colored paints with a bright contrasting mat (black and white works well)
- Enlarge all student edition pages
- Use a larger slate for capitals and numbers (11" x 17")
- Use a window guide to grade the size of handwriting
- Double lines can work well for children with poor vision
- Enlarge or thicken lines with a marker until the child is comfortable with the chosen size
- Provide a texture on the lines to help the child locate the line position.

Cerebral Palsy

To help a child with cerebral palsy, begin by establishing good positioning. If the child is in a wheelchair, try using a lap tray during writing time for support and stability of the arms and shoulders. If the child only has use of one extremity, clamp down paper and other materials using a clipboard clamp screwed into the lap tray. Once good writing position has been established, try these tips for writing success:

- If the child has problems with muscle tone, try an adapted pencil grip for more control of the pencil.
- Children with cerebral palsy may do better initially writing in capitals, which are developmentally easier to read and write.
- If the child has perceptual or visual problems, it may help to enlarge the worksheets and darken the print.

Dyslexia

Dyslexic children typically struggle with organization and using language effectively. Often, they struggle with writing because letter formation is not automatic. The teaching techniques help the child develop good habits: starting at the top with letter formation; learning a left-to-right flow in the sequence of reading and writing; and learning consistent, child-friendly terminology when learning letter formation. Help a child with dyslexia in the following ways:

- Use the Slate and Gray Blocks to correct letter and number reversals.
- Introduce Wood Pieces to teach correct formation of all capital letters.
- Use the double lines to teach consistency in placement of letters on the lines.
- Teach letters in groups of similar strokes, as taught in the student editions.
- Provide many opportunities for review and mastery lessons.

Strategies for Children with Special Needs

Dysgraphia

Children with dysgraphia have trouble producing written language due to poor motor planning. They may struggle with organizational skills and movements that need to be in an automatic and specific order, such as the formation of letters for writing. This can cause handwriting to be illegible or contain irregular and inconsistent letter formations. Children with dysgraphia can be scattered in their writing habits. For example, their writing is sometimes a mixture of lowercase and capital letters. You can help organize these children in the following ways:

- Teach the shapes (parts and pieces) of the letters using the Wood Pieces Set and the Mat for Wood Pieces.
- Use the Slate Chalkboard and Gray Block Paper to correct capital letter and number reversals. The smiley face will become a consistent reminder of the starting corner and will orient the child to the left side of the Slate Chalkboard.
- Provide visual models for the child to follow. Refer the child to the pictures in the student editions that give additional visual cues for letter formation.
- Provide many practice sessions to develop patterns for letter formation.
- Teach the letters in the recommended groups of similar strokes to help develop consistent patterns of letter formation.

Handwriting Standards for Written Production

Handwriting instruction must adhere to developmental principles to ensure success for all children. Yet, educational guidelines often are limited to one standard in the English Language Arts standards—"produces legible handwriting." When students fail to meet this standard, teachers have no means for examining which skills are lacking. To review standards visit our website: **LWTears.com/freeresources**.

Handwriting is an essential skill for both children and adults (Feder and Majnemer 2007). Even in the age of technology, handwriting remains the primary tool of communication and knowledge assessment for students in the classroom. The demands for handwriting are great, whether in the classroom or beyond. A 1992 study (McHale and Cermak) found that 85 percent of all fine motor time in second-, fourth- and sixth-grade classrooms was spent on paper and pencil activities. A more recent study (Marr, Cermak, Cohn and Henderson 2003) noted that kindergarten children are now spending 42 percent of their fine motor time on paper and pencil activities. The addition of handwritten components to many state standardized assessments and of a handwritten essay to the College Board SAT further emphasize the importance of handwriting. Furthermore, good handwriting is important long after graduation. In *Script and Scribble* (2009), Florey writes in reference to handwritten job applications, "Like it or not, even in our machine-driven world, people still judge you by your handwriting."

Research literature extensively documents the consequences of poor handwriting on early literacy and academic performance. Children who experience difficulty mastering this skill [handwriting] may avoid writing and decide they cannot write, leading to arrested writing development (Graham, Harris and Fink 2000). Handwriting is critical to the production of creative and well-written text (Graham and Harris 2005) affecting both fluency and the quality of the composition. Handwriting instruction must adhere to developmental principles to ensure success for all children. According to the National Association for the Education of Young Children, newborn to eight-year-old children learn best from methods that are consistent with developmentally appropriate practice (1998). However, due to a general lack of professional development in the area of handwriting, educators are not always aware of the specific objectives to be addressed at various age and grade levels.

Seeing the need for a more specific analysis of skills, a team of occupational therapists and educators developed a set of handwriting standards. We hope it serves as an example to educators and curriculum decision-makers and brings increased attention to this crucial, yet often overlooked, area of education.

Handwriting Standards for Written Production

Readiness Skills

K.1 Concept Development
Students will demonstrate emergent literacy skills needed for writing. Each student will:
- **A.** Identify basic shapes (e.g., squares, circles, and triangles)
- **B.** Recognize simple size differences (e.g., big and little)
- **C.** Understand position words (e.g., top/bottom, front/back, up/down, in/out)
- **D.** Demonstrate print awareness
    1. Position a book or page correctly for coloring, writing, or reading
    2. Track pictures, symbols, or letters from top to bottom and left to right
    3. Understand that printed words represent spoken words
- **E.** Identify printed symbols used for communication
    1. Identify capital letters
    2. Identify lowercase letters
    3. Identify numbers
- **F.** Use drawings and symbols to convey meaning and share ideas
    1. Draw simple shapes (e.g., squares, circles, and triangles)
    2. Draw a person
    3. Use letters to approximate words

K.2 Physical Development
Students will demonstrate physical development needed for writing. Each student will:
- **A.** Use a correct and efficient pencil grip for writing
- **B.** Stabilize paper with the non-writing hand while drawing/writing
- **C.** Position writing paper appropriately
- **D.** Maintain sitting posture for writing/coloring/drawing

Handwriting Standards for Written Production

Printing Skills
K.3 Letter Skills
Students will demonstrate skills in printing letters and numbers from memory. Each student will:
- A. Demonstrate correct formation of letters and numbers
    1. Start capital letters at the top
    2. Start numbers at the top
    3. Start lowercase letters (except **d** and **e**) at the top
    4. Follow standard formation sequence for letters and numbers
- B. Orient letters and numbers correctly (with few reversals)
- C. Place letters and numbers on a base line (within 1/8" above or below)
- D. Write letters and numbers in a grade-appropriate size
- E. Follow the writing guidelines of various styles of paper (triple, double, and single lines)

K.4 Word Skills
Students will write letters together to form words. Each student will:
- A. Write his/her name
    1. Begin with a capital letter
    2. Form each letter in a name, moving left to right

References

Boyd, Judi, W. Steven Barnett, Elena Bordova, Deborah J. Leong, and Deanna Gomby. 2005. "Promoting Children's Social and Emotional Development Through Preschool Education." New Brunswick, NJ: National Institute for Early Education Research.

Dennis, Julie L., and Yvonne Swinth. 2001. "Pencil Grasp and Children's Handwriting Legibility During Different-Length Writing Tasks." *American Journal of Occupational Therapy* 55 (2): 175–183.

Dolch, Edward William. 1948. *Problems in Reading*. Champaign, IL: The Garrard Press.

Feder, Katya P., and Annette Majnemer. 2007. "Handwriting Development, Competency, and Intervention." *Developmental Medicine & Child Neurology* 49: 312–317.

Florey, Kitty Burns. 2009. *Script and Scribble: The Rise and Fall of Handwriting*. New York: Melville House.

Florida International University. 2012. "Good Handwriting and Good Grades: FIU Researcher Finds New Link." *FIU News*, January 18. http://news.fiu.edu/2012/01/good-handwriting-and-good-grades-fiu-researcher-finds-new-link/34934.

Gesell, Arnold. 1940. *The First Five Years of Life: A Guide to the Study of the Preschool Child*. New York: Harper and Brothers.

Graham, Steve, and Karen R. Harris. 2005. "Improving the Writing Performance of Young Struggling Writers: Theoretical and Programmatic Research from the Center on Accelerating Student Learning." *Journal of Special Education* 39 (10): 19–33.

Graham, Steve, Karen R. Harris, and Barbara Fink. 2000. "Is handwriting causally related to learning to write? Treatment of handwriting problems in beginning writers." *Journal of Educational Psychology* 92: 620–633.

Knapton, Emily. 2011. "Exploring the Levels of Emergent Literacy." *Indiana Reading Journal* 43 (2): 16–18.

Lust, Carol A., and Denise K. Donica. 2011. "Effectiveness of a Handwriting Readiness Program in Head Start: A Two-Group Controlled Trial." *American Journal of Occupational Therapy* 65 (5): 560–568.

Marr, Deborah, Sharon A. Cermack, Ellen S. Cohn, and Anne Henderson. 2003. "Fine Motor Activities in Head Start and Kindergarten Classrooms." *American Journal of Occupational Therapy* 57 (5): 550–557.

McHale, Kathleen, and Sharon Cermak. 1992. "Fine Motor Activities in Elementary School: Preliminary Findings and Provisional Implications for Children with Fine Motor Problems." *American Journal of Occupational Therapy* 46, 10: 898–903.

National Association for the Education of Young Children & International Reading Association. 1998. "Learning to Read and Write: Developmentally Appropriate Practices for Young Children." *Young Children* 53 (4): 30–46. http://www.naeyc.org/files/naeyc/file/positions/PSREAD98.pdf.

National Governors Association Center for Best Practices and Council of Chief State School Officers. 2010. *Common Core State Standards*. Washington, D.C.: National Governors Association Center for Best Practices, Council of Chief State School Officers. www.corestandards.org.

Sousa, David. 2011. *How the Brain Learns*, 4th ed. Thousand Oaks, CA: Corwin Press.

Strickland, Dorothy S., and Judith A. Schickedanz. 2009. *Learning About Print in Preschool*, 2nd ed. International Reading Association: Newark, DE.

Tompkins, Gail E. 2010. *Literacy for the 21st Century: A Balanced Approach*, 5th ed. Boston, MA: Pearson.

Full list of references available on **LWTears.com**.

Index

A
A, 60
a, 80
active teaching, 4
activity design, 8
adaptive devices, 185
Air Writing, 170
alphabet knowledge, 20
A+Worksheet Maker, 75, 92, 98, 173
assessments, 14, 184
autism spectrum disorder, 194

B
B, 49
b, 103
Blackboard with Double Lines, 11, 176
body parts, 112, 132, 155, 158
building, 10, 20, 154

C
C, 58
c, 72
Capital Letter Cards for Wood Pieces, 10, 161
capitals, 41–65, 120. *See also Wood Pieces Set for Capital Letters*
    Center Starting Capitals (C, O, Q, G, S, A, I, T, J), 27, 44, 58–63, 165
    Frog Jump Capitals (F, E, D, P, R, N, M), 26, 44, 46–51, 166
    Learn & Check, 44
    lowercase letters vs., 42
    Magic C Capitals, 44
    remediation tips, 187
    Starting Corner Capitals (H, K, L, U, V, W, X, Y, Z), 27, 44, 52–57, 162–163, 165
Capitals for Me, 64
Capitals on the Door, 163
Center Starters. *See capitals*
cerebral palsy, 195
child development, 6, 198
    stages of learning, 20–24
child friendly language, 6
A Click Away, 5, 15, 182
coloring, 11, 20
comparisons, 126
conducive learning environment, 191
cooperative learning strategies, 192
counting, 72
Cross-Curricular Connections, 7, 9
    Language Arts, 45, 47, 51, 53, 56, 57, 60–63, 65, 75–83, 85, 87, 89–92, 97, 99, 101–105, 113, 115, 116, 118, 122, 124, 125
    Math, 50, 52, 54, 59, 61, 72, 95, 112, 127, 132, 134–137, 139, 141–144
    Music, 107
    Science, 46, 48, 55, 58, 88, 94, 98, 109, 114, 119, 138
    Social Studies, 49, 54, 64, 73, 74, 84, 86, 93, 96, 100, 106, 108, 117, 120, 121, 123, 126, 128, 140
curves. *See Wood Pieces Set for Capital Letters*

D
D, 48
d, 81
decoding, 19
demonstration, 21
descending letters, 7, 10, 42, 65, 68–70, 167, 175
developmental teaching order, 6, 19, 42, 44
diagonals, 50, 149, 160
dictated, 21
differentiated instruction, 9, 15, 193. *See also Cross-Curricular Connections*
Digital Products Portal, 12
Digital Teaching Tools, 172, 173
direct instruction, 21
directionality, 7, 152–153
Diver Letters. *See lowercase letters*
Door Tracing, 163. *See also tracing*
double lines, 7, 11, 68, 69, 79, 89
Down Syndrome, 194
drawing, 11
    development, 20, 198
    Mat Man® (draw a person), 155
dysgraphia, 196
dyslexia, 195

E
E, 47
e, 89
encoding, 19
English language learners (ELLs), 15, 191–193
enrichment, 9, 15. *See also Home Links*
Eraser Challenge, 186
exclamation point, 118, 125

Index

F
F, 47
f, 104
feedback, 193
fine motor skills, 194, 197
FLIP Crayons®, 11, 39
Flip the Pencil Trick, 37
Frog Jump Capitals. *See capitals*

G
G, 59
g, 82
Get Set for School Pre-K Workshops, 184
Gray Blocks, 7, 43, 44
grip, 11, 18, 22, 34, 37–39, 185
guided practice, 21

H
H, 52
h, 102
the Hand Activity, 84, 175
handedness, 185
hands-on materials, 147, 194
handwriting and reading integration, 19
handwriting process, 18
handwriting sequence, 22–23
handwriting standards, 197–201
helper hand, 186
Home Links, 51, 52, 56, 59, 62, 78, 82, 95, 103, 108, 182
horizontal, 160

I
I, 61
i, 88
IDTT, *See Interactive Digital Teaching Tool*
imaginary play, 10
imitation, 20–21, 39
indenting for paragraphs, 121
independent writing, 21–23
informative text, 116, 126
Interactive Digital Teaching Tool, 13, *See also IDTT*
instructional design, 21

J
J, 62
j, 95

K
K, 52
k, 92
Kick Start Kindergarten, 20

L
L, 53
l, 90
labels, 112, 116
language arts, 183. *See also Cross-Curricular Connections*
laser letters, 163, 171
left-handed, 6, 36, 73, 79, 107
letter lesson design, 9
letters, 11
    building, 20
    capitals – teaching order, 42, 44
    directionality, 7, 152–153
    formation, 10, 19, 44, 152–153, 164–166, 172–174. *See also individual letters*
    Learn & Check, 44, 71
    lowercase – teaching order, 42, 70
    orientation, 10, 18, 42, 44
    positioning, 160
    printing skills standards, 199
    reversals, 7, 18, 43, 44, 169, 195
    singing, 152, 166–167
    stories, 168–169
Letters and Numbers for Me **student edition**, 11, 20, 43, 71
letter-sound, 19, 120, 151, 164
Letter Stories, 168–169
lines, 7
    Double lines, Triple lines, 7, 11, 68, 69, 79, 89
    Wood Pieces Set for Big Lines, Little Lines, 157, 158, 160, 162
lines for poems, 125
literacy, 19, 197
Little Chalk Bits, 8, 39, 132, 164–165, 176
Little Sponge Cubes, 8, 39, 132, 164, 176
lowercase letters, 65, 67–109
    capitals vs., 42
    Diver Letters (p, r, n, m, h, b), 30, 70, 96–103
    Final Group (f, q, x, z), 30, 70, 104–109
    Learn & Check, 71
    Magic c Letters (a, d, g), 28, 70, 80–83
    multisensory activities and, 168–169, 175–176
    remediation tips, 188–189
    Same as Capitals and t (c, o, s, v, w, t), 28, 70, 72–79
    teaching guidelines for, 28–30
    Transition Group (u, i, e, l, k, y, j), 29, 70, 86–95

Index

M

M, 50
m, 100
Magic c. *See lowercase letters*
Magic C Bunny, 10, 177
Magic C Capitals. *See capitals*
matching, 142
Mat for Wood Pieces, 10, 20, 161–162
Mat Man®, 20
   Build, 154
   Draw, 155
   labels, 112
   sing, 20
measurement, 50
memory skills, 22–23
modeling, 193
models, 6
movement, 10, 35, 179
multisensory activities, 147–179
   air writing, 170
   A+ Worksheet Maker, 173
   building, 154
   capital letters, 161–164, 166
   cues, 148
   curves & circles, 159
   digital letter & number formations, 172
   drawing, 155
   Hand Activity, 175
   laser letters, 163, 171
   letter games, 151, 154–155
   letter positioning, 160
   letter stories, 168–169
   lowercase letters, 167, 176
   mystery letters, 165
   shaking hands, 150
   songs, 149, 152–154, 166–167, 178
   syllables, 179
   teaching guidelines, 26–31
   voices, 177
   Wet-Dry-Try, 164, 174, 176
   Wood Pieces Set, 156–162
multisensory instruction, 21, 192
music, 10, 20, 38, 107, 149, 152–154, 166–167, 178
My First School Book, 20
Mystery Letters, 49, 51, 83, 165
"My Teacher Writes", 189

N

N, 50
n, 99
names of children, 45, 151
   teaching guidelines for, 26
   in title case, 45
narrative writing, 121, 127
numbers, 7, 11, 22–23, 131–144
   Numbers for Me, 144
   numerals, 134–143
   remediation tips, 188
   stories, 133
   teaching guidelines for, 26–27
   Wet-Dry-Try, 132
   writing/formation, 133, 172, 173

O

O, 58
o, 73
online resources, 12. *See also Digital Teaching Tools*
order, 6, 19, 42, 44, 70

P

P, 48
p, 96
paper placement, 22, 34, 36
paragraphs, 121
parental involvement, 15. *See also Home Links*
pencil grip, 11, 18, 22, 34, 37–39
   quadropod grip, 37
   remediation tips, 185–186
   tripod grip, 37
pencil pressure, 186
pencil size, 11, 37
poems, 125
portal for digital products, 12
position words (e.g., up, down, under, over), 158, 198
posture, 22, 34, 35
practice, 67
Pre-K Assessments, 184
prepositions. *See position words*
pre-strokes, 22–23
pre-writing, 11, 20
primary skills, 22–23
printing, 22–23, 199
The Print Tool®, 184
prior knowledge activation, 191
professional development, 15

Index

punctuation
    comma, 128
    exclamation point, 118, 125
    period, 118, 121, 126
    question mark, 118, 119, 123

Q
Q, 59
q, 106
question & answer, 119, 123
quotations, 128

R
R, 49
r, 98
readiness, 14, 20, 26, 33–39, 149, 198
remediation, 15, 184–190
repetition, 192–193
resources, 181–199
reversals. *See letters*
review and practice, 7
rhymes, 124
right and left discrimination, 20, 150
Rock, Rap, Tap & Learn album, 10, 166–167. *See also music*
rubber band trick, 185

S
S, 60
s, 74
Same as Capitals and t. *See lowercase letters*
school-to-home connections, 15, 182. *See also Home Links*
Scope & Sequence of Printing, 22–23
Screener of Handwriting Proficiency, 14, 182, 184
secondary skills, 22–23
sensory motor skills. *See multisensory activities*
sentences, 113, 115, 117, 127–128, 183
    Learn & Check, 71
    practice, 67
    Sentences for Me, 85
    "Sentence Song," 167, 178, 190
    standards for skills, 199
    Words & Sentences for Me, 29, 68, 87, 91, 93, 97, 101, 105, 109
Sentence School, 183
shaking hands, 20, 150

shapes, 24, 198
    circle, 159, 198
    rectangle, 137
    square, 198
    triangle, 198
sharing, 20
Show Me Magnetic Pieces for Capitals™, 161
sign language, 121, 123
size, 23–24, 198
Slate Chalkboard, 11, 20, 43, 164–165
smiley face, 5, 15, 131, 162, 163, 169
social skills, 20
songs. *See music*
sound. *See letter-sound*
spacing, 7, 22–23, 43, 190
spatial organization, 7, 43
special needs strategies, 194–196
stages of learning, 20–24
standards for handwriting, 197–201
Starting Corner capitals. *See capitals*
student materials, 4, 10–11
syllables, 10, 114, 179

T
T, 61
t, 78
teacher education, 15
teacher support, 4, 14–15
teaching guidelines, 14, 25–31
teaching order capitals, 42, 44
teaching order lowercase, 42, 70
technology, 172–174. *See also Digital Teaching Tools*
thematic instruction, 192
title case, 45
title – for poem, 125
tracing, 163, 170, 171, 192
Transition Group. *See lowercase letters*

U
U 53
u, 86
uppercase. *See capitals*

Index

V
V, 54
v, 76
vertical, 42, 160
visual problems, 195
Voices activity, 177
vowels, 29, 122

W
W, 54
w, 77
Wet-Dry-Try, 8, 20, 132, 164, 174, 176. *See also Slate Chalkboard*
whiteboard, 13, 172
Wood Pieces Set for Capital Letters, 10, 20, 43, 156–162
    for Big Lines, Little Lines, 157, 158, 160, 162
    for curves & circles, 157, 159
words, 120
    Learn & Check, 71
    practice, 67
    standards for skills, 199
    Words for Me, 79
    Words & Sentences for Me, 29, 68, 87, 91, 93, 97, 101, 105, 109
student edition design, 6–7, 43, 68
writing
    big and little curves, 157, 159
    big and little lines, 44, 157, 158
    developmental stages, 11, 22–23
    lowercase letters, 67
    numbers, 131
    process, 18
    readiness. *See readiness*
    support, 14–15
writing activities, 30–31, 111–128
    comparisons, 126
    labels, 112, 116
    paragraphs, 121
    poem, 125
    punctuation, 118
    question & answer, 119, 123
    rhymes, 124
    sentences, 113, 115, 117, 127–128
    syllables, 114
    vowels, 122
    words, 120

X
X, 55
x, 107
y
Y, 55
y, 94
Z
Z, 56
z, 108